Jesus, Lazarus, and the Messiah

Unveiling Three Christian Mysteries

For Doris Jameson

Who has heard about
this book from the very
beginning! With gratitude
for all you do for our
beloved Cathedral.

Charles Stilwell
May 17, 2005
Washington National Cathedral

Jesus, Lazarus, and the Messiah

Unveiling Three Christian Mysteries

Charles S. Tidball

IN COLLABORATION WITH
Robert Powell

SteinerBooks
2005

Published by SteinerBooks
400 Main Street, Great Barrington, MA 01230

www.steinerbooks.org

Library of Congress Cataloging-in-Publication Data

Tidball, Charles S.
  Jesus, Lazarus, and the Messiah : unveiling three Christian
mysteries / Charles S. Tidball in collaboration with Robert Powell.
    p. cm.
  ISBN 0-88010-558-5
  1. Incarnation. 2. Jesus Christ–Biographyy–Sources. 3. Jesus
Christ–Historicity. I. Powell, Robert, 1947-II. Title.

BT220.T53 2005
299'.935--dc22

                                                      2005004217
           10 9 8 7 6 5 4 3 2 1

Printed in the United States of America

CONTENTS

PART ONE
DEVELOPING AN UNDERSTANDING

PART TWO
THE MYSTERY OF THE TWO JESUS CHILDREN

PART THREE
THE MYSTERY OF THE BELOVED DISCIPLE

PART FOUR

THE MYSTERY OF THE INCARNATION
OF THE CHRIST BEING

LIST OF FIGURES

LIST OF TABLES

FOREWORD

STRANGELY, interest in Christian origins has never been more intense. I say "strangely" because, since the end of Christendom and the rise of scientific materialism and enlightenment rationalism, the meaning of Christ's incarnation, death, and resurrection has been progressively called into question. Today, for many, the question itself is meaningless. Nevertheless, it continues to provoke controversy, and is clearly still a living issue that speaks to a heart's need, if an unconscious and unarticulated one.

Until recently, however, even among scholars, there has been little unanimity on the subject. Clearly something happened in Palestine in the 30s of the era we now call "common," but exactly what happened remains ambiguous. Skipping over the unbelief of the nineteenth century, we may say that New Testament experts have moved from "demythologization" (Rudolf Bultmann) to the apparently near-futile search for the "historical Jesus" (Robert Funk, John Crossan, and the Jesus Seminar), while the most recent textual research more or less confirms the reality of the canonical texts as written. In "The Resurrection of the Son of God," the last volume of his trilogy on *Christian Origins and the Question of God*, N.T. Wright, for instance, sees no compelling early evidence *not* to accept the experienced reality of Christ's rising from the dead. Larry Hurtado's *Lord Jesus Christ: Devotion to Jesus in Earliest Christianity* likewise confirms that acceptance of Jesus as Messiah goes back to the very first Jesus community.

Academic scholars, of course, are not the only interested parties. A whole industry of counter-scholarship now exists that interprets the Event in Palestine from a range of approaches including Jesus as "pagan god," "mason," "gnostic," and even the last of the "Egyptians."

The past century has also been particularly rich in theological approaches to the mystery of Christianity and the meaning of the Christ event. One need mention only, for instance, the Protestant Karl Barth, the Orthodox Sergius Bulgakov, and the Roman Catholics Karl

Rahner and Hans Urs von Balthasar. Though brilliant, profound, existential, and abounding in relevant and living insights, these theologians nevertheless remain expositors of tradition, rather than bearers of new revelation.

Charles Tidball falls into none of the above categories. He is neither a new testament scholar, a New Age Gnostic, nor a theologian, but falls somewhere in between. This makes his book hard to classify. Dr. Tidball is a scientist, whose field is medicine and computers. He is a Christian, a person of faith, a believer in the Incarnation in the full sense of the word. But he is also a seeker—a questioning soul who seeks evidence for what he knows in his heart. As such, an esotericist and a student of Anthroposophy and Rudolf Steiner. To understand his approach, therefore, several factors must be considered.

At the heart of the Christian mystery is the being of Christ Jesus, the Lord or Messiah. This is to say that, although Christianity is in some sense a "Religion of the Book" like Judaism or Islam, at its heart lies not a text, but an event: the event of the incarnation, death, and resurrection of the Messiah. When we seek to understand Christianity, therefore, we are not seeking to interpret words, though the words are saving, but to understand through them an *event*—something that actually happened—and happened to people who *witnessed it.* Understanding for Christians is witnessing. Hence the elevated status of martyrs or witnesses. There is a paradox here.

As Rudolf Steiner never tired of repeating, though the incarnation actually happened and was a true earthly event—Jesus was actually born on Earth in human form, walked, ate, talked, taught, healed, was crucified, and rose from the dead, and thence ascended from Earth to Heaven—this event was a *divine cosmic* event, a moment (as Steiner puts it) in the liturgy of the gods. As such, it was spiritual and supra-sensory—which is why it is so difficult to find historical traces of it and why, if we pay attention, we shall find that subsequent witnesses witnessed it supra-sensorily or in spiritual vision. Steiner in fact affirms that, even if we lost all evidence of what he called "the Mystery of Golgotha," including the New Testament itself, we could reconstitute it through direct supra-sensory perception.

This reality is evident in the early Christian centuries. From the so-called gnostics of the first and second centuries to the Montanist heresy of the third century, we find everywhere evidence of the spiritual witnessing of Incarnation and its spiritual consequences. Following Montanus, however, as part of its institutional centralization of political power, the Church banned private or personal visions—which is not to say, of course, that saints, visionaries, and mystics did not continue to witness the event in the spiritual world. The Church, however, was powerful enough to ensure that they had little effectiveness. On the basis of this—unfortunate—historical reality, many people now oppose the orthodox, institutional view to the visionary one, rather than see the two as complementary. Thus Elaine Pagels in her new book *Beyond Belief* sets the Gospel of John against the Gospel of Thomas. Readers must chose one or the other—but the situation is more complex.

To understand it we need something like an idea of Christian "Midrash." In Jewish tradition there is the Torah (the Bible) and the so-called "oral" Torah or Midrash, which is an extensive, six thousand page collection of koan-like paradoxical commentary, interpretation, and collateral narratives. Since the heart of Judaism is a text, the Midrash are textual and have to do with hermeneutics or how to read the text. In Christianity, where the central fact is an event, there are not readers, but witnesses. First the canonical witnesses—Matthew, Mark, Luke, John, and Paul—then the cloud of non-canonical witnesses, ranging from the first so-called Gnostics through the long two millennium line of mystics and visionaries (such as Hildegard of Bingen, Brigitta of Sweden, Jacob Boehme, Emmanuel Swedenborg, Anne Catherine Emmerich, to name a few)—up to and including the contemporary spiritual science of Rudolf Steiner. Viewed as Midrash, these witnesses are not in opposition to the canonical documents, but rather amplify, corroborate, and continually extend in surprising and fulfilling ways our understanding of the event witnessed. For this reason, as Rudolf Steiner said, and Dr. Tidball cites at the very beginning of his book, the Evangelists should be viewed as "mediators" whose revelation is to be unveiled and understood only gradually as humanity progresses.

Dr. Tidball is what might be called a second-order witness—a witness by faith and understanding. He is not himself a visionary, but by his faith and understanding he is able to bear witness to those whose witness is more direct. Taking as his starting point the account of the Christ event given by the canonical witnesses, the Evangelists, his faith uncovers three mysteries that seem to be crucial to any deeper understanding of the

JESUS, LAZARUS, AND THE MESSIAH

meaning of Christ's coming: first, the birth of Jesus, of which two quite different accounts are given (with quite different genealogies); second, the identity of the Beloved Disciple of St. John's Gospel, a riddle that textually seems connected to the person of Lazarus; and, finally, overshadowing and determining these, the nature, being, and function of the Messiah. To amplify into these, he turns to the evolving cloud of Christian witnesses. Rudolf Steiner's spiritual research provides the initial basis and all-important context, which itself is then amplified and illuminated by historical witnesses like Brigitta of Sweden and Anne Catherine Emmerich, as well as by contemporary students of spiritual science like Alfred Heidenreich, Karl König, Robert Powell, and Irene Johanson. The result is a new and profound unveiling of Jesus as Messiah or Christ.

Such work is necessarily "esoteric." The word itself simply means "inner" (while its converse, "exoteric," means "outer"). This is often explained by recourse to the analogy of a wheel, whose rim represents the exoteric or outer and whose spokes, connecting the rim to the center, represent the esoteric. That is to say, the esoteric is the way in, as well as the progressive interiority leading to the hub or center that determines all. On this account, reality is like an onion. In the sensory-physical world we live in the outer skin, but as we peel away layer after layer we move from sensory to supra-sensory realities, from "matter" to "spirit."

This being so, Dr. Tidball begins by describing briefly how a material world and a physically incarnate humanity evolved from a spiritual world and a spiritual humanity. The central ideas here are metamorphosis and reincarnation—not only at a human level, but also at a cosmic and spiritual level. Of a different order entirely is the incarnation of the Godhead in human form. It is this fact that the Gospels reveal, but, as Dr. Tidball establishes, to understand it we need the esoteric view of cosmic evolution and reincarnation.

To demonstrate this and to unveil their mysteries, he then turns to the questions in hand: the Jesus children, Lazarus/John and the incarnation of the Messiah, which of course is the overriding focus of this unique, fascinating work. Without revealing its substance, which is naturally the author's prerogative and privilege, I must say that the picture that Dr. Tidball presents will surprise, enlighten, and inspire not only anthroposophists, who will be familiar with some of the material, but also any Christian who is willing to contemplate with an open mind and heart the intricate and delicate working of God's purpose.

*   *   *

While the primary "maker" of *Jesus, Lazarus, and the Messiah*, Charles Tidball is not its only author. In connection with those witnesses on whom Dr. Tidball draws, I have mentioned Robert Powell. Dr. Powell is an esotericist, anthroposophist, and the learned author of books on Astrology, Christology, and Sophiology. In his *Chronicle of the Living Christ*, he was able to demonstrate how truthfully Anne Catherine Emmerich's visions elucidate the Christ event. In this work, having established birth dates for the Jesus children, Powell lays out a day by day account of Christ's ministry (some of this may be found in the Appendix). In some sense, it was Robert Powell's work, understood in the context of Rudolf Steiner's magisterial spiritual insight and research, that provided the initial impetus for this book. But Powell's presence is more pervasive still. He contributes two fundamental chapters—on the John Mystery and the Johannine Tradition—that buttress the argument in extraordinary ways, which I leave to readers to discover for themselves.

When we add to Robert Powell's contribution his translation of the extract from Irene Johanson's *Die Drei Jünger Johannes (The Three Disciples Called John)* and Anne Catherine Emmerich's "chronicle" (both added as Appendices), we realize that we have before us a remarkable phenomenon. We have a chorus of witnesses, if not of one voice, harmonizing at once with the Gospel testimony, and with Rudolf Steiner's anthroposophical spiritual science. In other words, something is going on—to which, if we are anthroposophists, institutional Christians, or just seeking to understand the Mystery of Golgotha, we would do well to attend.

CHRISTOPHER BAMFORD

ACKNOWLEDGMENTS

THIS BOOK IS DEDICATED to the memory of U. Christof Linder, M.D., who introduced me to the writings of Dr. Rudolf Steiner, and thus to the world of anthroposophy, some 60 years ago. In his youth Dr. Linder had been a worker on the original Goetheanum, in Dornach, Switzerland, and was present for the lectures Dr. Steiner gave to the workers in those days. Dr. Linder was exceedingly generous to me. Not only did he supply me with reading materials, he made it possible for me to spend an entire week in Dornach on my first visit in 1948. In the following year, he facilitated a summer position as a Laboratory Assistant to Dr. Ehrenfried Pfeiffer at the Threefold Farm, in Spring Valley, NY.

The most important acknowledgment is to Dr. Robert Powell. Through his *Chronicle of the Living Christ*, he provided much of the original research material for this book. Further, he wrote chapters 11 and 12, and translated relevant materials from German language sources for those chapters. When I started this effort, I had no idea that he would become a collaborator. I have been effusive in his praise at various points in the text. Without question, his ability to provide us an improved set of dates for the events that occurred two thousand years ago, marks a turning point in our understanding of the most momentous event to occur in the Earth planetary cycle of evolution—the incarnation of the Christ Being in human form. But, along with Robert, I must acknowledge his two primary sources: Dr. Rudolf Steiner and the Blessed Anne Catherine Emmerich. Without the understandings of spiritual science provided by the former and the details enunciated by the latter, none of the further unveiling of mysteries attempted here would have been possible. Now that Robert has become a collaborator, I marvel at what we have accomplished without a face-to-face visit. It is a testament to the wonders of the Internet and the support we have enjoyed from our word processors (which, incidentally, are not the same). I must also recognize that Robert is a superb e-mail correspondent.

Beyond that it is a pleasure for me to acknowledge the following: Bonnie Hedges sent me materials that I would not have been able to find very easily and made valuable suggestions relating to the earliest drafts of the manuscript; the Reverend Robert Davenport, with no previous exposure to anthroposophical materials, kept an open mind and helped to encourage me in the earliest days; the Reverend Canon Michael Wyatt made an important contribution when he helped me to understand that I was dealing not with one book but two; and Professor Penny Gill, at a late stage in the process, encouraged me to become familiar with the visions of Saint Brigitta of Sweden.

At SteinerBooks, I am grateful for the enthusiasm shown from the outset for this effort. It has been a pleasure to meet Gene Gollogly who manifests a genuine interest in his authors; Christopher Bamford not only permitted us to keep the footnotes on the text pages, but he was kind enough to write the Foreword where he heaped more praise on Robert and me than we deserve; Sarah Gallogly had an eagle eye and a gentle hand in the copyediting effort; and Mary Giddens contributed the cover design as well as thoughtful typesetting for the entire volume.

My final appreciation goes to Dr. M. Elizabeth Tidball, my wife of over fifty years. The subject matter of this volume is at a remove from her formal seminary experience and her alignment with Anglicanism. Also, the many hours I spent at the word processor did interfere with some of her legitimate needs. But, throughout this lengthy gestation period, she has been a paragon of patience and tolerance. She even proofread the final manuscript and made many suggestions for its improvement. Needless to say, I could not have produced this volume without her unflagging support.

CHARLES S. TIDBALL
Washington, D.C.
March 2005

INTRODUCTION

THE INTERRELATIONS

. . . humanity as a whole produced evangelists as mediators who provided revelations that can be understood only gradually. These scriptures will be understood more and more as humanity progresses.

—RUDOLF STEINER, 1911

THE ABOVE QUOTATION from Dr. Rudolf Steiner (1861–1925), see Appendix 1, has been used as a point of departure for the present effort.[1] It encourages humanity to continue in the incremental process begun by others, substantially influenced by Dr. Steiner himself, already extended in the interval between Dr. Steiner's death and the present day, and unquestionably to be continued in the years to come. The three *Christian* mysteries identified in the subtitle can be considered "interrelated" for four reasons: 1) each *mystery* belongs to the realm of the *esoteric*, 2) prior unveilings of the background required to appreciate these mysteries has already taken place, 3) various methodologies have been used to enhance understanding, and 4) all three mysteries contribute to an appreciation of the importance of the coming of the *Messiah*.[2]

THE REALM OF THE ESOTERIC

To say it another way, knowledge is in the realm of the esoteric when it is not generally known. At the outset, the evidence to support the view of important Christian events developed in this book was

---

1. Rudolf Steiner *The Spiritual Guidance of the Individual and Humanity: Some Results of Spiritual-Scientific Research into Human History and Development* (trsl. Samuel Desch, Hudson, NY: Anthroposophic Press, 1991) p. 22.
2. Many single words and a few word groups shown in *italic* font when they first occur may be found in the Glossary, where clarifications of meanings and usage are presented.

present—but appreciated by only a very few. As will become clear in Chapter 1, the *spiritual world* has taken a long time to create an environment in which humanity can undertake to evolve in a spiritual dimension. The concept of *reincarnation* applies not only at a *human* level, where existence in the spiritual world alternates with life in the *material world*, but also at a *cosmic* level where one *planetary cycle of evolution* succeeds another as the human entity becomes more complex in its organization. The incarnation of the *Godhead* in human form is *the most significant event ever to have occurred.* It was prepared in much more detail than has been reported in the New Testament. Understanding this fact requires an extensive background in *lore* that has not previously been widely disseminated.[3]

UNVEILING THE FOUNDATIONS

The three mysteries are interrelated because they concern the foundations of Christianity. It was part of Dr. Steiner's lifelong mission to unveil these deeper mysteries. Dr. Powell (b. 1947), see Appendix 1, put it this way, "Filled with the Holy Spirit, this *initiate* revealed the cosmic mystery of the seven days of creation, the human mystery of reincarnation, and the most sacred mystery of all: the Christ Mystery."[4] As the result of the prolific writings and lectures of Dr. Steiner, that lore has now been revealed. Yet, strange as it may seem, these details of the workings of the spiritual world have largely been ignored by most theological scholars.

Why is this so? For the most part, scholarship is based on the availability of documents. Since esoteric lore comes from initiates who have more direct access to the spiritual world than ordinary human beings, there has been some skepticism about accepting their insights. In the past, this lore was not written down, which explains the absence of written documents that would be helpful for the scholarly inclined.

---

3. The word lore has been used in the sense of "a body of knowledge." It was intended as a neutral term and should be accepted without preconceptions relating to validity. It does refer to the "realm of the esoteric," as mentioned in an earlier paragraph.
4. Robert Powell *Christian Hermetic Astrology: The Star of the Magi and the Life of Christ* 1991, reprinted (Hudson, NY: Anthroposophic Press, 1998) p. 45.

Also for many, the concept of reincarnation, which is so fundamental to an understanding of this lore, has become a stumbling block. Reincarnation is not a new concept. In their monumental anthology, Joseph Head and S. L. Cranston document the views of literally hundreds of thinkers on this subject. They use the immortal phoenix in the subtitle of their book because for millennia it has been a symbol of rebirth.[5]

There is no doubt that Dr. Steiner considered that reincarnation operated as far as his own life was concerned. On the title page of his *Autobiography*, he added the following words.

> Because I entered this world with defined soul predispositions, and because the course of my life, as expressed in my biography, is determined by those predispositions, as a spiritual human being I must have existed before my birth. As a being of spirit, I must be the repetition of someone through whose biography mine can be explained. In each life the human spirit appears as a repetition of itself with the fruits of experiences during previous lives.[6]

Dr. Steiner has also always been clear on the importance of the concepts of reincarnation and *karma* as prerequisites to an appreciation of his offerings. A good example of his approach is found in an appendix to *The Spiritual Guidance of the Individual and Humanity*, where the "Introductory Comments to the Lecture Cycle" provide a concise summary of how he felt about setting the stage for speaking on these matters on June 5, 1911.

> We have to ask…why are we incarnated again and again? We find this meaning when we learn through [*anthroposophy*] that every time we see all the wonders of this world with new eyes in a new body, we get a glimpse of the divine revelations veiled by the sensory world. Or, with our newly formed ears, we can listen to the divine revelation in the world of sound. Thus, we learn that in every new incarnation we can and should experience

---

5. *Reincarnation: The Phoenix Fire Mystery* (eds. Joseph Head and S. L. Cranston, New York: Crown Publishers, 1997) p. 17.
6. Rudolf Steiner *Autobiography: Chapters in the Course of My Life: 1861–1907* (trsl. Rita Stebbing, ed. Paul M. Allen, Hudson, NY: Anthroposophic Press, 1999) p. 3.

something new on earth. We understand that some people are destined by karma to announce prophetically what all of humanity will gradually, bit by bit, accept as the meaning of an epoch. ...Thus in every epoch we have to meet anew what is revealed to us out of the spiritual [world].[7]

For those who have come to anthroposophy more recently, there is some assurance provided by the fact that this lore has been carried for centuries in the *mystery schools*. A brief review of this background can be found in the Introduction to Dr. Steiner's *Christianity As Mystical Fact* written by Andrew Welburn of New College, Oxford.[8] Furthermore, as shall be presented, the existence of such lore has been confirmed more recently by other thinkers. Even the rediscovered ancients texts, whose contents are only now being disseminated, are generating a broader view of the events that occurred in the Holy Land some two thousand years ago.[9]

IMPROVING OUR UNDERSTANDING

The methodologies that have been used to enhance understanding of these early events are interrelated. In this regard, it is important to identify the role of the Blessed Anne Catherine Emmerich (1774–1824), the Augustinian nun who, among other visions, beheld the life of the *Christ Being*, from the baptism in the Jordan River to the crucifixion, in interior visions on a day-to-day basis during the last several years of her life, see Appendix 1.[10] Similarly, it is essential to acknowledge Clemens Brentano (1778–1842), who devoted some five years of

7. Steiner 1991 pp. 80–81.
8. Rudolf Steiner *Christianity As Mystical Fact* (trsl. Andrew Welburn, Hudson, NY: Anthroposophic Press, 1997) pp. xviiff.
9. Andrew Welburn *The Beginnings of Christianity: Essene Mystery, Gnostic Revelation and the Christian Vision* (Edinburgh: Floris Books, 1991).
10. On July 7, 2003, the second and critical step in the beatification of Anne Catherine Emmerich took place. "On this Monday, in the Sala Clementina at the Vatican, in the presence of Pope John Paul II, the decree *Super Miro* was promulgated through those responsible for the Congregation of Beatification and Sanctification, so that the beatification process of the servant of God, Anne Catherine Emmerich, was brought to a successful conclusion...." *Emmerickblatter* 47(2):3–4 (trsl. Robert Powell). The beatification took place in October of 2004.

his life to making a daily record of her visions, see Appendix 1. However, without the meticulous scholarship of Dr. Powell, it would not
have been possible to convert this rich information source into actual
dates.[11]

THE COMING OF THE MESSIAH

Finally, the three mysteries interact in that each contributes to developing an understanding of the events surrounding the first coming of
the Messiah. All this is in preparation for a second coming of the Messiah, not at the end of time for the last judgement but more proxi-
mately, in our very own time. As has been reviewed by another
contemporary, this second "coming" will be different from that of two
thousand years ago.[12] The Christ Being will not come again in human
form. Rather, it is humanity that will evolve new *organs* of seeing and
hearing that will enable all individuals to encounter the Christ Being in
the spiritual world which is his natural environment.[13]

O TASTE AND SEE

Come, enter this world of new ideas. Permit yourself to be stretched
in the realms of epistemology, cosmology, and Christology. As James
Wetmore states in the Foreword to Dr. Powell's *Chronicle of the Living
Christ*, "... [T]here exists no community of colleagues or experts in the
field who could be drawn upon to assess the work within a larger context. *It is unique both in its contents and its conclusions; and it should be
read with an open mind*" (emphasis added).[14] So too with this book.
Similarly, that perspective is projected at the end of Elaine Pagels' latest
book.

---

11. Robert Powell *Chronicle of the Living Christ The Life and Ministry of Jesus Christ: Foundations of Cosmic Christianity* (Hudson, NY: Anthroposophic Press, 1996) and Powell
1998.
12. Peter Tradowsky *Christ and Antichrist: Understanding the Events at the End of the Century and Recognizing Our Tasks* (trsl. John M. Wood, London: Temple Lodge, 1998).
13. Rudolf Steiner *The Etherization of the Blood: The Entry of the Etheric Christ into the Evolution of the Earth* (trsl. Arnold Freeman and D. S. Osmond, London: Rudolf Steiner Press,
1971) p. 26.
14. Powell 1996 p. 11.

Christianity has survived for thousands of years as each generation relives, reinvents, and transforms what it received. The act of
choice...leads us back to the problem that orthodoxy was
invented to solve: How can we tell truth from lies?... Orthodoxy tends to distrust our capacity to make such discriminations
and insists on making them for us. Given the notorious human
capacity for self-deception, we can, to an extent, thank the
church for this. Many of us, wishing to be spared hard work,
gladly accept what tradition teaches. But the fact that we have no
simple answer does not mean that we can evade the question.
Most of us, sooner or later, find that, at critical points in our
lives, we must strike out on our own to make a path where none
exists.[15]

Professor Pagels goes on to suggest that the diversity of Christian
religious traditions and the communities that sustain them provide
encouragement to seek—and to find.

---

15. Elaine Pagels *Beyond Belief: The Secret Gospel of Thomas* (New York: Random House,
2003) pp. 184–85.

PART ONE

DEVELOPING
AN
UNDERSTANDING

* * *

IN THIS INITIAL SECTION, preliminary fundamentals are presented in order to set the stage for dealing with the more didactic material that makes up the rest of the volume. In Chapter 1, four time-dependent frames of reference are provided:

1) the great cosmic cycles of planetary evolution;
2) the ages within the current Earth evolution;
3) the epochs within the post-Atlantean age; and
4) the years within the fourth post-Atlantean epoch. More specifically, the time period of special interest is from 50 *B.C.E.* to 50 *C.E.* with a special emphasis on the years of the Incarnation of the Christ Being from 29 C.E. to 33 C.E.

An additional perspective has been added to this chapter; it is not time-dependent but concerns the essential nature of the human being. In Chapter 2, the primary sources used for this discourse are identified. In chronological order of their original appearance, they include:

1) the New Testament (circa 100 C.E.);
2) paintings from the fourteenth to the sixteenth centuries;
3) translations from the original German of the visions of the Blessed Anne Catherine Emmerich as reported to Clemens Brentano (1820–24);
4) translations from the original German of various books and lecture cycles by Dr. Rudolf Steiner (1909–14);
5) two monographs by Dr. Robert Powell (1991 & 1996); and
6) an essay by Dr. Karl König originally delivered in 1962 but only recently published in English by Camphill Books (2000).

Chapter 3 is concerned with significant methodologies represented in the resources cited. Topics discussed include: revelation; biblical comparison; integration of multiple sources; and dealing with visions. In addition, at the close of the volume there are five appendices, followed by a glossary in which are defined many of the unusual words used in this book, a complete bibliography, and a comprehensive index. The perspectives offered by these resources not only provide a brief review of anthroposophical fundamentals but also establish a consistent vocabulary for the entire volume.

CHAPTER 1

FRAMES OF REFERENCE

IN ANY INTELLECTUAL effort it is desirable to establish a "frame of reference" to guide those who desire to understand just where the focus will be. This is especially true of *spiritual science*.[1] Dr. Steiner was often criticized for dealing with the cosmic settings for a subject at the outset of a lecture cycle. At the risk of garnering similar disapprobation, it is intended to provide—in a very rudimentary way—an understanding of two kinds of frames of reference. The first frame of reference sets a time line for this discourse with particular attention to where along that time line can be found the further unveilings that are to take place in this volume. The second frame of reference indicates the essential nature of the human being, taking into account spiritual elements. Interestingly, these two topics are related because it is the nature of spiritual evolution that the various *constitutional components* of the human being have been the products of the evolutionary stages and their sub-cycles described below.

TIME-DEPENDENT FRAMES OF REFERENCE

1. Planetary Cycles of Evolution

In Chapter IV of *An Outline of Occult Science*, Dr. Steiner presents the great cosmic planetary cycles of evolution.[2] These planetary evolutions then, become the first frame of reference. Because they bear names that are the same as those given to planetary bodies in the current

---

1. Rudolf Steiner *Theosophy* (trsl. Catherine E. Creeger, Hudson, NY: Anthroposophic Press, 1994) p. 18.
2. Rudolf Steiner *An Outline of Occult Science* (trsl. Maud and Henry B. Monges and revised by Lisa D. Monges, Hudson, NY: Anthroposophic Press, 1972) pp. 108ff.

solar system, it has been customary to precede the name with the word "Old" when referring to the cosmic planetary cycles of evolution that existed prior to the present planetary cycle of evolution, which is called *Earth.* It should be emphasized, as will be detailed in Chapter 6, that planetary cycles before the current one did not have the same physical conditions that are now present. Thus, a total of seven such cycles were identified by Dr. Steiner: *Old Saturn, Old Sun, Old Moon,* Earth, Jupiter, Venus and Vulcan. Details of the involvement of various categories of spiritual beings in this evolutionary process can be found in *The Spiritual Hierarchies and the Physical World.*[3]

2. The Earth Evolution

At the second frame of reference, which is really a level of detail, Dr. Steiner designated seven ages within the Earth Evolution. These bear the following names: Polarian, Hyperborean, Lemurian, Atlantean, Post-Atlantean, and a sixth and seventh age without specific names. Humanity is currently in the *Post-Atlantean Age,* which likewise has been divided into seven epochs.

3. The Post-Atlantean Age

At the following frame of reference, Dr. Steiner designated seven epochs within the Post-Atlantean Age. These are titled by number as well as by geographical sphere of influence: First Post-Atlantean – Ancient Indian Epoch; Second Post-Atlantean – Ancient Persian Epoch; Third Post-Atlantean – Egypto-Chaldean Epoch; Fourth Post-Atlantean – Greco-Roman-Christian Epoch; Fifth Post-Atlantean – European-American Epoch; and two additional epochs numbered sixth and seventh but not further characterized. Humanity is currently in the *Fifth Post-Atlantean Epoch,* which is characterized by a European-American sphere of influence. Dr. Robert A. McDermott in his *The Essential Steiner* has also provided the duration in years. For further details, see Figure 1, which has been reprinted with permission.[4]

---

3. Steiner 1996 pp. 77ff.
4. Robert A. McDermott, ed. *The Essential Steiner: Basic Writings of Rudolf Steiner* (New York: HarperCollins, 1984) p. 173.

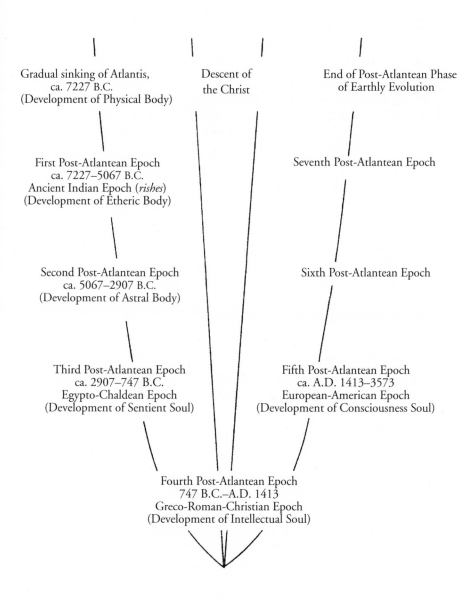

Gradual sinking of Atlantis,
ca. 7227 B.C.
(Development of Physical Body)

Descent of
the Christ

End of Post-Atlantean Phase
of Earthly Evolution

First Post-Atlantean Epoch
ca. 7227–5067 B.C.
Ancient Indian Epoch (*rishes*)
(Development of Etheric Body)

Seventh Post-Atlantean Epoch

Second Post-Atlantean Epoch
ca. 5067–2907 B.C.
(Development of Astral Body)

Sixth Post-Atlantean Epoch

Third Post-Atlantean Epoch
ca. 2907–747 B.C.
Egypto-Chaldean Epoch
(Development of Sentient Soul)

Fifth Post-Atlantean Epoch
ca. A.D. 1413–3573
European-American Epoch
(Development of Consciousness Soul)

Fourth Post-Atlantean Epoch
747 B.C.–A.D. 1413
Greco-Roman-Christian Epoch
(Development of Intellectual Soul)

FIGURE 1

**The Evolution of Human Consciousness through
Seven Post-Atlantean Epochs**

4. The Fourth Post-Atlantean Epoch

Thus the final time-dependent frame of reference is the Gregorian calendar in current use. Although the entire Post-Atlantean Age covers a period of approximately 15,000 years, each of the epochs covers only about 2,200 years. We have been in the Fifth Post-Atlantean Epoch since the beginning of the fifteenth century, but the time period that this volume will concentrate on is primarily found in the middle of the *Fourth Post-Atlantean Epoch*, also called the Greco-Roman-Christian Epoch, which took place between 747 B.C.E. and 1413 C.E. Using this time frame, the events that are to be detailed in this discourse occurred, approximately, in the 150 year period from 50 B.C.E. to 100 C.E. with special emphasis on the years of the *Incarnation* of the Christ Being from 29 C.E. to 33 C.E.[5]

THE ESSENTIAL NATURE OF THE HUMAN BEING

In Chapter 1 of *Theosophy*, Dr. Steiner begins his presentation of this subject with a quotation from Goethe that draws attention to three elements: first, the *objects* recognized by human senses; second, the *impressions* they make; and third, the *knowledge* they impart as they reveal the secrets of what they are and how they work.[6] From this beginning, Dr. Steiner defines the terms *body, soul,* and *spirit*, but he cautions *not* to associate any preconceived ideas with these terms but only to permit them to indicate three different domains of our human nature. As he develops the theme further, a total of nine "members" are indicated; but since in earthly human beings two pairs are said to be in unity, only seven constitutional components remain:[7]

---

5. For some it may seem strange to restrict the period of the Incarnation of the Christ Being in this manner, but there is some biblical support for such a view. An alternate translation of the words spoken by a voice from heaven at the time of the baptism in the Jordan River [Luke 3:22] is, "You are my son, this day have I begotten you." This subject will be taken up in greater detail in the chapters that follow.

6. Steiner 1994 pp. 21ff.

7. For a more detailed discussion, see Clopper Almon *A Study Companion to an Outline of Esoteric Science* (Great Barrington, MA: Anthroposophic Press, 1998) pp. 26ff.

1. Physical body
2. Ether body (also called life body or etheric body)
3. Astral body—includes the sentient soul and the intellectual soul (also called mind soul)
4. The individuality as the central core of a human being (also called Ego or "I")
5. Spirit self as transformed astral body —includes the consciousness soul
6. Life spirit as transformed ether body
7. Spirit body as transformed physical body

The significance of the frame of reference used in this discourse is to make a distinction between a) the materialistic perspective, which acknowledges "consciousness" as a function of the mind related to the physical brain in ways that are not yet understood by scientists who deny the existence of the spiritual world, and b) the view of spiritual science, which posits a relationship between consciousness and the higher constitutional components mentioned above.

In an Addendum that concludes the chapter previously cited, Dr. Steiner indicates that "at death our three lower constitutional components unite with the makeup of the perishable [material] world, while our four higher members unite with the eternal."[8] At this point, it is important to recall the words of the Introduction, where it was put forth unequivocally that the concept of reincarnation, by which is meant repeated, alternate embodiments in the spiritual world and in the material world, is fundamental to this entire treatise.

---

8. Steiner 1994 p. 62

CHAPTER 2

PRIMARY SOURCES

THE MYSTERY OF THE TWO JESUS CHILDREN

THERE ARE *three* time periods concerning the above named mystery. First, there is the interval of approximately 1,800 years when evidence was present but appreciated only by a very few. This esoteric period begins at the close of the first century, when the various portions of the New Testament were written, and continues to the beginning of the twentieth century. Then, with the advent of the revelations by Dr. Steiner, a second interval began in which this knowledge was no longer confined to the esoteric realm. As the result, a *qualitative* understanding of the mystery began to circulate, at least within anthroposophical circles. Now less than a hundred years later, with Dr. Powell's careful investigations, a third interval can be defined. This latest time period can be characterized as a *quantitative* understanding of the mystery, because today the actual dates when the real life events took place may well be at hand. Thus for the esoteric period, reliance will be made on Matthew's Gospel and Luke's Gospel using the New Revised Standard Version of the Holy Bible. Such a review is reinforced by the work of Dr. Adolf Arenson (1855–1936), an early member of the Theosophical Society,[1] and Dr. Alfred Heidenreich (1898–1969), a priest of the *Christian Community*.[2] The works of five artists from the Middle Ages will be described to reveal that at least some of these painters seemed to be aware of certain elements that have only more recently been brought to light.

---

1. Adolf Arenson *The History of the Childhood of Jesus: A Study of the Spiritual Investigations of Rudolf Steiner* (trsl. and ed. H. Collison, London: Anthroposophical Publishing, 1922).
2. Alfred Heidenreich *The Unknown in the Gospels* (London: Christian Community Press, 1972).

For the anthroposophical perspective, or the qualitative period, a synthesis of understandings will be drawn from several lecture cycles by Dr. Steiner, which were originally delivered during the period from 1909 to 1915.

The quantitative period is based on the multifaceted scholarship of Dr. Powell revealed in two of his publications: *Christian Hermetic Astrology* (1991, reprinted in 1998) and *Chronicle of the Living Christ* (1996). Dr. Powell made extensive use of information from the Steiner sources as well as from the visions of Sister Emmerich in developing this new perspective. Material on the authentication of this source can be found in Appendix 2. A proper sequencing of these visions required corrections for errors introduced by the editor of Brentano's manuscripts, which could only be accomplished after the original handwritten notes were published in 1980, 1983 and 1985. For more details on the methods and sources used by Dr. Powell, see Chapter 3.

THE MYSTERY OF THE BELOVED DISCIPLE

For this mystery, the lecture cycle known as *Christianity As Mystical Fact* delivered by Dr. Steiner in 1901–02, rewritten and issued in book form in 1902, provides the initial background.[3] This effort has been summarized and extended by Karl König (1902–1966) in the concluding essay of *The Mystery of John and the Cycle of the Year*. Although this work was published in German in the period between 1941 and 1965, it has only been generally available in English since 2000.[4] This mystery has also been brought up to date by Professor Welburn, who used his broad acquaintance with the strands that created the environment in which the Christ Being incarnated and blended that information, not only with the insights of Dr. Steiner, but also with the revelations from the old documents recently recovered at Qumran and Nag Hamadi.[5]

An additional source has been provided through an analysis of the visions of Sister Emmerich as published in Dr. Powell's *Chronicle of the*

---

3. Steiner 1997.
4. Karl König *The Mystery of John and the Cycle of the Year* (trsl. G. F. Mier, ed. Gregg Davis and Nicholas Poole, Great Britain: Camphill Books, 2000).
5. Andrew Welburn *The Beginnings of Christianity: Essene Mystery, Gnostic Revelation and the Christian Vision* (Edinburgh: Floris Books, 1991).

Living Christ. This compilation is presented in Appendix 4 under the title "Selected Entries from 'Chronicle of Christ's Ministry.'" Among other entries, each of the daily visions that mentions either John the son of Zebedee or Lazarus of Bethany appears verbatim as set forth by Dr. Powell.

THE MYSTERY OF THE INCARNATION

For this mystery, the primary source is the previously mentioned volume *Chronicle of the Living Christ.* The visions of Sister Emmerich provide the equivalent of a daily journal of the activities of *Christ Jesus* from the baptism in the Jordan River to the crucifixion. The daily journal is not complete, as discovered by Dr. Powell; nevertheless, it creates a background for understanding elements of the Savior's life which differ from their more abbreviated treatment in the canonical gospels. From these selected excerpts a new understanding of "the Incarnation" of the Christ Being emerges.

The focus has been on how the Christ Being spent the majority of his time during his three and one half years on earth. Therefore, no attempt has been made to deal with the Mystery of Golgotha mentioned so frequently in Dr. Steiner's writings, because the latter concerns cosmic issues related to the Incarnation as opposed to the daily events detailed in the visions. Those who desire a new perspective on these matters are referred to the final chapter of Professor Welburn's *The Beginnings of Christianity.*[6] It must be acknowledged that one can hardly appreciate the subtleties in those last pages without having read the entire book.

---

6. Welburn 1991 pp. 294ff.

CHAPTER 3

SIGNIFICANT METHODOLOGY

AS HAS BEEN SUGGESTED earlier, the sources for this volume vary considerably. When the concern is with material from the New Testament, the way in which these books came into the canon is well-documented and the commentaries abound. However, when dealing with esoteric lore, it is not so easy to validate information. This is true of the lecture cycles from Dr. Steiner, which were not reviewed by the lecturer with the same care as his classic monographs. Possibilities of error are also present regarding the visions of Sister Emmerich. Brentano did well in transcribing this material, but it required Dr. Powell's multifaceted research to put the fragments in a proper order. In the sections below, examples of methodologies appropriate to each of these areas are presented.

REVELATION

Dr. Steiner is very clear on the methodology he used to derive information for his approach to the events of the early Christian era.

> Today we can choose between two means of acquiring information about the past. We can look at physical records—historical documents if we want to learn about outer events or religious documents if we want to learn about spiritual circumstances—or we can ask what *seers* behold when the eyes of the spirit are opened to the everlasting chronicle we call the *Akashic record*, that mighty tableau where everything that ever happened in the evolution of the cosmos, the earth, and human kind is written in an unchangeable script.[1]

---

1. Rudolf Steiner *According To Luke: The Gospel of Compassion and Love Revealed* (trsl. Catherine E. Creeger, Great Barrington, MA: Anthroposophic Press, 2001) p. 27.

The Akashic record has been well-known among *esotericists* for centuries. The word *Akasha* comes from the Sanskrit language and refers to a "celestial ether or astral light that fills all space...."Every thought and action which takes place in the material world is recorded in this akashic medium...." [2] A key phrase in Dr. Steiner's comment is, "when the eyes of the spirit are opened." This means that only those whose spiritual evolution has proceeded to a level where they have developed organs of spiritual vision are able to experience the Akashic record. According to Dr. McDermott, "Although the ability to read the Akasha is very rare in the modern West, it is not rare in traditional cultures and was not at all rare in the ancient world." [3] In fact, Dr. Steiner has indicated that the Evangelists used this resource in developing their compilations of the life of Jesus Christ; but he also made clear that there are various levels of this ability which account for differences between the synoptic gospels and John's Gospel.

During an extended discussion of access to the Akashic record, Dr. Arenson makes the point that there are "two indispensable conditions ... without which it is impossible to become an investigator in spiritual realms." [4] These conditions, as has been reinforced by other authors on this subject, are: 1) full maintenance of consciousness during investigation and 2) a thorough acquaintance with modern scientific knowledge, especially natural science and mathematics.

Before leaving the subject of using the Akashic record as a source, it is worth noting an extensive discussion of the difficulties in this method as indicated by Dr. Steiner. [5]

In the lecture cycle entitled *According To Luke,* Dr. Steiner used four lectures to set the stage for an understanding of the Mystery of the Two Jesus Children. An edited version of his own summary of that material is now inserted here.

The beginning of the Christian era was full of strange and significant happenings leading to the greatest event in humankind's

---

2. Frank Gaynor *Dictionary of Mysticism* (New York: Philosophical Library, 1953).

3. Robert A. McDermott "Introduction: Approaching Rudolf Steiner's Lectures on the Gospel of Luke" in Steiner 2001 pp. 1–14.

4. Adolf Arenson *The History of the Childhood of Jesus: A Study of the Spiritual Investigations of Rudolf Steiner* (trsl. and ed. H. Collison, London: Anthroposophical Publishing, 1922) pp.1–7.

5. Steiner 2001 pp. 28–31.

evolution. These are only some of the facts that allow us to understand the wonderful mystery of Palestine. We must consider other aspects in order to understand what gradually led to this great event.... The Gospels always tell the truth; there are no conundrums to be solved.... Among the ancient Hebrews, all those "of the house and lineage of David" were descended from a common ancestor, David. The Bible tells us that David had [many sons, two being] Nathan and Solomon (2 Samuel 5:14). Two lines of descent, the Nathanic line and the Solomonic line, counted David as their common ancestor.... [We] can say that descendants of both the Nathanic line and the Solomonic line lived in Palestine at the beginning of our era. One descendant of the Nathanic branch of the house of David was a man named Joseph, a native of Nazareth. His wife's name was Mary. Surprisingly enough, a native of Bethlehem descended from the Solomonic branch was also named Joseph, and he too was married to a woman named Mary. Thus at the beginning of the Christian era there were two couples named Joseph and Mary living in Palestine. One couple [who resided in Bethlehem] was descended from the Solomonic branch of the house of David, that is from the kingly lineage, while the other couple in Nazareth were descendants of the Nathanic branch or priestly branch.... The [first] couple, not originally from Nazareth—we must take the Gospels literally—lived in Bethlehem as described by the author of the Matthew Gospel (Matthew 2:1).... [They will be called the *Solomon Joseph* and the *Solomon Mary*.] A son, ...named Jesus, was born to this Solomonic couple, and his body... supported the incarnation of a mighty individuality.... [T]he Nathanic couple, [who will be called the *Nathan Joseph* and the *Nathan Mary*] left Nazareth to go to Bethlehem "to be enrolled," as Luke says (Luke 2:4–5).... [While they were there, they had a son and also named him Jesus.].... As you see, we find part of the truth in Matthew and the other part in Luke. We must take them both literally, because the truth of the cosmos is complicated.[6]

------

6. Steiner 2001 pp. 95ff.

BIBLICAL COMPARISON

Once the clue has been given, a different methodology emerges. Now it is a matter of tabulating differences in the two gospel texts and correlating this with information from other sources. Qualitatively, this has been done very well by Arenson, Heidenreich, and König. This approach will be further documented in Chapters 4 and 9.

INTEGRATION OF MULTIPLE SOURCES

The next step is more difficult. Dr. Powell describes the dilemma with great precision.

> Christianity has its basis in *the historical fact* of the life, death, and resurrection of Christ Jesus. Although Christianity rests squarely on this historical event, and it is unique among religious traditions in this regard, the *dates* of Christ's birth and death were not transmitted—at least no record of them has yet been discovered.... The early Church fathers were faced with solemnizing an historical fact for which they had no exact date. They wished, quite naturally, to celebrate the birth and death of the Messiah each year. But in the absence of any transmitted dates how could they proceed? [7]

Converting qualitative suggestions to a quantitative record required that additional information be brought to bear on the effort. Dr. Powell employed such a strategy to determine the date of the crucifixion.

First he used Matthew's Gospel to fix the hour of Jesus' death to 3 p.m. (Matthew 27:46, 27:50); then he determined from John's Gospel that the day, defined as the Day of Preparation for the Festival of the Passover, was a Friday (John 19:14, 19:31). In terms of the Jewish calender then in use, this translated to Nisan 14; but it was still necessary to clarify the actual year. The crucifixion occurred when Pontius Pilate was procurator of Judea. Using Josephus, the Jewish historian, as an alternate source, the range of years must have been between 26 to 36 C.E. But this particular Nisan 14 occurred at the time of a full moon, and astronomical records indicated that such had only taken place in

---

7. Powell 1996 pp. 23–24.

the years 27, 30, 33, and 36. Adding additional information from the gospel narratives relating to the length of the ministry of *John the Baptizer*, Dr. Powell narrowed down the year to 33. This translated to Friday, April 3, 33 C.E.—a date that had been independently corroborated by three sources: Dr. Steiner in 1912; J. K. Fotheringham, a biblical scholar, in 1934; and, more recently, from interpreted data based on the visions of Sister Emmerich.[8]

The date of the birth is more complicated. Those details will be reviewed in Part 2 of this work. Nevertheless, to illustrate one aspect of Dr. Powell's multifaceted methodology, compare the English translation of Brentano's rendition of a vision by Sister Emmerich to what Dr. Powell derives from that same information.

> At the hour when the Child Jesus was born I saw a wonderful vision which appeared to the three holy kings. These kings were star-worshipers and had a tower shaped like a pyramid with steps. It was made partly of timber and was on the top of a hill; one of them was always there, with several priests, to observe the stars. They always wrote down what they saw and communicated it to each other. On this night I think I saw two of the kings on this tower. The third, who lived to the east of the Caspian Sea, was not with them. They always observed one particular star, in which they saw various changes; they also saw visions in the sky. Last night I saw the picture which appeared to them; there were several variations of it. They did not see it in one star, but in a figure composed of several stars, and these stars were in motion. They saw a beautiful rainbow over the moon, which was in one of its quarters. Upon the rainbow a Virgin was enthroned; her right foot was resting on the moon.[9]

Dr. Powell indicates the following about the text above.

> [Sister Emmerich] goes on to describe a wondrous vision of the spirit of a child coming forth from a chalice in front of the Virgin.

---

8. Powell 1996 pp. 443–44.
9. Anne Catherine Emmerich *The Life of the Blessed Virgin Mary* (trsl. Sir Michael Palairet, Springfield, IL: Templegate, 1954a; also reprinted, Rockford, IL: TAN Books, 1970) pp. 200–01.

But the main point here, according to [Sister Emmerich's] description, is that at the birth of the Solomon Jesus, as witnessed in the stars by the three kings, the Moon was in the constellation Virgo, and "was in one of its quarters." Normally this could be interpreted as signifying First Quarter or Last Quarter; but, reading [Sister Emmerich's] vision more closely, we find that she speaks of a "transparent disk" above the child, which makes her think of the Eucharistic wafer.

The whole impression conveyed by her vision is that of the Full Moon, and her statement that the Moon was visible in one of its quarters, I believe, is meant in the sense that it was in one of its main visible phases: First Quarter, Full Moon, or Last Quarter. (At the New Moon, of course, the Moon is not visible.)[10]

Dr. Powell then consulted astronomical tables to determine in which years before 2 B.C.E. the Moon was full while located in the constellation Virgo. That led him to the March 5/6, 6 B.C.E., which is exactly four years *before* his previously determined conception of the Nathan Jesus! *Thus the two Jesus children were born four years and nine months apart!*

DEALING WITH VISIONS

The life of Sister Emmerich is presented in Appendix 1. Because her visions are used as data by both Dr. Powell and in this volume, it is appropriate here to state some methodological issues relating to such use. In the preface to the first German edition of the *Dolorous Passion*, Brentano declared the following.

Though the accounts of these visions, among many similar fruits of the contemplative love of Jesus, may appear in some degree remarkable, they solemnly reject the slightest claim to bear the character of historic truth. All that they wish to do is to associate themselves with the countless representations of the Passion by artists and pious writers, and to be regarded merely as a pious nun's Lenten meditations imperfectly comprehended

10. Powell 1996 p. 71.

and narrated and also very clumsily set down. She herself never attached to her visions anything more than a human and defective value, and therefore yielded to an inner admonition to communicate them only in obedience to the repeated commands of her spiritual directors and after a hard struggle with herself.[11]

It is not easy to resolve, at this distance in time, whether this was a statement in keeping with cultural norms, or whether it should be taken literally. One clue is provided by the reverse of the title page, where there is printed the "Imprimatur," an indication that the book had been reviewed by an official of the Roman Catholic Church and found not to contain material against its doctrine. Perhaps, the disclaimer quoted above was the price for publishing this rich source; the visions do not always conform to traditional understandings derived from the New Testament.

In reviewing some of the material from these earlier visions, which do not adhere to a time line as well as the visions concerning the life of Jesus Christ, one finds a great wealth of detail. The frequent corroborations that occur in the notes surprised Brentano, yet gave him a sense of validity for much of this visionary material.[12] There is more documentation on authentication in Appendix 2.

AN ADDITIONAL VISIONARY SOURCE

After this volume was essentially completed, a suggestion was made to consider adding material from the visions of Saint Birgitta of Sweden (1303–1373), see Appendix 1. Without question, hers is an amazing life! Due to fortunate circumstances an extensive record of her 700 interactions with the spiritual world was compiled during her lifetime. The complexities of transferring visions to the spoken word, then having them translated from Old Swedish to Latin, and eventually through several redactors to English have been documented by one of her translators.[13] He concludes, "In my opinion, the rhythm and flow of the Birgittine writings springs not from the calculated designs of a

---

11. Emmerich 1954a p. viii.
12. Ibid. pp.16ff.
13. Albert Ryle Ketzel "Translator's Foreword" in *Birgitta of Sweden: Life and Selected Revelations* (ed. Marguerite Tjader Harris, New York: Paulist Press, 1990) pp. 59ff.

committee, but from an individual life vigorously lived. I see no reason to doubt that we are reading the experiences of the woman Birgitta." Other sources are less certain. Morris concludes, "In the end, however, scholars are agreed that the original formulation of her vision[s] cannot easily be prised out of the existing texts or her voice heard through all the levels of textual transmission." [14] Another source makes the point, "As was the case with other mediaeval women writers, Birgitta's texts for publication were transcribed and edited by male mentors." [15]

Some material from her visions will be incorporated here to provide another rich source of visionary material. Although most of her visions deal with contemporary issues in her life, she visited the Holy Land and at that time experienced visions of the nativity and the crucifixion that are germane to this discourse and will be referenced in appropriate places.

CONSISTENT NOMENCLATURE

Another methodological issue relates to the use of multiple sources of information. Regrettably, not all authors use the same names. One solution to the problem of multiple names for the same individual, often used by Dr. Steiner, is to use more than one name in any particular discourse. An alternative solution, which seems especially attractive for this treatise, is to apply names consistently in an intentional way and to avoid the use of duplicate names. This is especially important when changes in names accompany changes from conventional understandings, such as inserting the word Solomon or the word Nathan before Jesus, or when changes in names signify a change in status, such as adding the word Apostle in front of the names of those who were only disciples prior to *Pentecost*. This is important, too, when quotations from earlier works do not have the desired context. There are also disadvantages to this approach. One is that it is labor intensive for an author to produce the emendations in all direct quotations; another is that it may be distracting for the reader to encounter the more bulky additions. To facilitate this *Consistent Nomenclature*

---

14. Bridget Morris *St Birgitta of Sweden* (Woodbridge, Suffolk, UK: Boydell Press, 1999). p. 8.
15. Kirsi Irmeli Stjerna *St. Birgitta of Sweden: A Study of Birgitta's Spiritual Visions and Theology of Love* (Unpublished doctoral dissertation, Boston University, Graduate School, 1995). p. 9.

effort, two tables have been provided where changes in names for the same individuals are presented on a chronological basis. Also, all the important names are listed in the Glossary at the back of the volume.

TWO RHETORICAL QUESTIONS POSED BY POWELL

Before posing these two rhetorical questions, it is necessary to recall that Sister Emmerich did not distinguish between the *Solomon Jesus* and the *Nathan Jesus*. When she related her visions to Clemens Brentano, while on the whole she recounted the visit of the Magi (to the Solomon Jesus) quite separately from the shepherds' adoration (of the Nathan Jesus), she sometimes mixed together elements of the two. Since the fact of the birth of two Jesus children was not revealed to her, it is quite natural that her accounts were somewhat tangled. So Dr. Powell asks, "Why was the fact of two births and two holy families concealed from her?" and the follow-up question, "Why did this mystery have to wait until the time of Rudolf Steiner to be revealed?"[16]

Dr. Powell answers his two rhetorical questions as follows:

During the period (1819–24) that [Sister Emmerich] was telling her visions to Clemens Brentano, there was virtually no knowledge of reincarnation in the West. It would therefore have been something quite inexplicable, and very confusing, if she had spoken of two Jesus children.... [As has been established already, an appreciation of reincarnation is essential in order to comprehend the basis for two Jesus children.] Almost a hundred years had to elapse, until the time of Dr. Steiner's teaching activity (1900-25), before this mystery could be unveiled; for it was in the context of reincarnation that Dr. Steiner spoke of this mystery, referring to the Solomon Jesus as the reincarnation of Zarathustra and the Nathan Jesus as the reincarnation of the [Special Individuality who can be likened to] the "sister soul" of Adam.[17]

Before leaving this question entirely, there is an interesting revelation that has to do with the two Jesus children, one from the Solomon

---

16. Powell 1996 p. 80.
17. Ibid. pp. 80–81.

line and the other from the Nathan line. This occurs in visions of Sister Emmerich where she joins the Solomon Mary, when she is a very young child, with two young boys whom she calls prophets. This was not an isolated vision but one that occurred on more than one occasion. The difference in the ages and demeanor of the two "prophets" is consistent with what we have learned from Dr. Steiner and Dr. Powell about the Solomon Jesus and the Nathan Jesus. In her visions, Sister Emmerich "sees" the two "Jesus" children many years before either was born.[18]

---

18. Emmerich 1954a pp. 95–96.

PART TWO

THE
MYSTERY
OF THE
TWO JESUS
CHILDREN

* * *

THERE ARE SEVERAL LINES of evidence that support the concept that there were *two different families* each with a Joseph from the Davidic line, a Mary, and a child named Jesus. In Chapter 4, the first of these lines of evidence is developed. It springs from a careful reading of the New Testament texts as found in the works of Dr. Adolf Arenson and Dr. Alfred Heidenreich. An example of the "code language" used in John's Gospel is presented; the genealogies of Jesus found in Matthew's Gospel and Luke's Gospel are compared and contrasted; and other differences between the two nativity narratives are analyzed. In Chapter 5, the second line of evidence is reflected in the works of artists from the Middle Ages. Paintings by Meister Frank (Hamburg), by an unknown master of the Flemish School (Cambridge), by Raphael (Berlin), by a work attributed to van Orley (San Francisco), and by Borgogni (Milan) are presented and interpreted. In Chapter 6, the third line of evidence is set forth based primarily on the writings of Dr. Rudolf Steiner. It deals with the extensive preparation made by the spiritual world for "the Incarnation of the Christ Being," which is not mentioned in the canonical gospel accounts. Additionally, details from the lives of both the Solomon Jesus and the Nathan Jesus are set forth from the visions of Sister Emmerich and St. Birgitta of Sweden. In Chapter 7, the final chapter of this part, special emphasis is placed on those elements included in the unveiling of this mystery and how they differ from the viewpoint of "mainstream" Christianity. The four elements of the Chicago-Lambeth Quadrilateral of 1888 are used as a distillation of that belief. Further discussion of the Messianic prophecies, the selection of the Solomon Joseph to be the spouse of the Solomon Mary by the priests of the Temple in Jerusalem, the concept of the Virgin Birth, and a comparison between resurrection and reincarnation are included. In Appendix 3 can be found a summary of the significant dates, as developed by Dr. Robert Powell, for the events relating to this mystery.

CHAPTER 4

BIBLICAL EVIDENCE

AN EARLY SOURCE on Dr. Steiner's approach to biblical analysis is Adolf Arenson (1855–1936). He uses a portion of the first chapter of John's Gospel to illustrate that some biblical passages are written in a form of code that is not obvious to the average reader and even to many biblical scholars.

> Philip found Nathanael and said to him, "We have found him about whom Moses in the law and also the prophets wrote, Jesus son of Joseph from Nazareth." Nathanael said to him, "Can anything good come out of Nazareth?" Philip said to him, "Come and see." When Jesus saw Nathanael coming toward him, he said of him, "Here is truly an Israelite in whom there is no deceit!" Nathanael asked him, "Where did you get to know me?" Jesus answered, "I saw you under the fig tree before Philip called you." Nathanael replied, "Rabbi, you are the Son of God! You are the King of Israel!" [John 1:45–49]

Dr. Arenson indicates that "the plea for the sudden conversion of Nathanael is altogether insufficient. We cannot pass by the question: What really happened to change a sceptic into a disciple [in such a short period of time]?"[1] He goes on to explain what *spiritual science* has to say about this passage. Apparently, Nathanael was an initiate of the "Eastern Mysteries." In those Mysteries there were seven grades of initiation which, in Persian nomenclature, were called: Raven, Occultist, Combatant, Lion, Persian, Sun-Hero, and Father. Nathanael was an

---

1. Adolf Arenson *The History of the Childhood of Jesus: A Study of the Spiritual Investigations of Rudolf Steiner* (trsl. and ed. H. Collison, London: Anthroposophical Publishing, 1922) pp. 9–11.

initiate of the fifth grade. If he had been from Persia, he would have been called a Persian; since he was from Israel, his occult name was Israelite, which no one outside the Mysteries would have known. When Nathanael saw Christ Jesus for the first time, he did not recognize him as an initiate, much less as a supreme spiritual being. However, Christ Jesus, as the "Master of All-Comprehending Wisdom," [2] could recognize Nathanael as an initiate; and when Christ Jesus spoke to him in the mystery-language that only the two of them understood, Nathanael realized that he was in the presence of an initiate of a very high degree. Then Christ Jesus said to Nathanael, "I saw you under the fig tree before Philip called you." The fig tree was the symbol of initiation in the Egypto-Chaldean epoch. Thus, Christ Jesus revealed to Nathanael that he had seen him spiritually at the time of his initiation. This gave Nathanael the certainty that he was in the presence of the Godhead; for to such alone was it permitted to read the occult status of another individuality. It is no longer striking that Nathanael, shaken and overwhelmed, broke out in the words, "Rabbi, you are the son of God!"

THE CONTRASTING STORIES

The late Dr. Alfred Heidenreich, a priest of the Christian Community, carefully reviewed the contrasting stories of the childhood of Jesus for a series of lectures delivered during the spring of 1967. As is indicated in the Editor's Foreword, Dr. Heidenreich was both a skilled speaker and a published author. Regrettably, this is a typescript of the taped lecture that has neither the charm of the spoken word nor the precision of the written word had he been able to rewrite the transcripts. But his material is well organized and that sequence has been followed in the current presentation.

First, Dr. Heidenreich acknowledges that for the general public, "the problem of these two remarkably contrasting stories is mostly glossed over by what one might call a 'merger,' because generally the story in [Matthew's Gospel] of the kings and the story in [Luke's Gospel] of the shepherds are combined." [3] This happens in great paintings by

---

2. Using the terminology of this volume, the word "Godhead" is an appropriate synonym for "Master of All-Comprehending Wisdom" as used by Arenson.
3. Alfred Heidenreich *The Unknown in the Gospels* (London: Christian Community Press, 1972) p. 26.

famous artists as well as in humble Christmas cards. An exception was the German-Austrian Oberufer Cycle, a Christmas pageant performed on an island in the Danube River in what was once called Hungary. This spectacle brought out the contrast between the two Nativity stories in the two Gospels in a unique way. There, on one evening, was the Kings' Play taking place in a substantial house with Mary, the Queen of Heaven, holding court. All was solemn. The pageant included the three kings who came in pomp to visit the child and to bring him their gifts. And there was a counterplot—the wicked King Herod being outwitted by the Magi, his terror bringing about the Massacre of the Innocents; until, with great relish, Herod was disposed of by the devil. Then, on a separate evening, the Shepherds' Play was staged. It was set in a stable and depicted a more modest Maiden and the simplicity of the shepherds with their humble faith, piety, and sly humor.

A second element has to do with the timing. The death of King Herod occurred after the birth of the kingly Messiah but before the birth of the priestly Messiah. In Dr. Heidenreich's time the best that one could do was to put the death of King Herod somewhere about 4 B.C.E. The nativities of the two different Jesus children then occurred: one before the death of Herod and the other after the death of Herod at the time when Cyrenius was appointed governor of Syria as documented in *The Gospel According to Luke* [Luke 2:2]. This is of some import, as Dr. Steiner pointed out, because both John the Baptizer and the younger of the two Jesus children would have been killed in the Massacre of the Innocents, if they had not been born well after that event.[4]

THE TWO GENEALOGIES

Without question, the two genealogical charts presented in the canonical gospels are different. At one level, they are different in their starting point: the chart in Matthew's Gospel starts with Abraham and works forward in time to Jesus, whereas the chart in Luke's Gospel starts with Jesus and works backward in time to his antecedents. When the two charts are presented in the same direction, see Table 1, it becomes more obvious that the progenitors are also different. The

4. Steiner 2001 pp. 102–03.

Matthew chart starts with Abraham, but the Luke chart goes back
another twenty-one generations to God. In Chapter 6, a rationale for
this starting point will be presented. In one sense, the differences
identified above relate to presentation and may be considered superfi-
cial. A more substantive difference is the sequence of names after King
David. The Matthew chart goes from David to *Solomon* and then
through the necessary generations to a Jacob, the father of Joseph,
who is indicated as "the husband of Mary, of whom Jesus was born,
who is called the Messiah." [Matthew 1:16] By contrast the Luke
chart goes from David to *Nathan* and then through an entirely different sequence of names, including several more generations, to a Heli,
the father of Joseph, of whom Jesus was the son. Another substantive
difference is the number of generations between David and the two
Jesus children.

TABLE 1 : *The Two Genealogies*[5]

Adapted from Matthew 1:1-17

1. Abraham	15. SOLOMON	29. Salathiel
2. Isaac	16. Rehoboam	30. Zerubbabel
3. Jacob	17. Abijah	31. Abiud
4. Judah	18. Asaph	32. Eliakim
5. Perez	19. Jehoshaphat	33. Azor
6. Hezron	20. Joram	34. Zadok
7. Aram	21. Uzziah	35. Achim
8. Aminadab	22. Jotham	36. Eliud
9. Nahshon	23. Ahaz	37. Eleazar
10. Salmon	24. Hezekiah	38. Matthan
11. Boaz	25. Manasseh	39. Jacob
12. Obed	26. Amos	40. Joseph
13. Jesse	27. Josiah	41. Jesus
14. David	28. Jechoniah*	

*Symmetry indicated in Matthew 1:18 requires Jechoniah to be
counted twice!

5. Arenson 1922 pp. 24–25.

Adapted from Luke 3:23-38

1. God	21. Terah	41. Jonam	61. Josech
2. Adam	22. Abraham	42. Joseph	62. Semein
3. Seth	23. Isaac	43. Judah	63. Mattathias
4. Enos	24. Jacob	44. Simeon	64. Maath
5. Cainan	25. Judah	45. Levi	65. Naggai
6. Mahalaleel	26. Perez	46. Matthat	66. Esli
7. Jared	27. Hezron	47. Jorim	67. Nahum
8. Enoch	28. Aram	48. Eliezer	68. Amos
9. Methusalah	29. Amminadab	49. Joshua	69. Mattathias
10. Lamech	30. Nahshon	50. Er	70. Joseph
11. Noah	31. Salmon	51. Elmadam	71. Jannai
12. Shem	32. Boaz	52. Cosam	72. Melchi
13. Arphaxad	33. Obed	53. Addi	73. Levi
14. Cainan	34. Jesse	54. Melchi	74. Matthat
15. Shelah	35. David	55. Neri	75. Heli
16. Eber	36. **NATHAN**	56. Shealtiel	76. Joseph
17. Peleg	37. Mattatha	57. Zerubbabel	77. Jesus
18. Reu	38. Menna	58. Rhesa	
19. Serug	39. Melea	59. Joanan	
20. Nahor	40. Eliakim	60. Joda	

One can distinguish between these two Jesus children by appending the name of their Davidic ancestor in front of their names. Thus there are twenty-seven generations between David and the Solomon Jesus. By contrast, the number of generations between David and the Nathan Jesus is forty-two.

Emil Bock has made a thoughtful study of these genealogies. He concludes:

> ... W]hat does the Gospel express by the silent gesture of placing two such irreconcilable domains side by side? ... [T]he Gospels compel us ... to the realization that we are dealing in Matthew and Luke with the birth of two different children who come from different families and lineages and confront quite contrasting social milieus.[6]

---

6. Emil Bock *The Childhood of Jesus: The Unknown Years* (trsl. Maria St. Goar, Edinburgh: Floris Books, 1997) p. 49.

THE OTHER DIFFERENCES

Once one has become alerted to the presence of differences, a number of other items emerge. These have been listed in Table 2 where the biblical citations are also noted. Thus, the possibility of dealing with two entirely different stories becomes more plausible.

TABLE 2 : *Other Differences* [7]

Item	Matthew	Luke
1. Start of narrative	Bethlehem	Nazareth
2. Annunciation made to	Joseph	Mary
3. Residence of father	Bethlehem	Nazareth
4. Locus of birth	Bethlehem	Bethlehem
5. Birth location	House	Stable
6. Year of birth	Before 4 B.C.E.[8]	After 4 B.C.E.
7. Visitation of the Magi	Only in Matthew	
8. Flight to Egypt	Only in Matthew	
9. Massacre of the innocents	Only in Matthew	
10. Visit to Elizabeth		Only in Luke
11. Census requiring registration		Only in Luke
12. Visitation by the shepherds		Only in Luke
13. Presentation to the Temple		Only in Luke
14. Return to Nazareth	From Egypt (some years after birth)	From Jerusalem (right away)

Although the starting point for the nativity narrative is well documented in each case—Bethlehem for the Matthew story of the Solomon Jesus and Nazareth for the Luke story of the Nathan Jesus— some of the comparisons are arrived at by inference. There is support for such inferences in the visions of Sister Emmerich; however our current focus is the biblical evidence, therefore such considerations will be deferred to a later chapter.

---

7. Heidenreich 1972 pp. 28–29.
8. Based on the death of Herod the Great. See page 46 for a later, improved estimate.

Regarding the birth location of the Solomon Jesus, Matthew's Gospel has this to say.

> ... [the Magi] set out; and there, ahead of them, went the star that they had seen at its rising, until it stopped over the place where the child was. When they saw that the star had stopped, they were overwhelmed with joy. On entering *the house*, they saw the child with Mary his mother; and they knelt down and paid him homage (emphasis added). [Matthew 2:9–10]

This is in clear contrast to the birth location of the Nathan Jesus which is described as follows:

> And she gave birth to her firstborn son and wrapped him in bands of cloth, and laid him in *a manger*, because there was no place for them in the inn. (emphasis added) [Luke 2:7]

In each case the reader must make an inference. Since the Solomon Joseph had a house in Bethlehem, it is reasonable to imagine that the Solomon Jesus was born in that house. Regarding the Nathan Jesus, since there was no room for the visiting couple from Nazareth in the Bethlehem inn, for generations the inference has been made that he was born in a stable because of the mention of a manger.

Two other segments where the biblical narratives clearly differ have to do with the timing of the births. Obviously, the Solomon Jesus was born before the death of King Herod since Herod figures prominently in the Matthew narrative; however the decree from the Emperor Augustus that all the world should be registered [Luke 2:1] occurred after the death of Herod. Also, the return of the Nathan Jesus and his parents to Nazareth occurred soon after the birth and the presentation to the Temple in Jerusalem, whereas the return of the Solomon Jesus and his parents was from Egypt and at a longer interval from the actual birth. However, instead of returning to their original residence in Bethlehem, the Solomon parents set up a new residence in Nazareth as the scriptures say, "And being warned in a dream, [the Solomon Joseph] went away [from Bethlehem in Judea where the son of Herod was now ruling] to the district of Galilee. There he made his home in a town called Nazareth." [Matthew 2:19–23]

A SPECIAL SITUATION

One occurrence in which there is biblical support related to the mystery of the two Jesus children occurs later in the lives of the two youths. A better understanding will be developed in a subsequent chapter, but here the biblical data will be presented without the detailed explanation. Remember that, at this point in the sequential development of the stories of the two children, both the Solomon Jesus and the Nathan Jesus are living with their parents in Nazareth, except that the Solomon Joseph has recently died, see Appendix 3. The narrative concerning the visit of the twelve-year-old Nathan Jesus to Jerusalem at the time of the Passover, which occurs only in Luke, is reproduced below in its entirety.

> Now every year [the] parents [of the Nathan Jesus] went to Jerusalem for the festival of the Passover. And when [the Nathan Jesus] was twelve years old, they went up as usual to the festival. When the festival had ended and they started to return, the boy Jesus stayed behind in Jerusalem, but his parents did not know it. Assuming that he was in the group of travelers, they went a day's journey. Then they started looking for him among their relatives and friends. When they did not find him, they returned to Jerusalem to search for him. After three days they found him in the Temple, sitting among the teachers, listening to them and asking them questions. And all who heard him were amazed at his understanding and his answers. When his parents saw him they were astonished; and his mother said to him, "Child, why have you treated us like this? Look, your father and I have been searching for you in great anxiety." He said to them, "Why were you searching for me? Did you not know that I must be in my Father's house?" But they did not understand what he said to them. Then he went down with them and came to Nazareth, and was obedient to them. His mother treasured all these things in her heart. [Luke 2:41–51]

Dr. Heidenreich summarized what occurred as follows, "[The two youths] are taken to Jerusalem. There the event takes place, initially so startling to modern minds, which is both revealed and concealed in the story of the twelve-year-old [Nathan Jesus] in the Temple: the fantastic transformation when the boy is suddenly wise. His parents do not recognize him any more; he can answer, and he himself can ask, searching questions." [9] Dr. Steiner has provided the clue to this "fantastic transformation." The individuality of the Solomon Jesus departed from the Solomon Jesus and entered the Nathan Jesus.[10] That *Zarathustra* individuality, which had reincarnated many times, was the source of the sophisticated "child" who was unable to be recognized by his birth parents. Nevertheless, as the Holy Bible says, he returned to Nazareth with them "and was obedient to them." From this time forward, the critical elements of the two Jesus children had merged. The two streams were joined; the preparation for the Incarnation of the Christ Being had made a significant step forward.

*   *   *

Although this is not biblical evidence, Dr. Heidenreich closes his chapter on the contrasting stories of the childhood of Jesus with a "brief archaeological epilogue." It is a personal tale of his visit to the Holy Land and some observations about Bethlehem and Nazareth. It is repeated here because it is an expression of a thoughtful traveler who had a broad perspective on these events of long ago.

If you go to Bethlehem, you visit, of course, the Church of the Nativity and see the cave, and in the cave the great silver star which shows where the Child was born. But then (a place which you are not shown but can hear about), in another street is the house of Joseph. Naturally, the house that stands there today is not the house in which Joseph lived, but the oriental mind is very retentive, and if, apart from the grotto of the Nativity, they speak in Bethlehem of the house of Joseph, it is not impossible to suggest that here the memory lives that the house of David, the royal family, had a house in Bethlehem, and that it was this house, and not the grotto, where the Magi paid homage. Now we come to Nazareth. There is the so-called Shrine of the Incarnation in an enormous church which the Franciscans have built over the place

---

9. Heidenreich 1972 p. 40.
10. Steiner 2001 pp.115–16.

where Mary was supposed to have received the Annunciation. There is an excavation not very far from it of what is called "the workshop of Joseph." Then, also, there is the convent of nuns of the Congregation of Nazareth, under which was excavated at the beginning of [the twentieth] century a large Byzantine basilica of about the fourth century which was later destroyed in the Moslem invasion of the seventh century. In that big underground basilica there is "The Jewel," a little house of the first century, almost intact; it is supposed to be the house of the Holy Family. The interesting thing is that there are *two* places. Is it likely that Joseph had a workshop at a distance from his house? Or were there, perhaps, two families, the remnants of which are still there? Moreover, of that house in the basilica there is even part of the garden left, and in that garden there is a tomb. When that tomb was opened, it was found to contain relics of the first century, and it smelt of incense. The nuns say, "We have the grave of a saint." They believe, hoping they are right, that it was Joseph's. This is not very likely; it was not customary that a man was buried in his own garden. The Jews at that time either had rock tombs, like the one in which Christ was buried, or they had cemeteries, to which reference is made in the [New Testament]—(St. Matthew, Chapter 8). Who was likely to be buried in the garden next to the house? Of course, I do not know, but is it impossible to think that perhaps…the Matthew child was buried there? I do not know. But with all the new light thrown on these things at various times by Rudolf Steiner, everything looks different, even established archeological data.[11]

The tale speaks for itself, but like the biblical evidence, if one approaches certain findings with a new perspective and an open mind, then it is possible to find confirmation for even what does not seem very plausible at the outset.

---

11. Heidenreich 1972 pp. 43–44.

CHAPTER 5

ARTISTIC EVIDENCE

ONCE AGAIN, a debt to Dr. Alfred Heidenreich should be acknowledged; he was careful to include an artistic perspective in his comparison of the two contrasting stories of the birth narratives for the Solomon Jesus, as presented in Matthew's Gospel, and the Nathan Jesus, as brought forth in Luke's Gospel. Accepting that the story of the kings in Matthew's Gospel and the story of the shepherds in Luke's Gospel were usually combined, he went on to say:

> It is only fair to say that there are some earlier artistic presentations where the contrast also is brought out. I think especially of a wonderful altarpiece (now in a public gallery in Hamburg), painted by Meister Franke at the beginning of the fourteenth century, where both stories are told side by side. In the picture of the Luke story, Mary is painted as a young girl in a white garment with a golden hem, in a kind of natural cave, with the shepherds in the background against the star-studded sky. Next to it is shown a royal lady in a red dress, blue mantle, and wedding ring, in the setting of a house, with the kings coming in; the royal Mary is holding court and receiving homage and presents on behalf of the young prince to whom she has given birth." [1]

Another source for such images is a compilation by Olive Whicher that includes a pair of paintings from the Flemish School that currently

---

1. Alfred Heidenreich *The Unknown in the Gospels* (London: Christian Community Press, 1972) pp. 29–30.

FIGURE 2

reside at Cambridge University in the United Kingdom.[2] This pair of paintings is especially interesting because of a detail that is not always present. In the Nathan Jesus version (on the right of Figure 2) there is only one lone shepherd in view, although many angels are present; and the child, an obvious newborn, is very small. In the Solomon Jesus version (on the left in Figure 2) the child is seated on his mother's lap with head held erect, an infant, not a newborn. This is consistent with the timing provided by Dr. Powell, who affirms that the visit of the Magi occurred some nine months after the birth of the Solomon Jesus, see Appendix 3 for the actual dates.

A third source for artistic images is a compilation by Hella Krause-Zimmer with the intriguing title *Die Zwei Jesuknaben In der Bildenden*

---

2. Olive Whicher *Sun Space: Science at a Threshold of Spiritual Understanding* (London: Rudolf Steiner Press, 1989) p. 90.

FIGURE 3

Kunst (*The Two Jesus Children in Pictorial Art*). [3] Plate 34 in this volume
is called the *Terranuova Madonna* and was painted c. 1505 by Raphael;
it currently resides at the Staatliche Museen zu Berlin, Gemaldegalarie,
Berlin, Germany. Although Raphael painted many Madonnas—some
without child, some with one child, and some with two children—this
painting is unusual in that there are three children in it. When there are
two children in a depiction of the Madonna, it is usually easy to recognize that one of the children is the young John the Baptizer, because he
generally has a staff with a cross on the top of it. Here with three children, this particular artist has something special to communicate (see
Figure 3).

---

3. Hella Krause-Zimmer *Die Zwei Jesuknaben in der Bildenden Kunst* (*The Two Jesus Children in Pictorial Art*) (Stuttgart: Verlag Freies Geistesleben, 1969) plate 34.

FIGURE 4

And Raphael is not alone. Plate 38 from the above volume depicts a holy family scene that also has three young children in it. To the left is a seated child writing on a scroll at a little desk looking up at a second child in the central figure's lap. The third child to the right is obviously John the Baptizer since he holds a lamb in his hands and has a staff with a cross on it. There are also five adults in this image: from left to right, there is a female with a white veil and a wimple, there is a male who is partially bald and has a beard, there is the central female figure, there is a younger male without a beard, and finally another female with a white veil but no wimple. The identity of these persons is more difficult than those of the three children, but it may be possible to discern relationships by the grouping of the figures. If the child on the left is the Solomon Jesus, then the couple on the left would be the Solomon Mary and the Solomon Joseph, who may have been older than the Nathan Joseph. The central female with the child on her lap and the younger male would be the Nathan Mary, the Nathan Jesus, and the Nathan Joseph. And the final right-hand female would be Saint Elizabeth, the mother of John the Baptizer who stands in front of her. This

FIGURE 5

painting is attributed to Bernart van Orley; but there is a question mark which suggests that this is not certain. The original is currently in San Francisco (see Figure 4).

Finally, Dr. Heidenreich tells of a Renaissance painting by Borgognoni currently found in one of the side chapels in the church of San Ambrogio in Milan, Italy.[4] This image is also present in the previously cited reference (see Figure 5).

It depicts, in the foreground, a young boy with golden hair and a halo, wearing a red robe, seated on a raised chair. He is surrounded by older men who are paying close attention to what the young boy is saying. At the left of the painting is a young boy of similar appearance who also has blond hair and a halo, in the same dress, but the colors are faded. A young woman folds her garment about the lad and leads him away. She too wears a halo, suggesting that she is the Nathan Mary, the mother of the Nathan Jesus. This idea is reinforced by the presence of a

---

4. Heidenreich 1972 p. 41.

bearded man behind her who also wears a halo. The artist has depicted the moment in time when the anxious parents of the Nathan Jesus have found the son whom they had lost coming home from the Festival of the Passover in Jerusalem. But instead of the quiet, simple, and loving child whom they were accustomed to, he had been transformed into a scholar who could hold his own with the elders of the Temple. Of course, from the perspective of the current discourse, this occurred because the individuality of Zarathustra had been transferred from the Solomon Jesus to the Nathan Jesus, who now had all the accumulated wisdom of the "Radiant Star."[5]

Recently, another scholar has brought forward evidence for there being two Jesus children.[6] Ovason reviews not only the literary tradition but also the artistic one. He suggests that Renaissance artists were walking a fine line between wanting to depict the two Jesus children that the literary tradition presented and trying to avoid being accused of heresy.[7] He affirms that the use of the accepted attributes for John the Baptizer was a device "to disguise the heretical Two Jesus theme." His volume is extensive; the 412 pages of text, with many excellent line illustrations, are buttressed by 45 pages of notes in fine print. He seems to have arrived not only at an acknowledgment of the legitimacy of the concept of the two Jesus children that is independent of Dr. Steiner's formulation, which however he does acknowledge, but he also has developed a rationale for why there should have been more than one Jesus child. Since it is consistent with the rationale presented in this discourse, it seems worthwhile to quote the last paragraph of his concluding chapter.

> Stripped of all its arcane literature, and divorced from the rich heritage of art to which *The Two Children* have given rise, the story we have just examined seems reasonable. It is reasonable that, for a God to descend into a living body, a supporting power would have to descend from the heavens much like a falling star. It is reasonable that, for a perfect earthly body to be prepared as a

5. Rudolf Steiner *From Jesus To Christ* (trsl. Charles Davy, Sussex, England: Rudolf Steiner Press, 1991) p.134.
6. David Ovason *The Two Children: A Study of the Two Jesus Children in Literature and Art* (London: Century, 2001).
7. Ibid. pp. 286ff.

temporary housing for this God, whole generations should have been involved in its making. It is reasonable that, in the final phase of this operation, when the long-awaited Messiah was poised to descend into flesh, the two perfections of Stars and Earth should combine their wisdom and their power. In such a way, human flesh was quickened by a stellar light, to be a worthy receptacle for a God who died, and was resurrected, and who promised to stay with humanity until the end of time.[8]

Dr. Powell's *Chronicle of the Living Christ* was published five years before *The Two Children*. Ovason, apparently, was not aware of this earlier source. Had he been able to incorporate Dr. Powell's definitive dates into *The Two Children,* it would have enabled him to present his argument in a more compelling manner.

---

8. Ovason 2001 p. 412.

CHAPTER 6

PREPARATION FOR
THE INCARNATION

IN ORDER TO comprehend the full extent of the preparation for the Incarnation of the Christ Being it will be necessary to delve deeper into the esoteric lore that was alluded to in Chapter 3. Therefore, as a prelude to addressing the title subject, it would seem appropriate to set out some understandings that are fundamental to that perspective.

ANTHROPOSOPHICAL VERITIES

1. **The primacy of the spiritual world** ~ The spiritual world existed before the material world was created and will remain after the material world is no more.

2. **The great cosmic planetary cycles of evolution** ~ There are three kinds of cycles: 1) the three that have previously occurred, called Old Saturn, Old Sun, and Old Moon; 2) the current one, called Earth; and 3) the three cycles that are yet to come, called Jupiter, Venus, and Vulcan. The former planetary cycles brought forth warmth, gases, and liquids, respectively. Solids are a manifestation of the current planetary cycle, which is called Earth; they will be absent from subsequent cycles. Liquids will be absent from Venus and Vulcan; gases will not be present in Vulcan, only warmth.

3. **The purpose of the material world** ~ The material world was created as an environment for the spiritual development of humanity. As used here, humanity must be understood on more than one level. Usually, the word humanity refers to creatures of

flesh and blood in the Earth planetary cycle of evolution, but the key to that humanity is that portion of the human being known as the individuality and the other three higher elements: spirit self, life self, and spirit body. In earlier planetary cycles of evolution, the word humanity has been used where once again it referred to the individuality, or its equivalent, even if the conditions were very different from those in our current planetary cycle.

4. The nature of the human being ⁓ The present earthly human being consists of seven elements: a physical body, an ether body, an astral body, an individuality, a spirit self, a life spirit, and a spirit body.

5. The fundamentals of reincarnation ⁓ At the time of a death in the material world, the first three elements of the human being—the physical body, the ether body, and the astral body—unite with the make-up of the perishable material world; the four higher elements—the individuality, the spirit self, the life spirit, and the spirit body—unite with the eternal spiritual world. Thus, a death in the material world is a birth in the spiritual world; and a death in the spiritual world is a birth in the material world. This process is repeated many times for every individual member of humanity.

6. The nature of the Christ Being ⁓ The Christ Being is at the highest level in the spiritual world.[1] His three-and-one-half-year incarnation in the material world is the most important event that has ever happened! There will be a "Second Coming," but the Christ Being will not come into the material realm again; it is humanity that will develop new organs of vision and hearing to seek him, to find him, and to interact with him in the realm of the ether body. This will happen relatively soon and certainly before the Day of Judgment, which is still many centuries into the future.[2]

1. For a discussion of the highest levels in the spiritual world, see Rudolf Steiner *The Spiritual Hierarchies and the Physical World: Reality and Illusion* (trsl. R.M. Querido and Jann Gates, Hudson, NY: Anthroposophic Press, 1996) pp.151–52.
2. For a sense of how far into the future the Day of Judgment will be, see Figure 1.

THE PREPARATION

The Incarnation of the Christ Being was a unique event. The spiritual world prepared for this occurrence by making sure that the human vehicle for the Incarnation was properly suited. The usual incarnation consists of a single individuality attaching itself to the same physical body for an entire life in the material world. In this instance, at the outset, an individuality that was a representative of the *kingly* tradition incarnated in the physical body of the Solomon Jesus. Then several years later a second individuality that was a representative of the *priestly* tradition incarnated in the physical body of the Nathan Jesus. After a suitable period of maturation, the individuality of the Nathan Jesus was joined by the individuality of the Solomon Jesus, which entered the prepared vehicle of the Nathan Jesus. After further maturation, that joined individuality departed to make way for the Incarnation of the Christ Being. Without this elaborate preparation, an ordinary human entity would not have been able to tolerate the presence of the Christ Being as its individuality.

The spiritual world prepared for this event in ways that extend well beyond any single faith tradition. In fact, the influences of the ancient Indian, ancient Persian, and ancient Egypto-Chaldean traditions were incorporated into the preparation. Additionally, the Hebrew people were selected as the vehicle for the Incarnation because a number of elements in their tradition were a reasonable approximation of spiritual reality. A review of some of these elements now follows.

Hebraic Traditions

1. **Belief in a monotheistic God** ~ This is reasonably straightforward. The first of the Ten Commandments is a condensed version of this concept: "I am the Lord your God who brought you out of the land of Egypt, out of the house of slavery; you shall have no other gods besides me." [Exodus 20:2–3]

2. **Belief that God created the earth** ~ Once again the Old Testament provides the fundamentals. It is important to acknowledge that "Yahweh's creative work was understood in a completely different sense from the creation beliefs among Babylonians, Egyptians, or Canaanites." [3]

---

3. *The Interpreters Dictionary of the Bible* (Nashville, TN: Abingdon,1962) vol. 1, p. 725.

3. Belief that our earliest ancestors brought about an alienation *(the Fall)* **between God and humanity** ⁓ Although the story of Adam, Eve, and the serpent can be presumed to be an allegory, it does suggest that human behavior brought about such an alienation. The interpretation of that event has varied over time. "Where earlier generations of Jews and Christians had once found in Genesis 1–3 the affirmation of human freedom to choose good or evil, Augustine, living after the age of Constantine, found in the same text a story of human bondage." [4]

4. Belief that the children of Israel were favored of God ⁓ The history of the Hebrew people as found in the Old Testament abounds with examples to support that belief: the preservation from the flood (Genesis), the deliverance at the Red Sea (Exodus), and the redevelopment of Jerusalem after the exile to Babylon (Ezekiel).

5. Belief in a role for prophets ⁓ Once again, the Old Testament abounds with support. In earlier times, the Hebrew scriptures were referred to simply as the Law and the Prophets. [Matthew 32:36]

6. Belief in a role for priests ⁓ At Sinai, Aaron and his sons, of the tribe of Levi, were appointed to the priesthood; the office became hereditary and restricted to that family. [Exodus 28:1; 40:12–15]

7. Belief in a role for kings ⁓ Although the Hebrew people resisted the idea of a king for some time, eventually, with God's concurrence, a regal dynasty was established. [1 Samuel 9–11]

8. Belief in the coming of a Messiah ⁓ The future hope of Israel was set forth in the prophecies of Isaiah and Micah. [Isaiah 11; Micah 7:13–20]

With these fundamentals in mind, it is time to present, in greater detail, the nature of the two individualities that were involved in the preparation for the Incarnation of the Christ Being.

THE "RADIANT STAR" INDIVIDUALITY

In Dr. Steiner's own words:

The individuality that we know as the Zarathustra of ancient Persian culture reincarnated in the [Solomon Jesus].... To the Persians, Zarathustra proclaimed the existence of Ahura Mazda,

---

4. Elaine Pagels *Adam, Eve, and the Serpent* (New York: Vintage Books, 1989) p. 97.

who would later be called the Christ. In Zarathustra's time, this being did not yet walk the earth. Zarathustra could only point to the Sun, saying, "He lives there and is gradually approaching the earth; one day he will inhabit an earthly body...."[5]

Zarathustra had two pupils, the individuality who later reappeared as the Egyptian Hermes and the [individuality] who later reappeared as Moses.... We must recognize that Zarathustra's astral body reincarnated in the Egyptian Hermes to allow all the outer science that Zarathustra had absorbed to reappear in the material world. Moses received Zarathustra's ether body. Because everything that [is related to the concept of] time is linked to the ether body, Moses...was able to awaken temporal processes in the great and mighty images we encounter in Genesis. Thus the power of Zarathustra's individuality worked on, inaugurating and influencing [not only the Persian culture but also] the [ancient] Egyptian and the ancient Hebrew cultures.[6]

Dr. Steiner makes it clear that such an individuality who lived as Zarathustra was destined for further greatness. An individuality who learns to give away his original astral and ether bodies is always able to consecrate another astral body and strengthen another ether body. Thus, about six hundred years before the beginning of our era, Zarathustra was reborn as Zaratas, who became a teacher in the Chaldean mystery center. In fact, he was the teacher of Pythagoras. Everything that Zaratas taught targeted the outer world and attempted to imbue it with order and harmony. Thus his pupils were not only great initiates but also kings. They called their leader "Radiant Star" because in him they saw reflected the glory of the sun. *Their master's reappearance in Bethlehem could not remain hidden from their profound wisdom.* Led by their star, these kings traveled across the desert to bring him outer tokens of the gifts he had given to human beings. This wisdom was symbolized by gold, frankincense, and myrrh. That is, gold for thinking, frankincense for feeling, and myrrh for willing. [7]

---

5. Steiner 2001 pp. 103ff.
6. Ibid. p. 107.
7. Ibid. p. 108.

This then is an approximation of the nature of the Radiant Star individuality that incarnated in the Solomon Jesus. Before turning to the second nativity story, it is appropriate to establish some dates regarding the events related to the Solomon Jesus.

SIGNIFICANT DATES IN THE LIFE OF THE SOLOMON JESUS [8]

Date of Birth

According to Dr. Powell, a key to establishing the birth date of the Solomon Jesus is the "Star of the Magi" spoken of in Matthew's Gospel.

In the time of King Herod, after Jesus was born in Bethlehem of Judea, Magi from the East came to Jerusalem, asking, "Where is the child who has been born king of the Jews? For we observed his star at its rising, and have come to pay him homage. [Matthew. 2:1–3]

The German astronomer Johannes Kepler (1571–1630 C.E.), in his work *De Stella Nova* (The New Star), indicated that the Star of the Magi was bound up with three conjunctions of the planets Jupiter and Saturn that occurred in 7 B.C.E. The birth of the Solomon Jesus took place *shortly after* the last of these three conjunctions when Mars joined the conjunction with Jupiter and Saturn.

Next, it must be determined more precisely what "shortly after" means. Dr. Powell takes more than two pages in a meticulous review of relevant scholarly sources to suggest that the date of the birth of the Solomon Jesus was March 5, 6 B.C.E. Dr. Powell then uses information from his two clairvoyant sources, Sister Emmerich and Dr. Steiner, to confirm that this is the correct date.[9]

Presentation of the Solomon Jesus at the Temple

Unlike the presentation at the Temple described in great detail in Luke, Matthew does not mention such an occurrence for the Solomon Jesus. It is inconceivable that persons as devout as the Solomon Joseph

---

8. For a summary of significant dates, as developed from data by Powell, see Appendix 3.
9. Powell 1996 pp. 68ff.

and the Solomon Mary would have failed to fulfill the obligation to present their first-born male child at the Temple as required by Hebrew Law. It seems strange that the author of the Matthew gospel did not catalog that event. Sister Emmerich provides some information that is attributable to this subject, and Dr. Powell has been able to derive from it a date for this event. It is April 17, 6 B.C.E., which is based on the forty-third day after the birth of the Solomon Jesus.[10] In her vision, Sister Emmerich sees the Solomon Mary giving to the Temple "five triangular pieces of gold from the [Magi's] gift." *There is a problem here.* The presentation to the Temple occurred well before the visit of the Magi.

Dr. Powell and the author have had some correspondence on this matter.[11] The best explanation may be that the Solomon Holy Family made a second visit to the Temple before they went to Egypt; and Sister Emmerich had a vision of this visit that was somehow confused in her mind with the earlier visit to the Temple for the presentation.

Date of the Visit of the Three Kings and Related Events

Although the Magi observed unusual stellar configurations that told them that their leader was about to incarnate again, they were far away from Bethlehem. It took time for the one furthest away "across the Caspian Sea" to join the other two and make the long journey by camel to Bethlehem. They did not arrive until December 26, 6 B.C.E., some nine and one half months after the birth of the Solomon Jesus.

A related event is the Flight into Egypt. Although Matthew suggests that this happened soon after the visit of the Magi, according to Dr. Powell it did not actually occur until February 29, 5 B.C.E., when the Solomon Jesus was almost one year old.

A second related event is the Massacre of the Innocents. Here, too, there was some delay. It did not occur until about September 15, 5 B.C.E., when the Solomon Jesus was approximately one and a half years old. This explains why all male children in Bethlehem up to two years of age were killed by Herod's soldiers.

A third related event is the Death of King Herod. The date favored by Dr. Powell is January 28, 1 B.C.E.[12] This date is somewhat later than

---

10. Powell 1996 n. 2.
11. Robert Powell (Personal communication dated October 10, 2001).
12. Powell 1996 pp. 67ff

earlier sources suggested, but once again Dr. Powell has used various authorities to arrive at that date, which is supported by Edwards.[13] That date is also consistent with the return from Egypt of the Solomon Holy Family, which will be taken up next.

Return from Egypt

When the family of the Solomon Jesus came back from Egypt in 2 C.E., rather than returning to Bethlehem where they had originally lived, they settled in Nazareth.

> When Herod died, an angel of the Lord suddenly appeared in a dream to Joseph in Egypt and said, "Get up, take the child and his mother, and go to the land of Israel, for those who were seeking the child's life are dead." Then Joseph got up, took the child and his mother, and went to the land of Israel. But when he heard that Archelaus was ruling over Judea in place of his father Herod, he was afraid to go there. And after being warned in a dream, he went away to the district of Galilee. There he made his home in a town called Nazareth, ... [Matthew 2:19–23]

By this time, the Nathan Jesus had been born in Bethlehem, and the Nathan Holy Family had returned to Nazareth. Thus it came about that the Solomon Jesus and the Nathan Jesus grew up in the same village.

THE "SPECIAL INDIVIDUALITY" OF THE NATHAN JESUS

Now consider the second nativity story and see what sort of an individuality was sent for that portion of the mission. Dr. Steiner says:

> Old [individualities] that have worked on themselves through many incarnations accomplish great deeds on behalf of human-ity and teach great ideas, but they sacrifice youthful freshness and strength for the sake of this progress.[14]

---

13. Ormond Edwards *When was Anno Domini?: Dating the Millennium* (Edinburgh: Floris Books, 1999) p. 46.
14. Steiner 2001 pp. 91ff.

Dr. Steiner goes on to explain that the Special Individuality that was to incarnate in the Nathan Jesus:

> …came from the great mother lodge of humanity, led by the great Sun initiate Manu. A great individual force, lavished with care and attention in the great mother lodge, was sent down into the [Nathan Jesus] who was born to the couple the Luke Gospel calls Joseph and Mary. This child received the best and strongest of the individualities fostered by the Sun oracle.

In a subsequent lecture, Dr. Steiner clarified that a suitably ennobled human body could not have been produced without incorporating the etheric substance taken from the sister soul of Adam, which, having never incarnated, had been untouched by the Fall, into the ether body of the Nathan Jesus.[15] This explains why, in the genealogy as recorded in the Luke gospel (see Table 1), the paternity of the Nathan Jesus is traced back to God rather than only to Abraham as in the genealogy of the Solomon Jesus.

In a lecture cycle delivered in Leipzig in 1913–14, Dr. Steiner made clear that this Special Individuality had been previously "enlivened by the Christ Being on three different occasions."[16] The first of these occurred in the Lemurian Age at a time when the forces of *Lucifer* and *Ahriman* were attempting to prevent the proper development of the sense organs of the human physical body (seeing, hearing, smelling, tasting, and touching). The second of these occurrences took place in the Atlantean Age at a time when once again the forces of Lucifer and Ahriman were attempting to prevent the proper development of the vital organs of the human ether body (respiration, circulation, and digestion). And finally, at a later time in the Post-Atlantean Age when the soul powers of the human astral body (thinking, feeling, and willing) were in jeopardy from Luciferic and Ahrimanic forces, the Christ Being once more called on this Special Individuality, whose intervention assured that "human thinking, feeling, and willing took an orderly course."

---

15. Steiner 2001 122.
16. Rudolf Steiner *Christ and the Spiritual World: The Search for the Holy Grail* (trsl. C. Day and D. Osmond, London: Rudolf Steiner Press, 1963) pp. 54ff.

This, then, is an approximation of the exalted nature of the Special Individuality that incarnated in the Nathan Jesus. Now it is necessary to review how this birth related to the Ancient Indian tradition.

Adoration of the Shepherds

In the second lecture of the cycle titled *According to Luke*, Dr. Steiner indicates some results from an investigation of the Akashic record that relate to the conversion of spiritual streams. He says:

> ... [The] power and urgency of love [is unfolded to a greater extent in Luke's Gospel] than in any other Christian document.... A wonderful passage in the Luke Gospel tells us that an angel appeared to the shepherds out in the fields and proclaimed the birth of the "Savior which is Christ the Lord."... As strange as it may sound, if we trace the angel's revelation to the shepherds back through the Akashic record to earlier times, we come to the enlightenment of the great Buddha.... The Buddha was a bodhisattva before he became a buddha.... [T]his being was the Bodhisattva who taught us love, compassion, and all related virtues.... Once the bodhisattva became the Buddha, he no longer needed to return to earth. Since then, he has existed as a purely spiritual being, influencing events on earth from the spiritual world. As the most important event in earthly evolution approached, ["a multitude of the heavenly host"] appeared in the spiritual heights to the shepherds out in the fields.... What was this host? The image that appeared to the shepherds was the transfigured Buddha, the spiritual figure of the bodhisattva of ancient times, the being that brought the message of love and compassion to human beings for millennia. Now that this being had completed his final earthly incarnation, he hovered in spiritual heights and appeared to the shepherds besides the angel who proclaimed what was to happen in Palestine.... This power worked toward the greatest event of all time as it shone above the [Nathan Jesus] and prepared him to take his rightful place in the evolution of humanity.[17]

---

17. Steiner 2001 pp. 37ff.

SIGNIFICANT DATES IN THE LIFE OF THE NATHAN JESUS

Date of Birth

Determining the actual date of birth of the Nathan Jesus was a masterpiece of scholarly research by Dr. Robert Powell. It has already been detailed how Dr. Powell arrived at the date of the crucifixion (see Chapter 3) which is an important starting point in arriving at the date of birth of the Nathan Jesus. Now it is time to retrace the remainder of the logical sequence.

The visions of Sister Emmerich, as recorded by Clemens Brentano in *The Life of the Blessed Virgin Mary,* include information that can be used to derive that date of birth.[18] According to this description, the birth took place around midnight on the day after the Sabbath. As Dr. Powell elaborates, "Since the Jewish Sabbath falls on Saturday, and the Jewish day begins at sunset, the Sabbath day extends from sunset Friday to sunset Saturday. The birth took place, therefore, around the midnight between Saturday and Sunday."[19] From that same source, it was also possible to determine that the birth took place during the Jewish month of Kislev. The visions of Sister Emmerich permit a greater precision. The proximity to the Feast of the Dedication of the Temple, which extended the days between the birth and the circumcision by one day, makes it possible to say that the birth occurred on the twelfth day of Kislev.[20]

Dr. Powell has become an expert on the intricacies of the Jewish calendar in use in this era. In his Appendix II he devotes three and a half pages to describing the Babylonian origins of the Hebrew Lunar calendar and how the extra days were distributed to reconcile it with the annual calendar based on the Sun.[21] The next appendix is devoted to a "Reconstruction of the Hebrew Calendar for the Time of Christ's Ministry Based on Anne Catherine Emmerich's Calendar Indications."[22] Without discussing this content in detail (some additional material in Appendix 2 of the current volume is devoted to

18. Emmerich 1954a pp. 191–93.
19. Powell 1996 p. 28.
20. Emmerich 1954a pp. 240–41.
21. Powell 1996 pp. 444–47.
22. Ibid. pp. 447–55.

authentication) it is clear that Dr. Powell is convinced that Sister Emmerich's "calendar indications are in fact virtually completely consistent—mutually supporting—in accord with the actual months of the Hebrew calendar for the period of [Sister Emmerich's] description of the ministry of Christ Jesus—on the whole, historically accurate indeed." [23]

Having an hour, day, and month, however, is not sufficient. It is necessary to determine the year. For that, Dr. Powell turns to another vision of Sister Emmerich that relates to the length of the life of Jesus Christ. She states, "Christ reached the age of thirty-three years and three times six weeks. I say three times six [weeks] because that figure was in that moment shown to me three times one after the other." [24] So now all falls into place. With the previously established date of the crucifixion as Friday, April 3, 33 C.E., it is possible to work backward and state that the birth occurred around midnight on Saturday/Sunday of Kislev 12 in 2 B.C.E., which converts to December 6/7 2 B.C.E. Dr. Powell provides a comparison of other proposed dates and rationalizations as to why his date should be preferred. [25] It should be noted that this birth date of the Nathan Jesus occurred *four years and nine months after* the birth of the Solomon Jesus as described earlier in this chapter.

Details of the Birth of the Nathan Jesus

From the English translation of Sister Emmerich's visions we have the following details.

When [the Nathan] Mary told [the Nathan] Joseph that her time was drawing near and that he should now betake himself to prayer, he left her and turned toward his sleeping place to do her bidding. Before entering his little recess, he looked back once toward that part of the cave where [the Nathan] Mary knelt upon her couch in prayer, her back to him, her face toward the east. He saw the cave filled with the light that streamed from [the

23. Powell 1996 p. 455.
24. Emmerich 1954a p. 145.
25. Powell 1996 p. 34.

Nathan] Mary, for she was entirely enveloped as if by flames. It
was as if he were, like Moses, looking at the burning bush. He
sank prostrate to the ground in prayer, and looked not back
again. The glory around [the Nathan] Mary became brighter
and brighter, the lamps that [the Nathan] Joseph had lit were
no longer to be seen.... At that moment she gave birth to the
[Nathan] Jesus. I saw Him like a tiny, shining Child, lying on a
rug at her knees, and brighter far than all the other brilliancy.[26]

And from Saint Birgitta of Sweden, who experienced these visions
some 350 years earlier, a similar story.

When I was present by the manger of the Lord in Bethlehem, I
beheld a Virgin of extreme beauty wrapped in a white mantle
and a delicate tunic through which I perceived her virgin body
soon to be delivered. With her was an old man of great honesty,
and they brought with them an ox and a donkey. These entered
the cave, and the man, after having tied them to the manger,
went outside and brought to the Virgin a burning candle; having attached this to the wall, he went outside so that he might
not be present at the birth.... When all these things were
ready, then the Virgin, kneeling with great reverence, placed
herself in prayer, with her back to the crib, her face eastward,
raised to heaven.... And while she stood in prayer, I beheld her
Child move in the womb and at once, in a twinkling of an eye,
she brought forth her Son, from Whom such ineffable light
and splendor radiated that the sun could not be compared to it;
nor did the candle which the old man set in any manner give
light, because that divine splendor had totally annihilated the
material splendor of the candle,... I immediately beheld that
glorious babe lying naked and most pure on the ground,... [27]

26. Anne Catherine Emmerich *The Life of Jesus Christ and Biblical Revelations: From the
Visions of the Venerable Anne Catherine Emmerich as recorded in the journals of Clemens Bren-
tano* (trsl. anonymous, arr. and ed. The Very Reverend Carl E. Schmöger, C.SS.R., Fresno,
CA: Academy Library Guild 1954b; also reprinted, Rockford, IL: TAN Books, 1986) vol.
I, pp. 226–27.
27. Anthony Butkovich *Revelations: Saint Birgitta of Sweden* (Los Angeles Ecumenical
Foundation of America, 1972) p. 29.

Presentation at the Temple of the Nathan Jesus

This event is well-detailed in Luke's Gospel and there is no need to repeat that material here. But, for the sake of completeness, it should be indicated that the presentation occurred on January 15, 1 B.C.E.[28]

First Visit of the Nathan Jesus to the Temple for the Passover

It was the custom in Israel, in those days, to journey to the Temple in Jerusalem for the Festival of the Passover. At the Passover of 8 C.E., the Nathan Jesus, having attained the age of eight, for the first time accompanied his parents to Jerusalem, and he continued to do so in each subsequent year. "He was a pure and loving child but did not yet display any sign of genius."[29]

THE TWO BECOMING ONE

In an earlier work, Dr. Robert Powell describes how the two Jesus children became one. (Rather than paraphrase that language, it is inserted here verbatim except that emendations have been made to preserve the Consistent Nomenclature effort previously developed in this volume.)

> After the end of the [Festival] of the Passover in 12 [C.E.], the twelve-year-old [Nathan] Jesus parted company with his parents and set off on the return journey with other youth from Nazareth. But while still in Jerusalem, not far from the Mount of Olives, he took leave of his youthful friends, who thought he was going to rejoin his parents. It was at this moment in time that the two Jesus children became one. The decision on the part of the [Nathan] Jesus to separate from his parents and friends and return to Jerusalem came about through the union of the [Solomon] Jesus with him, an inner union whereby the [individuality] of "Radiant Star" separated from [the Solomon Jesus'] body and united with the [Special Individuality] to indwell the

---

28. Powell 1996 p. 102.
29. Powell 1998 p. 53.

[Nathan Jesus'] body. This was the joining together of the two lineages in Jesus—the kingly line from Solomon and the priestly line from Nathan. Two months after this occurrence, the body of the [Solomon] Jesus—now just seventeen years old—having [lost its individuality], was laid to rest.[30]

To acknowledge, in this discourse, the transformation of the Nathan Jesus, he will be referred to as Jesus of Nazareth until the next transformation. A table of Consistent Nomenclature has been provided, see Table 3. Dr. Powell continues the Jerusalem story and details how Jesus of Nazareth, imbued with the great wisdom of the "Radiant Star," went to one of the rabbinic schools and discoursed with doctors and scribes and astounded them with his questions and answers. The next day he repeated this at a second school, and on the morning of the third day again at a third school. By this time his parents, who had met up with the youths of Nazareth at a small village north of Jerusalem, had discovered his absence. They were greatly concerned for the boy's safety and set off back to Jerusalem to try to find him.

On the afternoon of the third day since his transformation, Jesus of Nazareth was in the great hall of Solomon in the Temple itself. There he sat upon a large chair surrounded by rabbis and many others who had gathered to listen to him and to dispute with him. The doctors and scribes intended to humble the youth, who had embarrassed them with his profound knowledge during the past three days. They put one question after another to him, not only of a theological kind but also concerning nature, art, and science. Jesus of Nazareth answered and taught. In reality the rabbis were confronted by the wisest of souls—"Radiant Star"—whose wisdom had been accumulated through numerous incarnations upon the Earth. Jesus of Nazareth discoursed with a facility beyond the reach of even the most learned rabbi, on astronomy, geometry, arithmetic, architecture, jurisprudence, medicine, agriculture, and every issue they put to him.

---

30. Powell 1998 p. 53.

TABLE 3 : *Consistent Nomenclature—Christ Jesus*

SOLOMON LINE   NATHAN LINE

Solomon Jesus
Born: March 5, 6 B.C.E.
Individuality: Zarathustra

Nathan Jesus
Born: December 6, 2 B.C.E.
Individuality: "Special" (see text)

First Transfer of Individuality
Jesus of Nazareth

Transfer: April 3, 12 C.E.
(At the time of the Festival of the Passover)
Individuality: "Special" + Zarathustra

Second Transfer of Individuality
Christ Jesus

Transfer: September 23, 29 C.E.
(At the time of the baptism in the River Jordan)
Individuality: Christ Being

After he had been teaching for some two hours, his parents entered the Temple and finally found him. They were quite awed and astonished at the remarkable transformation that had taken place in their son, for they saw he had increased in wisdom and stature. Great was their joy at finding him, but they were also perplexed at his new-found independent spirit, and they reprimanded him for causing them so much sorrow and anxiety. Obediently, he returned with them to Nazareth. From this time onwards he became a teacher among his companions, giving instruction when they walked or talked together.[31]

---

31. Powell 1998 pp. 54–55.

THE SECOND MERGER

In a lecture given in Oslo on October 5, 1913, Dr. Steiner indicated, "We also know that the two families had come together after the mother of the Nathan [Jesus] and the father of the Solomon [Jesus] had died and that Jesus [of Nazareth] who then also bore the Zarathustra [individuality] grew up in the combined family." [32] Dr. Powell adds a few more details.

The further life and destiny of the Solomon Mary after the birth of [the Solomon] Jesus was highly eventful: the visit of the Magi to the house of [the Solomon] Joseph in Bethlehem, the flight to Egypt, the return to Israel, the start of a new life in Nazareth, the birth of six further children, the death of her husband before the Passover 12 [C.E.], followed by the death of her seventeen-year-old [Solomon] Jesus in June 12 [C.E.]. A new life began for her when she married [the Nathan] Joseph of Nazareth, who had been left a widower with one child, the twelve-year-old Jesus of Nazareth, following the death of the Nathan Mary, August 4/5, 12 [C.E.].[33]

Strange as it may seem, Jesus of Nazareth, whose own mother never had any additional children, acquired four brothers—James, Joseph, Simon, and Judas—and two sisters whose names are not included in the gospel passages that describe these relationships. [Matthew 13:55–56] The combined family lived in Nazareth until the death of the Nathan Joseph which took place before the Passover of 29 C.E.[34] At that time the Solomon Mary moved to a house between Capernaum and Bethsaida, which is mentioned in both Sister Emmerich's visions and also the canonical gospels.

CHANGES AT THE TIME OF THE BAPTISM

The final chapter in the preparation for the Incarnation of the Christ Being occurs before the baptism in the River Jordan on September 23,

32. Rudolf Steiner *The Fifth Gospel: From the Akashic Record* (trsl. A.R. Meuss, London, Rudolf Steiner Press, 1995) p. 45.
33. Powell 1996 p. 133.
34. Emmerich 1954b vol. I, pp. 330–31.

29 C.E. There is still some of the mystery that is not completely explained. In *The Fifth Gospel*, Dr. Steiner devotes several pages to a conversation that Jesus of Nazareth had with the Solomon Mary shortly before the baptism.[35] This is also mentioned by Dr. Powell, who summarizes the conversation before using a direct quotation from Sister Emmerich regarding the very same conversation.[36] Then Dr. Powell goes on to quote Dr. Steiner's interpretation of the significance of that conversation. In spite of all this material related to the same event, there is still some confusion regarding what actually took place.

There is the individuality of Jesus of Nazareth, whether thought of as only the former Zarathustra individuality or a merger of that individuality and the Special Individuality that incarnated into the Nathan Jesus at birth, reviewing details of his life for his stepmother, the Solomon Mary, with whom Jesus of Nazareth had become very close since the merger of the two families some seven years before. In fact, the suggestion has been made that it was not just a conversation, but that portions of Jesus of Nazareth's individuality were actually transferred to the Solomon Mary. Dr. Steiner puts it this way: "We might say that the [Jesus of Nazareth's individuality] seemed to go across, as it were, though it did not in fact go across; it was merely that his [stepmother] felt she was given new life by those words."[37] At that time, the entire individuality had to leave Jesus of Nazareth in order for the Christ Being to be able to incarnate in that prepared vehicle, but the details of the actual transfer were not made clear in the cited sources. It is indicated that after the "conversation," Jesus of Nazareth felt compelled to seek out John the Baptizer and that he journeyed in a dreamlike state to the place of baptism.

Dr. Steiner also affirms that as a result of the aforementioned "conversation" another event of considerable importance took place. "The strange effect of this talk was that the *soul* of the [Nathan Mary] who had been the physical mother of the Nathan [Jesus] came down from the world of the spirit and united with the *soul* of the foster mother. After that talk, the *soul* of the Nathan [Jesus'] true mother had been received into [the Solomon Mary's] *soul*. Virginity was reborn, as it

---

35. Steiner 1995 pp. 122ff.
36. Powell 1996 pp. 107–08.
37. Steiner 1995 p. 129.

were." (There will be more on this subject in the next chapter.) In recognition of this change, the Solomon Mary will, in this discourse, be called the *Blessed Virgin Mary* from this moment forward in time, not only in the text but in the pertinent support materials in the appendices.

One final task remains—to confirm that the most important transfer of all time took place at the time of the baptism. For this purpose reliance is placed on the words of Dr. Powell, who says, "It was at this moment, when he was baptized, that the cosmic being of Christ descended to unite with Jesus of Nazareth." [38] This concept is also reinforced by Dr. Steiner, who says, "During the baptism the Christ *spirit* entered the body of Jesus [of Nazareth]." [39] But the most beautiful formulation comes from Sister Emmerich who put it this way:

> They were just mounting the steps when the voice of God came over Jesus [of Nazareth] who was still standing alone and in prayer upon the stone. There came from heaven a great, rushing wind like thunder. All trembled and looked up. A cloud of white light descended, and I saw over Jesus [of Nazareth] a winged figure of light as if flowing over him like a stream…. [He] was perfectly transparent, entirely penetrated by light. One could scarcely look at him. [40]

Only one additional element remains. The translation of the New Revised Standard Version of the New Testament indicates that the voice from the clouds said, "You are my Son, the Beloved; with you I am well pleased." [Luke 3:22] A footnote indicates: "Other ancient authorities read, 'You are my Son, today I have begotten you.'" Dr. Powell favors the alternate version. He says:

> The latter is, in fact, closer to the true significance of the moment of the baptism, for the baptism was at the same time the *birth* of Christ, that is, his union with the earthly Jesus [of Nazareth]. At this moment Jesus [of Nazareth] becomes *Christ Jesus.* [41]

Now the Preparation has been completed. The Incarnation of the Christ Being has begun.

38. Powell 1996 p. 109.
39. Steiner 1995 p. 129.
40. Emmerich 1954b vol. I, pp. 441–42.
41. Powell 1996 p. 109.

CHAPTER 7

ALTERNATIVE VIEWPOINTS

THE VIEWPOINTS in this book are not always consistent with those that have emerged from the perspective of Christian "belief" as it evolved at the outset and has been reinforced by subsequent tradition. To complete the inquiry into the Mystery of the Two Jesus Children, it seems desirable to summarize "mainstream" Christian belief and to delineate the specific areas where those views are not consistent with the further unveiling of the above mystery. Although it was an arbitrary choice, the source selected for the summary of "mainstream" Christian belief was *The Book of Common Prayer* (According to the use of The Episcopal Church in the United States of America).[1]

THE CHICAGO-LAMBETH QUADRILATERAL 1888

The period preceding the turn of the nineteenth century into the twentieth was one in which there was considerable interest in matters *ecumenical*. In 1886, a convention of the Protestant Episcopal Church in the United States of America was held in Chicago, IL. A resolution consisting of four "inherent parts," hence called a Quadrilateral, was adopted by the House of Bishops, but it was not enacted by the House of Deputies. Instead, it was referred for "study and action" to a newly created Joint Commission on Christian Union. The Quadrilateral had some twenty-eight lines of introductory and explanatory text to support the eleven lines of the four clauses. Two years later, at the Lambeth Conference of 1888, which took place in England, the gathering of the leaders of the worldwide Anglican Communion passed Resolution 11, which

---

1. *The Book of Common Prayer and Administration of the Sacraments and Other Rites and Ceremonies of the Church* (New York: Church Hymnal Corporation and Seabury Press, 1979) pp. 876–78.

consisted of the essentials of the American document, without the introductory and explanatory text and with **minor** revisions in wording of the
four clauses. The complete text of those **Articles** appears below.

> That, in the opinion of this Conference, the following Articles
> supply a basis on which approach may be by God's blessing
> made towards Home Reunion: [2]
>
> (a) The Holy Scriptures of the Old and New Testaments, as
> "containing all things necessary to salvation," and as being the
> rule and ultimate standard of faith.
>
> (b) The Apostles' Creed, as the Baptismal Symbol; and the
> Nicene Creed, as the sufficient statement of the Christian faith.
>
> (c) The two Sacraments ordained by Christ Himself—Baptism and
> the supper of the Lord—ministered with unfailing use of Christ's
> words of Institution, and of the elements ordained by Him.
>
> (d) The Historic Episcopate, locally adapted in the methods of
> its administration to the varying needs of the nations and peo-
> ples called of God into the Unity of His Church.

It is not intended to dissect each of the clauses in this historic document, but to provide an overview of the various elements that must go
into making even a simple statement of the articles of faith for a religious denomination.

There is no conflict between this discourse and the provisions of
Article (a) providing that it is acknowledged that the original texts of the
Old Testament and the New Testament were occasionally written in
"coded" language which is susceptible to different interpretations. Article (b) will be the source of most of the discrepancies that can be found
in both of the two creeds, and these will be detailed below. Article (c) is
concerned with "The two Sacraments ordained by Christ [Jesus] Himself—Baptism and the supper of the Lord." There is no issue between
this formulation and the substance treated in this volume. Similarly,
Article (d), "The Historic Episcopate," presents no problems; although
it should be acknowledged that once branches have occurred in The

---

2. Though not used today, Home Reunion signified bringing together all the separate
Christian denominations into a single body.

~~Historic Episcopate, it becomes difficult to reconcile the legitimacy of~~
multiple lists, e.g., Anglican, Eastern Orthodox, Lutheran, Methodist, and Roman Catholic. Also, for those denominations that do not have bishops, an affirmation of Article (d) will not come easily.

THE RELATIONSHIP TO THE MESSIANIC PROPHECIES

The major stumbling block with the creeds is the suggestion that Jesus Christ was conceived by the Holy Spirit. This would seem to deny the requirement of a descendant of David as the proper paternity for the Messiah. The importance of that view is enhanced when one realizes, as further unveiling of the Mystery of the Two Jesus Children is undertaken, that there was not only a Davidic antecedent for the Solomon Jesus who came first, but also a different Davidic antecedent for the Nathan Jesus who came four years and nine months later. This also relates to the Virgin Birth, and there will be more on this subject subsequently, but first some differences between the Solomon line and the Nathan line should be presented.

As has been previously noted, there are three major leadership roles in Hebrew history: prophet, priest, and king. There is ample documentation for the role of prophet throughout the time that the Hebrews recorded their history. With regard to the Christian era, John the Baptizer fulfills that role. The other two roles were either to have been incorporated into two different Messiahs or combined in one Messiah.[3] The latter appears to have been the case. Although the Solomon line is well identified with the kingly role and certainly the Magi reinforce that connection, the Nathan line is less compelling as a representative of the priestly role, since that was usually assigned to descendants of Levi. Yet Dr. Steiner clearly uses this designation in his characterization of the Nathan line.[4] To reject these substantial identifications with Hebrew traditions in order to support an extraordinary virgin birth seems, in one sense, a denial of, or at least a failure to appreciate, the careful preparation that the spiritual world went through to accomplish the Incarnation of the Christ Being.

---

3. Andrew Welburn *The Beginnings of Christianity: Essene Mystery, Gnostic Revelation and the Christian Vision* (Edinburgh: Floris Books, 1991) pp. 123ff.
4. Steiner 2001 p. 55.

THE SELECTION OF THE SOLOMON JOSEPH

The visions of Sister Emmerich provide a detailed account of how the priests of the Temple in Jerusalem went about finding the proper suitor for the Solomon Mary, who was about to leave the Temple after eleven years as a Temple Virgin.

[The Solomon] Joseph, whose father was called Jacob, was the third of six brothers. His parents lived in a large house outside Bethlehem, once the ancestral home of David.... He left the house at night in order to earn his living in another place by carpentry.... He might have been eighteen to twenty years old at that time.... Later still I saw him working in Tiberius for a master-carpenter. He might have been as much as thirty-three years old at that time.... [The Solomon] Joseph was very devout and prayed fervently for the coming of the Messiah.... [He] gave himself up to continual prayer, till he received the call to take himself up to Jerusalem to become by divine decree the spouse of [a Temple virgin].[5]

[The Solomon Mary] had reached the age of fourteen and was to be dismissed from the Temple along with seven other maidens to be married.... Then I saw that messengers were sent throughout the land and all unmarried men of the line of David summoned to the Temple.... [The Solomon] Mary was then presented to them.... I now saw that the high priest, in accordance with inner instruction he had received, handed a branch to each of the men present, and commanded each to inscribe his branch with his name and to hold it in his hands during the prayer and sacrifice. After they had done this, their branches were collected and laid upon the altar before the Holy of Holies, and they were told that the one among them whose branch blossomed was destined by the Lord to be married to [the Solomon] Mary.... After the appointed interval their branches were given back to them with the announcement that none had blossomed, and therefore none of them was the bridegroom destined by God for this

---

5. Emmerich 1954a pp. 118–23.

maiden…. I then saw the priests in the Temple making a fresh search in the ancestral tables to see whether there was any descendant of David's who had been overlooked. As they found that of six brothers registered at Bethlehem one was missing and unknown, they made a search for [the Solomon] Joseph…. On command of the high priest, [the Solomon] Joseph now came, dressed in his best, to the Temple at Jerusalem. He, too, had to hold a branch during the prayer and sacrifice, and as he was about to lay this on the altar before the Holy of Holies, a white flower like a lily blossomed out of the top of it, and I saw over him an appearance of light like the Holy Ghost. [The Solomon] Joseph was now recognized as appointed by God to be the bridegroom of [the Solomon] Mary.[6]

With this background in mind, there is a clarification of the importance of the descent from the Davidic line. The traditional view of the virgin birth completely eliminates a human male role which, of course, denies the ancient Hebrew prophecies that the Messiah would be a descendant of King David. If then there is to be an alternative viewpoint between Hebraic and Christian traditions, anthroposophy stands with the Hebraic. However, there is no denying that members of the worldwide Anthroposophical Society consider themselves as devout Christians as any persons can be.

VIRGIN BIRTH REVISITED

In the tradition of the Roman Catholic Church, Mary's virginity is characterized as follows:

From the first formulations of her faith, the Church has confessed that Jesus was conceived solely by the power of the Holy Spirit in the womb of the Virgin Mary, affirming also the corporeal aspect of this event: Jesus was conceived "by the Holy Spirit without human seed."[7]

6. Emmerich 1954a pp. 129-32.
7. *Catechism of the Catholic Church* (Saint Charles Borromeo Catholic Church web site, 2nd edition of the English translation, 1997). Paragraph 496.

(The portion in quotation marks at the end of this excerpt is foot-noted in the original as a deliberation of the Council of the Lateran, which was held in 641 C.E.) Obviously, the Mystery of the Two Jesus Children and the Mystery of the Incarnation are not consistent with this formulation. The essential thesis of this discourse, as informed by various authors from the anthroposophical tradition, suggests a more complex preparation by the spiritual world for the final incarnation of the Christ Being at the Baptism after the crucial elements of the two Jesus children had joined in the person of Jesus of Nazareth. Accordingly, some additional material relating to these events is appended below.

There is more to the story of the betrothal of the Solomon Mary and the Solomon Joseph in the Temple. Did the conception also take place at that time? Emil Bock indicates that just as the priests of the Temple arranged the "Temple marriage" of the Solomon Joseph and the Solomon Mary, so also the conception of the Solomon Jesus occurred in such a way that neither the Solomon Mary nor the Solomon Joseph was truly conscious of what had actually happened as a result of a "Temple sleep" brought about by the priests.[8] Dr. Steiner has also confirmed this matter of "Temple sleep," which is related to the "deep sleep" mentioned in Genesis.[9] Apparently, the conception of the Solomon Jesus occurred in the Temple when the Solomon Mary was betrothed to Solomon Joseph at the age of thirteen years and nine months, so that when the Solomon Mary left the Temple at the age of fourteen, she was already three months with child. This would explain the Solomon Joseph's attitude, referred to in Matthew's Gospel, where he was obviously perplexed to discover that the Solomon Mary was expecting a child.[10]

Some material relating to the Nathan Mary and the nature of her conception should be added here. Again Emil Bock is helpful. He has digested many of the non-canonical sources and identifies similarities and differences between the Temple environment of the Solomon Mary's conception and the Nazarene environment dominated by the Essene Order, which provided a similar protective setting where "No

---

8. Emil Bock *The Childhood of Jesus: The Unknown Years* (trsl. Maria St. Goar, Edinburgh: Floris Books, 1997) pp. 153ff and also p. 172.
9. Heidenreich 1972 p. 34.
10. Powell 1996 p. 132.

miracle in the sense of a violation of natural laws occurred here. Rather, it was the miraculous manifestation of celestial laws, laws of heaven that mankind generally had long since forfeited, laws in which they had once shared in paradisal primordial times."[11] Bock also emphasized differences in the maturity of the individualities of the Solomon Holy Family and those of the Nathan Holy Family, indicating that the Nathan Joseph "had such a childlike nature in his obedience to the will of God that he could not have experienced the doubts in which the Solomon Joseph became caught up."

FINE TUNING ON REINCARNATION

Both of the Christian creeds also touch on the resurrection. In the Apostles' Creed the modern wording is "the resurrection of the body"; in the Episcopal tradition, "resurrection of the body" is defined to mean "that God will raise us from death in the fullness of our being, that we may live with [the] Christ [Being] in the communion of the saints."[12] In the Nicene Creed it is put forth as "the resurrection of the dead," but there is no separate definition in the Catechism.

The relationship between reincarnation and resurrection is not straightforward. Authorities differ on whether reincarnation can be considered an "acceptable" belief for Christians. Valentin Tomberg has an extended discussion of this subject in his *Covenant of the Heart.* He makes the point that "[N]either the opinion that only one life is allotted to man, nor the view that man can live repeated lives on earth, belongs to the truths of salvation…. Therefore the first viewpoint cannot be maintained as a dogma, but only as a prevailing opinion; and the second view, correspondingly, cannot be considered an erroneous teaching or heresy."[13]

Tomberg goes on to review the traditional teachings of the Roman Catholic Church and suggests there are three different answers to the question, "Where does the soul of the newborn child come from?" The three concepts are: "creationism" which posits a new soul created by

---

11. Bock 1997 p. 155.
12. *The Book of Common Prayer* 1979 p. 862.
13. Valentin Tomberg *Covenant of the Heart: Meditations of a Christian Hermeticist on the Mysteries of Tradition* (trsl. Robert Powell and James Morgante, Rockport, MA: Element, 1992) p. 60.

God for each birth, "tradutionism" which affirms that the soul of the child issues from the soul of the father, and "pre-existentialism" which declares that the soul descends at birth out of existence in the spiritual world into earthly existence. All three positions have been held by various religious authorities at one time or another, but creationism is the current view of the Roman Catholic Church and has been so since Thomas Aquinas (1225 ? –75 C.E.).[14]

More importantly, Tomberg then makes assertions regarding the relation of reincarnation to resurrection. These are able, for some, to reconcile the creedal statements to the idea of reincarnation. Therefore a significant portion is included below verbatim.

> If the theme of reincarnation has been spoken of here, it is not to persuade anyone of its truth, but only to consider it in relation to the ideal of resurrection. Here it is the author's desire that those people who cannot do other than accept repeated earthly lives as true, should not believe themselves at variance with the cardinal truth of salvation, the resurrection; and that they see that their conviction in no way contradicts the redemptive truth of resurrection, but on the contrary, receives there from its significance and fulfillment. For reincarnation does not only mean repeated opportunities to gather experience and to overcome the trials of earthly life, but it signifies also the repetitions of the earthly constraints of suffering, sickness, and death. So it is not only an increased period of grace, but also a lengthened period of shouldering the burden of the cross.

> Resurrection, on the other hand, is also a reappearance in the body, but without the earthly constraints of suffering, sickness, and death, i.e., without the earthly necessities of destiny against which man struggles in each of his incarnations. Thus resurrection appears to be the crown and victorious fulfillment of the battle against constraint, suffering, and death which mankind fights ceaselessly both in the course of the gene rations and through repeated earth lives. . . . It is solely the hope for resurrection which makes it worthwhile to live many times on earth.[15]

---

14. Tomberg 1992 p. 62.
15. Ibid. pp. 62–63.

Anthroposophy is founded on the concept of reincarnation, which it defines in a sufficiently broad sense that it incorporates not only a process for the spiritual evolution of human beings but also cosmic processes for the planetary cycles of evolution as described in Chapter 1. It must be acknowledged that resurrection in the creedal statements is usually interpreted as a single event, rather than the cyclical alternating states that are implied by the concept of reincarnation. But Tomberg has expanded the process of reincarnation as a path toward the ideal of resurrection. Thus, both reincarnation and resurrection, as well as, the *eschaton,* can all be held in the same belief structure. This is especially true if one accepts the idea that the "day of judgment" may only lead to a new planetary cycle of evolution.

An additional perspective on reincarnation has been provided recently by Pietro Archiati. Relying heavily on Dr. Steiner's teaching on reincarnation and karma, he asserts the following:

In Rudolf Steiner's spiritual science Christianity is made the *basis for life* in a most real and practical manner. For either daily life becomes Christian or there is no such thing as Christianity. True Christianity cannot exist *alongside* life, it has to be *life* itself. Essential to this living Christianity is an awareness of reincarnation and karma which in itself does not remain only a theoretical dogma but which takes such possession of our hearts that every meeting with another person becomes a Christian sacrament.[16]

However, it is still necessary to deal with the concept of "the life everlasting." From the point of view of mainstream Christianity, "the life everlasting" is a new concept uniquely identified as a teaching of Christ Jesus and linked with the reality of his resurrection as an example. From the point of view of anthroposophy, reincarnation provides a continuity that has been present since the material world was created and, even earlier, in former planetary cycles of evolution. Thus, this is another example of an alternate viewpoint.

---

16. Pietro Archiati *Reincarnation in Modern Life: Towards a New Christian Awareness* Six lectures given in Rome 22–25 April 1994 (trsl. Pauline Wehrle, London: Temple Lodge, 1997) p. 94.

PART THREE

THE
MYSTERY
OF THE
BELOVED
DISCIPLE

* * *

THERE ARE SEVERAL LINES of evidence that support the concept that the disciple whom Jesus loved was Lazarus of Bethany rather than, as it has been assumed, John the son of Zebedee. In Chapter 8, three different sources are provided for information on Lazarus: 1) *The Gospel According to John,* 2) the visions of the Blessed Anne Catherine Emmerich as published in Dr. Powell's *Chronology of the Living Christ,* and 3) chapter 7 of the lecture cycle by Dr. Rudolf Steiner on the *Gospel of St. John.* In Chapter 9, the essay by Dr. Karl König (1902–1966) entitled "The Two Disciples Called John" has been used as a guide to the biblical evidence for the usage of the phrase "the disciple whom Jesus loved." Although this work by Dr. König was originally presented at Eastertide 1962, it has only recently been translated into English, then published, and become more generally available. The documentation is taken from primary sources in Dr. Steiner's writings. Such issues as the authorship of *The Gospel According to John,* the difference between a raising from the dead (as suggested in the Gospel) and the concept of an initiation (as suggested by Dr. Steiner), as well as the origins of the new personality of Lazarus after his initiation are brought to bear on the unveiling of this mystery. In Chapter 10, a more detailed analysis of the daily visions of Sister Emmerich for the period of the incarnation as published in Dr. Powell's *Chronology of the Living Christ* is undertaken. The data for this analysis have been reproduced in Appendix 4. This provides additional support for the important role that Lazarus played in the course of Christ Jesus' life and ministry. When it is realized that Lazarus is being mentioned in several places only by his code name, "the disciple whom Jesus loved," an understanding of his real importance is much enhanced. In Chapter 11, authored by Dr. Robert Powell, a contemporary account based on the views of The Reverend Irene Johanson, originally published in German, is presented. A translation by Dr. Robert Powell of several excerpts from her work can be found in Appendix 5. In Chapter 12, also authored by Dr. Powell, two biographies are set forth: one of John the son of Zebedee, who became the Apostle John; and the other of Lazarus, who became the Apostle Lazarus, then the Bishop of Marseille and, eventually, Presbyter John.

CHAPTER 8

THREE DIFFERENT VIEWS
ON LAZARUS

LAZARUS OF BETHANY is a shadowy figure in the New Testament. This is not a coincidence. As has been indicated before, much of the New Testament is written in such a way that it can be interpreted on more than one level. Dr. Karl König has made it clear in his significant essay, "The Two Disciples Called John," that a number of veils were deliberately cast over certain individuals when John's Gospel was written.[1]

LAZARUS AS SEEN BY *The Gospel According to John*

Lazarus of Bethany is not even mentioned in the synoptic gospels, and his appearance by name in John's Gospel is restricted to Chapters 11 and 12, as cited in one long segment and three short excerpts reproduced below.

Now a certain man was ill, Lazarus of Bethany, the village of Mary and her sister Martha. Mary was the one who anointed the Lord with perfume and wiped his feet with her hair; her brother Lazarus was ill. So the sisters sent a message to [Christ] Jesus, "Lord, he whom you love is ill." But when [Christ] Jesus heard it, he said, "This illness does not lead to death; rather it is for God's glory, so that the Son of God may be glorified through it." Accordingly, though [Christ] Jesus loved Martha and her sister and Lazarus, after having heard that Lazarus was ill, he stayed two days longer in the place where he was. Then after this he

---

1. Karl König *The Mystery of John and the Cycle of the Year* (trsl. G. F. Mier, ed. Gregg Davis and Nicholas Poole, Great Britain: Camphill Books, 2000) pp. 135–37.

said to the disciples, "Let us go to Judea again." The disciples said to him, "Rabbi, the Jews were just now trying to stone you, and are you going there again?" [Christ] Jesus answered, "Are there not twelve hours of daylight? Those who walk during the day do not stumble, because they see the light of this world. But those who walk at night stumble, because the light is not in them." After saying this, he told them, "Our friend Lazarus has fallen asleep, but I am going there to awaken him." The disciples said to him, "Lord, if he has fallen asleep, he will be all right." [Christ] Jesus, however, had been speaking about his death, but they thought that he was referring merely to sleep. Then [Christ] Jesus told them plainly, "Lazarus is dead. For your sake I am glad I was not there, so that you may believe. But let us go to him." Thomas, who was called the Twin, said to his fellow disciples, "Let us also go, that we may die with him."

When [Christ] Jesus arrived, he found that Lazarus had already been in the tomb four days. Now Bethany was near Jerusalem, some two miles away, and many of the Jews had come to Martha and Mary to console them about their brother. When Martha heard that [Christ] Jesus was coming, she went and met him, while Mary stayed at home. Martha said to [Christ] Jesus, "Lord, if you had been here, my brother would not have died. But even now I know that God will give you whatever you ask of him." [Christ] Jesus said to her, "Your brother will rise again." Martha said to him, "I know that he will rise again in the resurrection on the last day." [Christ] Jesus said to her, "I am the resurrection and the life. Those who believe in me, even though they die, will live, and everyone who lives and believes in me will never die. Do you believe this?" She said to him, "Yes, Lord, I believe that you are the Messiah, the Son of God, the one coming into the world."

When she had said this, she went back and called her sister Mary, and told her privately, "The Teacher is here and is calling for you." And when she heard it, she got up quickly and went to him. Now [Christ] Jesus had not yet come to the village, but was still at the place where Martha had met him. The Jews who were with her in the house, consoling her, saw Mary get up quickly and go out. They followed her because they thought that she was going to the tomb to weep there. When Mary came where

[Christ] Jesus was and saw him, she knelt at his feet and said to him, "Lord, if you had been here, my brother would not have died." When Jesus saw her weeping, and the Jews who came with her also weeping, he was greatly disturbed in spirit and deeply moved. He said, "Where have you laid him?" They said to him, "Lord, come and see." [Christ] Jesus began to weep. So the Jews said, "See how he loved him!" But some of them said, "Could not he who opened the eyes of the blind man have kept this man from dying?"

Then [Christ] Jesus, again greatly disturbed, came to the tomb. It was a cave, and a stone was lying against it. [Christ] Jesus said, "Take away the stone." Martha, the sister of the dead man, said to him, "Lord, already there is a stench because he has been dead four days." [Christ] Jesus said to her, "Did I not tell you that if you believed, you would see the glory of God?" So they took away the stone. And [Christ] Jesus looked upward and said, "Father, I thank you for having heard me. I knew that you always hear me, but I have said this for the sake of the crowd standing here, so that they may believe that you sent me." When he had said this, he cried with a loud voice, "Lazarus, come out!" The dead man came out, his hands and feet bound with strips of cloth, and his face wrapped in a cloth. [Christ] Jesus said to them, "Unbind him, and let him go." [John 11:1– 44]

Six days before the Passover [Christ] Jesus came to Bethany, the home of Lazarus, whom he had raised from the dead. There they gave a dinner for [Christ Jesus]. Martha served, and Lazarus was one of those at the table with him. [John 12:1–2]

When the great crowd of the Jews learned that [Christ Jesus] was there, they came not only because of [Christ] Jesus but also to see Lazarus, whom he had raised from the dead. So the chief priests planned to put Lazarus to death as well, since it was on account of him that many of the Jews were deserting and were believing in [Christ] Jesus. [John 12:9–11]

So the crowd that had been with him when he called Lazarus out of the tomb and raised him from the dead continued to testify. [John 12:17]

For some, using only these gospel passages was enough to suggest that Lazarus was in fact the Beloved Disciple. In an article published in 1949, Professor Floyd V. Filson of McCormick Theological Seminary suggests that the "Fourth Gospel" must be read on its own merits without the "benefit" of later commentaries and "patristic" accretions from post-first-century times. On this basis he decodes the Beloved Disciple to be Lazarus and even cites earlier writers who came to the same conclusion.[2]

LAZARUS AS SEEN BY SISTER EMMERICH

When the visions of Sister Emmerich are analyzed, an expanded picture emerges of the relationship between Lazarus and Jesus of Nazareth/Christ Jesus. In the excerpts below, which are abstracted from Dr. Powell's *Chronicle of the Living Christ*, the dates as provided by the author have been used as an organizing principle.[3] A more complete tabulation of this information can be found in Appendix 4, where the page citations to the original source are also available.

> *Tuesday May 31, 29 C.E.* Jesus [of Nazareth] arrived at Lazarus' castle in Bethany. After talking with Lazarus, Jesus [of Nazareth] and his two friends [Parmenas and Joanadab from Nazareth] visited the Temple in Jerusalem.

> *Wednesday Sep. 21, 29 C.E.* Then [Jesus of Nazareth] continued on his way, arriving that night at Lazarus' castle in Bethany. He was greeted not only by Lazarus but also by Nicodemus, John Mark, and the aged Obed (a relative of the prophetess Anna) who were guests of Lazarus in Bethany. Among the women gathered there as guests of [Lazarus' sister] Martha were Veronica, Mary Mark, and Susanna of Jerusalem. Jesus [of Nazareth] greeted them all, and they took a meal together before retiring for the night.

> *Thursday Sep. 22, 29 C.E.* During that morning, Jesus [of Nazareth] walked about in the courtyards and gardens of the castle, teaching those who were present.... At about half-past one, the [Solomon] Mary arrived accompanied by Mary Chuza, the widow Lea, Mary Salome, and Mary Cleophas. After a light meal, Jesus [of Nazareth] and [the Solomon] Mary, retired to talk

---

2. Floyd V. Filson "Who was the Beloved Disciple?" *Journal of Biblical Literature* 68:83–88, 1949.
3. Powell 1996 pp. 184–352.

to one another. In this conversation, Jesus [of Nazareth] told [the Solomon] Mary that he was now going to be baptized and that his real mission would begin with that event.... That evening, Lazarus gave a feast for all who were present.... The same night, Jesus [of Nazareth], accompanied by Lazarus, set off in the direction of Jericho to make his way to the place of baptism.

Friday Sep. 23, 29 C.E. Jesus [of Nazareth] went on ahead of Lazarus and arrived at the place of baptism [on the west side of the Jordan River south of Ono, near day-break] some two hours before him.... John [the Baptizer] felt Jesus' presence among the crowd. He was fired with zeal and preached with great animation concerning the nearness of the Messiah. Then he started baptizing. By ten o'clock he had already baptized many people. Jesus [of Nazareth] now came down to the baptizing pool where John [the Baptizer] was being helped by Andrew.... At the moment of baptism, a voice of thunder spoke the words, [YOU ARE MY SON, TODAY I HAVE BEGOTTEN YOU (Luke 3: 22)] and Christ Jesus became transparent with radiant light. Meanwhile, Nicodemus, Obed, John Mark, and Joseph of Arimathea had also arrived to join Lazarus in witnessing the baptism of [Christ] Jesus. John [the Baptizer] then told Andrew to announce the baptism of the Messiah throughout Galilee....

Sunday Sep. 25, 29 C.E. In the synagogue at Luz, [Christ] Jesus held a lengthy discourse, interpreting many things from the Old Testament.... Lazarus, who had accompanied [Christ] Jesus thus far, now parted company with him and returned to Bethany.

Saturday Oct. 8, 29 C.E. [Christ] Jesus remained for the Sabbath in Gilgal. Lazarus, Joseph of Arimathea, and some other friends arrived from Jerusalem to hear him preach. The mood was joyful, and as [Christ] Jesus was leaving the synagogue the crowd shouted, "The covenant is fullfilled!" Lazarus and the friends from Jerusalem left, and [Christ] Jesus sent a message through them to [the Blessed Virgin Mary] in Galilee that she should expect him at Great Chorazin (about ten miles from Capernaum) at the Feast of Tabernacles.

Thursday Oct. 20, 29 C.E. Toward evening, [Christ] Jesus and his disciples arrived at a hostel near Bethany that had been put at

their disposal by Lazarus. Lazarus came to greet them.... [Christ]
Jesus then took leave of [his disciples] and made his way to Lazarus' castle at Bethany, accompanied by Lazarus and the two
nephews of Joseph of Arimathea, Aram and Themeni. Here
many friends from Jerusalem were expecting him.

Friday Oct, 21, 29 C.E. [Christ] Jesus interpreted various passages
from the scriptures to the friends gathered together.... [Christ
Jesus] then set off in the direction of Jericho. For the first part of
the journey he was accompanied by Lazarus. Lazarus went with
[Christ] Jesus as far as a hostel (that he owned) close to the wilderness. Here they parted company, and [Christ] Jesus continued
on his way alone and barefoot....

Thus it can be seen that in less than six months, according to Sister
Emmerich, Lazarus was closely involved with Jesus of Nazareth/Christ
Jesus on eight occasions both before and after the baptism in the River
Jordan. A number of these involved hospitality, either at Lazarus' major
residence in Bethany, or at other properties that Lazarus owned. Subsequent to these visits, Lazarus attended the wedding at Cana, so it follows that he was both a close supporter of Jesus of Nazareth/Christ
Jesus and a person of wealth who had considerable standing in Jerusalem and the surrounding area. As other elements in the total story are
traced, it will be possible to determine other reasons why Lazarus was
considered by Christ Jesus to be a suitable individual to receive an
important change in his life status.

LAZARUS AS SEEN BY DR. STEINER

It is significant that Lazarus is featured in *Christianity As Mystical Fact*,
one of the earliest volumes based on lectures delivered by Dr. Steiner. The
original edition was published in 1902; in it Dr. Steiner devoted an entire
chapter to "The 'Miracle' of Lazarus." [4] There is no brief quotation that
provides a suitable summary of this volume; however, in the Introduction
to the latest edition, Professor Andrew Welburn does present a scholarly
treatment of the importance of that book. [5] To encapsulate what can be

4. Steiner 1997 pp. 110ff.
5. Andrew Welburn "Introduction" in Steiner 1997 pp. ix–xxi.

found in this volume, it must be acknowledged that there is a starting point in the ancient *mysteries*.

> The ancient testimonies to the Mysteries are at once revealing and yet full of ambiguity. The initiates were convinced that to tell what they knew would be sinful, and indeed that it would be sinful for the uninitiated to hear it.... A special mode of life was one of the requirements for a subsequent initiation. The senses were to be brought under the control of the spirit; fasting, isolation, ordeals, and certain meditative techniques were employed to that end.... The [one to be initiated] was to be conducted into the life of the spirit and behold a higher world order. Without the preparatory exercises and ordeals he or she would be able to form no connection with that world—and on that connection everything depended.[6]

Beyond that simple beginning, Dr. Steiner traces the mysteries through their origins in classical times, from pre-Socratic philosophers through Platonic perspectives to Egyptian and other Eastern mysteries. In a later chapter, he describes both the great Buddha and Jesus Christ as examples of the life of an initiate.[7] But then he comes to a chapter entitled "The Evidence of the Gospels," which he uses to set the stage for his view of the Lazarus "miracle." Dr. Steiner emphasizes the importance of the opening lines of John's Gospel.

> In the beginning was the Word, and the Word was with God, and the Word was God.... And the Word became flesh and lived among us, and we have seen his glory, the glory as of a father's only son, full of grace and truth. [John 1:1, 1:14]

Dr. Steiner goes on to say, "To begin a work in this way is quite obviously to claim that it has to be interpreted in a specially deep sense.... It is safe to suppose that in the instance of a man being raised from the dead—a case that poses the greatest challenge to the eye and ear and to the reasoning mind—the very deepest meaning lies concealed."[8] Dr. Steiner then makes a very important clarification:

---

6. Steiner 1997 p. 3.
7. Ibid. p. 91.
8. Ibid. pp. 110–11.

"Where would be the point of bringing someone back from the dead if after his resurrection he were just as he was before?" Beyond that, Dr. Steiner places the words of Christ Jesus in a context that addresses the change that had to come about in Lazarus as the result of this event: "I am the resurrection and the life. Those who believe in me, even though they die, will live, and everyone who lives and believes in me will never die." [John 11:25–26] Dr. Steiner interprets this in the following manner: "Through the process Lazarus is completely transformed. Previously the Word, the spirit, was not alive in him. Now it lives in him. The spirit has been born within him." [9]

In his review of the entire process, Dr. Steiner mentions how Lazarus was loved by Christ Jesus, not in the sense of personal affection, but in the sense of the mystery tradition between a teacher and a pupil. Christ Jesus found in Lazarus one who was sufficiently ripe that he could awaken "the Word" within him. There were already strong links between the family in Bethany and Jesus of Nazareth, as was reinforced by Sister Emmerich's visions. Not only was Lazarus a pupil of Christ Jesus, he was a pupil of whom Christ Jesus could be absolutely confident that his initiation would be accomplished. Because in fact, in the complete understanding of the tradition of the *mystery schools*, the raising of Lazarus was not a raising from the dead—it was an initiation.

From Dr. Steiner's lectures on John's Gospel it can be learned that after his initiation, Lazarus was destined to make an important contribution to early Christianity. He became the author of *The Gospel According to John*. Dr. Steiner further clarified that the first half of that account is really the story of John the Baptizer as he prepared the way for the coming of the Messiah; in the middle is the initiation of Lazarus, who is then given a new name: Lazarus-John.[10] The second half of the gospel is "the testimony of the *new* John whom the Lord Himself had initiated, for this is the risen Lazarus."[11]

In the next chapter, the scholarship of Dr. König will be used as a guide to follow the transitions that Lazarus-John made during the final days of Christ Jesus' earthly life.

9. Steiner 1997 p. 115.
10. Alfred Heidenreich "Preface" in Rudolf Steiner's *The Last Address* (London: Rudolf Steiner Press, 1967) p. 10; and Edward Reaugh Smith *The Disciple Whom Jesus Loved: Unveiling the Author of John's Gospel* (Great Barrington, MA: Anthroposphic Press, 2000)p. 27.
11. Rudolf Steiner *Gospel of St. John* (trsl. Maud B. Monges, Hudson, NY: Anthroposophic Press, 1962) p. 65.

CHAPTER 9

FROM THE SCHOLARSHIP
OF DR. KÖNIG

DR. KARL KÖNIG (1902–1966) has made a significant contribution to this subject in his essay entitled "The Two Disciples Called John."[1] In the Preface to this essay, Dr. König acknowledges that Dr. Steiner provided the key to resolving the Mystery of the Beloved Disciple, namely that the individuality that was present in the Hebrew prophet Elijah appeared again "at the most important moment of human evolution," first as John the Baptizer and then, after the death of the latter, with the raised Lazarus, who was therefore called Lazarus-John. The difference between "a raising from the dead" and "an initiation" has previously been set forth from the writings of Dr. Steiner. Here, it is intended to concentrate on biblical passages that Dr. König has catalogued as being related to Lazarus-John. It is important for the reader to appreciate that Dr. König does this in the context that there is a mystery regarding Lazarus-John and that both of the sons of Zebedee are implicated in that mystery.

THE RICH YOUTH

The passage identified by Dr. König is from chapter 10 of Mark's Gospel.

As he was setting out on a journey, a man ran up and knelt before him, and asked him, "Good Teacher, what must I do to inherit eternal life?" [Christ] Jesus said to him, "Why do you call

1. König 2000 p. 129.

me good? No one is good but God alone. You know the commandments: 'You shall not murder; You shall not commit adultery; You shall not steal; You shall not bear false witness; You
shall not defraud; Honor your father and mother.'" He said to
him, "Teacher, I have kept all these since my youth." [Christ]
Jesus, looking at him, loved him and said, "You lack one thing;
go, sell what you own, and give the money to the poor, and you
will have treasure in heaven; then come, follow me." When he
heard this, he was shocked and went away grieving, for he had
many possessions. [Mark 10:17–22]

Although there is nothing in this description to tie it to Lazarus-John,
Dr. König relates other passages from the canonical gospels to make the
connection.[2] In Matthew's Gospel the same scene is described, but there
are no clues as to the identity of the questioner. [Matthew 19:16–22]
However, in Luke's Gospel, there is another way of referring to this rich
youth; he is called "A certain ruler...." [Luke 18:18] This is important
because, in those times, a "ruler" was one who belonged to the circle of
the priesthood. Another instance in which that distinction occurs is in
John's Gospel where an unidentified disciple is designated as "being
known to the high priest." [John 18:15] Clearly, this cannot apply to
John the son of Zebedee, or any of the other disciples chosen by Christ
Jesus. However, as more details about Lazarus-John are identified, it can
indeed apply to him, for "he was of the high priestly caste of Israel." [3]

TWO DIFFERENT EVENTS

Dr. König makes a point of distinguishing two events that are often
thought to be the same: one took place in Bethany, in the castle belonging to Lazarus-John six days before the Passover. This is clearly *before*
the entry into Jerusalem, which occurred the following day. [John
12:1–12] The second event also took place in Bethany, but in the house
of Simon the leper, two days before the Passover, which was clearly *after*
the entry into Jerusalem. [Matthew 26:6 / Mark 14:1–3] The accounts
also differ because in John's Gospel the woman is identified as Mary

2. König 2000 p. 141.
3. Edward Reaugh Smith *The Disciple Whom Jesus Loved: Unveiling the Author of John's Gospel* (Great Barrington, MA: Anthroposophic Press, 2000) p. 31.

[Magdalene] and she anoints the feet of Christ Jesus; but in the other two descriptions, the woman is not identified by name and she anoints the head of Christ Jesus. Dr. König uses this example to reinforce that the gospels must be read carefully and that similar events occurring at different times are not the same. This assertion sets the stage for how carefully one should interpret the sequence of events relating to the Last Supper.

THE LAST SUPPER

Strangely, this important event is not described in its entirety in any one source. In particular, Dr. König relies on the visions of Sister Emmerich, which he considers to describe very fully certain portions, but not all, of the parts of the Last Supper.[4] In fact, he affirms, "From her description it becomes clear that this tremendous event must have lasted many hours, and that the three synoptic gospels tell us only about the beginning, while John's Gospel records the middle and end of these events." From his scholarly analysis, Dr. König identifies five segments in the following sequence:

1. The Festival of the Passover, its preparation and meal,
2. The sacramental inauguration of the Holy Mass,
3. The Washing of the Feet and the speeches connected with it,
4. The naming of the traitor and the question of Lazarus-John,
5. Finally, the great Farewell Discourses.[5]

Dr. König suggests that the first of these parts is described only by Sister Emmerich; the second can be found in the synoptic gospels but is absent from John's Gospel. The third part is described in detail by Sister Emmerich but is found only in John's Gospel. Elements of the fourth and fifth parts are found in more than one source.

The confusion is partially resolved in the restatement of Sister Emmerich's visions found in Powell. As he lays out each day in ways that are less obvious in the New Testament descriptions, it becomes

---

4. König 2000 p. 146.
5. Ibid. p. 147.

obvious that there was one meal in the house of Simon the leper of Jerusalem and, on the following day, a second meal in the *Coenaculum*. It is at the earlier of these two meals that Sister Emmerich tells of Mary Magdalene coming in to anoint Christ Jesus with the costly ointment. Following that scene, Sister Emmerich sees Judas in an agitated state rushing off to make his ill-conceived bargain with the Pharisees. Because Sister Emmerich does not describe "The sacramental inauguration of the Holy Mass," except to make reference to the Holy Gospels for further details, it is unclear at which of these two meals it occurred. But if the theological indication of Dr. König is employed, that "The sacramental inauguration of the Holy Mass" is performed for all including Judas—representing all future traitors—then Judas was present at that portion of the Last Supper.

There appears to be an inconsistency between the statement in John's Gospel, after the identification of the one who would betray him, when Christ Jesus says, "Do quickly what you are going to do" [John 13:27] and the vision of Sister Emmerich, who has Judas going to the Pharisees on the preceding day.[6] Of course, both occurrences can be reconciled if Judas went to the Pharisees two days before the crucifixion and was only going to fetch the band of soldiers on the night of the betrayal. This is consistent with a vision of Sister Emmerich that suggests that Judas had an even earlier interchange with Caiphas in the week before Judas betrayed Christ Jesus.[7]

Although Dr. König's list of five elements is helpful, it is not always synchronous with the various descriptions. The foot washing takes place during the supper in response to the argument mentioned in Luke's Gospel. Christ Jesus wants the disciples to know "I am among you as one who serves." [Luke 22: 24–27] However, in John's Gospel it is clear that Christ Jesus used the foot washing to set the stage for his new commandment, "Just as I have loved you, you also should love one another." [John 13:34] But this happens *after* Christ Jesus passes the piece of bread to Judas. [John 13:26]

Dr. König suggests why certain items do not appear in John's Gospel, which is considered by him to be the work of Lazarus-John. His analysis is based on the absence of any information on "the sacramental

---

6. Powell 1996 p. 349.
7. Ibid. p. 344.

inauguration of the Holy Mass" in the Johannine gospel. His conclusion is that Lazarus-John "bears witness only of those things in which he himself took part after his [initiation]."[8] Further, Dr. König determines that the moment when Lazarus-John joins the twelve is just before the foot washing begins. The John that Sister Emmerich mentions, in the visions that describe the washing of the feet, may really have been Lazarus-John. Here follows a review of some of the relevant sources. Dr. König suggests that there must have been an agreement between Christ Jesus and Lazarus-John not to have the latter enter the circle of the twelve until after the Festival of the Passover and the sacramental inauguration of the Holy Mass were completed.

Dr. König quotes a portion of Sister Emmerich's vision that is not present in Dr. Powell's edited version. (That in itself is not surprising. Sister Emmerich's vision of the last paschal supper consists of sixteen pages; the washing of the feet is described in three and one half pages; and the institution of the blessed sacrament takes another ten pages.[9] All this is summarized by Dr. Powell in less than one page, so that many details were not included.[10])

Dr. König goes on to suggest that the teaching of Christ Jesus that follows the washing of the feet is meant for all the disciples, but some of the words could only be understood by one who had been initiated by Christ Jesus. "The one who ate my bread has lifted his heel against me" [John 13:18] is interpreted by Dr. König to mean that Christ Jesus indicates that He is destined to be the spirit of the Earth. *The New Oxford Annotated Bible* suggests that Christ Jesus honors Judas "by seating him next to himself, handing him a piece of bread, concealing his treachery from all but [Lazarus-John]."[11] Dr. König goes on to say,

> When Judas expels himself from the circle of the apostles, Lazarus-John [is] a direct witness. Indeed, when prompted by Peter to put the direct question about the traitor he becomes almost the instrument for the execution of this act. As long as Judas was still one of those sitting around the table, [Lazarus-]John lay as the thirteenth on the bosom of Christ [Jesus]. Now, however,

---

8. König 2000 pp. 147–48.
9. Emmerich 1954b vol. IV pp. 48–63; 64–67; 67–77.
10. April 2, 33 (see Appendix 4)
11. *The New Oxford Annotated Bible* 1991, NT, p.148, n.13.21–30.

after Judas is gone, [Lazarus-John] is numbered among the twelve, and so both [Lazarus-John] and John [the son of] Zebedee are present at the table. *Metaphorically speaking, the Eagle, Lazarus[-John], has* now taken the place of the Scorpion, Judas. [Lazarus-John] does not enter in John *[the son of] Zebedee's stead, but in place of Judas Iscariot; he takes upon himself the yoke of the traitor, of the man who has become the deceiver. [Lazarus-John] is the only one who can do this because he has overcome death— none of the other eleven apostles would have been capable of this redemption* (emphasis added).

The circle of the twelve is now closed again. Both [Lazarus-John] and John [the son of] Zebedee are together in the circle of the other disciples, and both listen to the Farewell Discourses which Lazarus[-John] has conveyed to us in the Gospel of St. John.[12]

Dr. König then addresses a difficult question. Is Lazarus-John one of the three disciples whom Christ Jesus chose to keep watch with Him in this heaviest hour?

GETHSEMANE AND THE THREE DISCIPLES

Using the logic previously developed, Dr. König asserts that Lazarus-John could not have taken part in what happened to Christ Jesus *before* he was taken prisoner in Gethsemane: "[H]ad he done so, he would also have reported it in the Gospel of St. John."[13] Dr. König goes on to explain what went on in the Garden of Gethsemane in the words of Dr. Steiner.

Let us place ourselves with all humility—as we must within the soul of Christ Jesus, who to the end tries to maintain the woven bond linking him with the souls of the disciples.... This soul might well put to itself the world-historical question, "Is it possible for me to cause the souls of a least the most select of the disciples to rise to the height of experiencing with me everything that is to happen until the Mystery of Golgotha?" The soul of Christ [Jesus] itself is faced with this question at the crucial moment when Peter,

---

12. König 2000 p.149.
13. Ibid. p. 150.

James, and John [the son of Zebedee] are led out to the Mount of Olives, and Christ Jesus wants to find out from within Himself whether He will be able to keep those whom he has chosen. On the way he becomes anguished. Yes, my friends, does anyone believe, can anyone believe that Christ [Jesus] became anguished in the face of death, of the Mystery of Golgotha, and that he sweated blood because of the approaching event of Golgotha?...Why does [Christ Jesus become distressed? He does not tremble before the cross. That goes without saying. He is distressed above all in the face of this question, "Will those whom I have with me here stand the test of this moment when it will be decided whether they want to accompany me in their souls, whether they want to experience everything with me until the cross?"...So he leaves them alone to see if they can stay "awake," that is in a state of consciousness in which they can experience with Him what he is to experience...He comes back, and they are asleep; they could not maintain their state of wakeful consciousness...Certainly the world had the Mystery of Golgotha, but at the time it happened it had as yet no understanding of this event; and the most select and chosen of the disciples could not stay awake to that point.[14]

Dr. König uses this explanation as another proof that Lazarus-John was not one of the three chosen disciples who failed during this heavy hour. As one who had been initiated by Christ Jesus in the former manner of the ancient mysteries, Lazarus-John could no longer be overcome by spirit-sleep. So what was his role in these unfolding events? His office was to be consciously present at every event. Lazarus-John, having linked himself with the destiny of Judas, followed him to the palace of the High Priest. Thus it was also his duty to be present when Christ Jesus was taken prisoner. As Dr. König put it, "What came about through Judas had to be consciously experienced by Lazarus-John." This was essential so that in his capacity as the author of John's Gospel, Lazarus-John would have a double credibility: that of an initiate and also that of an eye-

---

14. König 2000 pp. 150–51. (The quotation from Dr. Steiner comes from the *Gospel of St. Mark* (trsl. Conrad Mainzer, ed. Stewart C. Easton, Hudson, NY: Anthroposophic Press, 1986) pp. 168–69.

witness. Now consider a final scene in which the confusion between Lazarus-John and John the son of Zebedee is substantial.

WHAT DISCIPLE WAS PRESENT AT THE CRUCIFIXION?

The interchange between Christ Jesus on the cross and a disciple designated only by the code language "the disciple whom he loved," is as follows.

> When [Christ] Jesus saw his mother and *the disciple whom he loved* standing beside her, he said to his mother, "Woman, here is your son." Then he said to the disciple, "Here is your mother." And from that hour the disciple took her into his own home (emphasis added). [John 19:26–27]

This passage is not found in any of the synoptic gospels. The interchange is described in the visions of Sister Emmerich in which she names the disciple as John the son of Zebedee. There will be more on this subject in the next chapter. The "disciple whom Christ Jesus loved" has already been confirmed not only to be Lazarus but, more importantly, after his initiation Lazarus-John. Of the original twelve disciples, he was one who could have been present at the crucifixion without fear of apprehension since he was a recognized leader of the community, as has been previously established. Similarly, he was the only one who had an actual "home" to provide. However, some of this is also interpretable on a totally different level, which has been done by Dr. Steiner and reviewed by Dr. König.[15] The next issue to be recapitulated deals with similarities and differences in the subsequent lives of John the son of Zebedee and Lazarus-John.

JOHN THE SON OF ZEBEDEE

Dr. König begins his discussion of John the son of Zebedee with an inquiry about his parents. Little is known about the father other than his name. With regard to the mother, even the name is not clear at first, but Dr. König does some biblical investigation and comes up with not only a name, but also a significant relationship. That inference is reinforced by a citation to a work published in 1896.[16] The name is Salome, who is not

---

15. König 2000 pp. 153–55.
16. Ibid. p. 158.

only the mother of Zebedee's sons, James and John, but also the sister of the Solomon Mary. This makes the brothers cousins of the Solomon Jesus, and one can assume that, as part of the narrower family circle of Jesus of Nazareth, they had known each other for some time.

There follows an extensive discussion of the relationships implied by the naming of the sons of Zebedee as "Sons of Thunder" by Jesus of Nazareth as indicated in Mark 3:17. This includes some explanations made by Dr. Steiner of the role of Thor as the Angel of Egohood for the Nordic people, and the parallel role of Elijah as the group soul of the Hebrew people. Thus the mission of James and John was to be as messengers of the annunciation of the individuality. As Dr. König puts it, "The Zebedee sons bear this special commitment. Therefore they leave their father, sever the bonds of the old blood relationship and follow the One who not only heralds the coming of [the awareness of the individuality] but who brings it about."[17] Dr. König goes on to explain how John the son of Zebedee fails by falling back into the old bondage. First, he condemns the one who drives out demons in the name of Christ Jesus but does not belong to the community of the disciples; second, sponsored by his mother, he asks for his seat in heaven; and finally, in the garden of Gethsemane, he fails again because he was not able to sustain spiritual consciousness in his individuality during the agony of that night.

Then Dr. König presents his own wisdom. His words, being too significant to paraphrase, are presented below.

But these [failures] are precisely the virtues of the growing [individuality], namely that it knows itself to be lonely, a voice in the wilderness, alone without brother or friend; that it does not flee in the face of death nor from the experience of agony and pain, but remains awake and maintains its consciousness.

Only then will the [individuality] become the bearer of love, of that *agape* of which [Saint] Paul says: "[Love is patient; love is kind; love is not envious or boastful or arrogant or rude.]" To acquire this love as the bearer of the [individuality] is the mission of John and James, the sons of Zebedee, who have become the "sons of thunder."

---

17. König 2000 p. 161.

Through all temptation and failure Christ [Jesus] remains true to them. Even when the other disciple "whom the Lord loved" appears in order to counterbalance what John, the child of thunder, could not fulfill, [Christ Jesus] takes them with Him to the Mount of Olives where He reveals to them the future of mankind; He takes them into the [C]oenaculum in order to hold the Last Supper with them, and to Gethsemane in order to let them take part with their [individualities] in His suffering. Only to Golgotha they can no longer follow, for to that place leads only that [individuality] which has gone through death. But the grace of the [Christ Being] takes them again unto Himself in the light of the Resurrection when he joins the disciples on Easter Sunday, and they are also present when He reveals Himself to them on Lake Genesareth.[18]

In a subsequent section entitled "Ascension," Dr. König reviews how in the four gospels the development of the post-resurrection appearances builds from a general picture in Matthew's Gospel through additional details in Mark's Gospel, to further clarification in Luke's Gospel, until in John's Gospel there is the highest degree of clarification, "dense with detail."

Dr. König also suggests that, "The precision that permeates the gospels and the clarity of their presentation should be more recognized." [19] This is said in the context of the use of eleven and twelve in the numbering of how many disciples were present. Dr. König has already made the point that Lazarus-John has taken the place of Judas so that, for a while, the complement of disciples is back to twelve. When the gospels speak of their being only eleven disciples present on the day of the Resurrection, it is Thomas who is absent. This confirms that Lazarus-John was part of the twelve disciples at that point in time. There follows a description of a painting that Raphael made as a design for a tapestry intended for the Vatican, which is the scene at the time of the Ascension. Lazarus-John says farewell to the disciples at this time as well. "For him, too, the forty days

---

18. König 2000 p. 162.
19. Ibid. p. 165.

of union with the other eleven disciples are over because his immediate mission is fulfilled. It is [Saint] Peter, not [Lazarus-]John who must undertake the office of succession...."[20] There remains now only a final section to review.

THE LATER DESTINIES OF THE TWO JOHNS

As Dr. König was aware, through Dr. Steiner it has been established that Lazarus-John was the author not only of *The Gospel According to John* but also of the *Letters of John* and of *The Revelation to John* and that he died in Ephesus at a very great age, at least ninety-five years.[21] Dr. König quotes Robert Eisler, who cites the church historian Eusebius as the source of a letter to Pope Victor, written about 196 C.E., from Polycrates, Bishop of Ephesus. In it he mentions "John who lay against the bosom of the Lord and was a priest who wore the golden petalon, who was a martyr and a teacher. He rests in Ephesus."[22] The use of the code language "lay against the bosom of the Lord" refers obviously to the Last Supper. From this source it can be affirmed that the one buried in Ephesus is Lazarus-John even if he is called by other names. Since *The Revelation to John* was written on the island of Patmos, it remains now to determine how Lazarus-John traveled from Jerusalem to Patmos and back to Ephesus.

Dr. König quotes Emil Bock as the source of the suggestion that Lazarus-John, whom Bock calls simply John, "appears to have gone to Greek towns on the coast of Asia Minor in order, like a sower of the word, to pass through the small Christian congregations that were forming everywhere."[23] Bock describes how about the year 95 or 96 C.E. "the fury of Domitian's persecution of the Christians afflicted the region of [Lazarus-]John's congregations in Asia Minor."[24] Bock also assumes that about that time Lazarus-John "was carried off to Rome to be tormented and tortured before finally being exiled to Patmos. There he received [*The Revelation to John*] and then, liberated after

20. König 2000 p. 167.
21. Steiner 1991 p. 99.
22. König 2000 p. 169.
23. Ibid. p. 169.
24. Ibid. p. 170

the violent death of Domitian, returned again to Ephesus. On June 24 in one of the following years he laid himself down to die in the grave which had been prepared long before" [25]

A similar story is told of John the son Zebedee that contributes to the confusion between these two mighty individualities. (So follow the footsteps of John the son of Zebedee for a moment.) Once again, Dr. König does the historical research. He now quotes Karl August Eckhardt, who in 1962 cited Tertullian for information about John the son of Zebedee and his deportation to a lonely island, that presumably was Patmos. As Eckhardt indicates, there is no good information about when and how John the son of Zebedee came to Rome, but he concludes, "It is not unlikely that he went to Rome with Saint Peter." [26] There are sources that point to the reign of Nero (54–68 C.E.) as the time of the banishment of John the son of Zebedee, when he was caught up in the persecution of Christians in Rome. As Dr. König emphasizes, "But what seems especially important is the fact that there are accounts of John [the son of Zebedee] returning from Patmos to Jerusalem and not to Ephesus." [27] This return occurred in a fashion similar to the return of Lazarus-John—"after the death of the tyrant"— but in this instance *some thirty years earlier.*

Dr. König acknowledges that the death of John the son of Zebedee is still shrouded in mystery. Eckhardt assumes that he met his death with many others during the destruction of the Temple after Jerusalem was conquered in the year 70 C.E. Dr. König prefers to leave that fact to be discovered by subsequent spiritual and/or historical investigation.

*   *   *

Finally, it is understandable that Lazarus-John and John the son of Zebedee have been confused. Although much of their personal history has been veiled, there are amazing similarities—and differences—in their travels. There is additional information in Dr. König's essay not only in the Epilogue but also in an Afterword. In the next chapter, the visions of Sister Emmerich will be used to see what further light can be shed on this subject.

---

25. König 2000 p. 170
26. Ibid. p. 171
27. Ibid. p. 171

CHAPTER 10

FROM THE VISIONS OF
SISTER EMMERICH

ROBERT POWELL has carefully unraveled the visions of Sister Emmerich in his significant work *Chronicle of the Living Christ.*[1] A most important part of his contribution was the ability to assign actual dates to most of the days of the Incarnation of the Christ Being. Using the availability of the handwritten notes of Clemens Brentano, written in German and only published in three releases during the 1980s, Dr. Powell was able to identify the actual number of days during which there were no recorded visions. In the last section of Chapter One in *Chronicle of the Living Christ,* entitled "The Gap in Anne Catherine Emmerich's Account of the Ministry," Dr. Powell provides a detailed account of the missing material.[2] He also has produced a table that gives an overview of six different periods related to these visions. The table is reproduced below; the dates included are the actual dates on which Sister Emmerich communicated information to Clemens Brentano.

In subsequent paragraphs, Dr. Powell refines the view to include overlaps and earlier periods when duplicate materials were revealed at other times. Included in the review is the analysis of how many Festivals of the Passover were attended by the Christ Being. Brentano and his posthumous editor, The Very Reverend Carl E. Schmöger, C.SS.R, thought there were only three Festivals of the Passover, which meant that only 15 days had been omitted from the entire record. A more careful reading of Brentano's original handwritten notes by Dr. Powell

---

1. Powell 1996.
2. Ibid. pp. 41–55.

established that the correct missing period was 313 days. Dr. Powell goes on to reconstruct as much of that period as possible from John's Gospel.[3]

TABLE 4 : *Overview of Visions (after Powell)*

Communications of Anne Catherine Emmerich

1. July 29, 1820–March 29, 1821 — The last eight months of the ministry, leading up to the crucifixion.

2. March 30, 182–June 1, 1821 — The crucifixion, the resurrection, and subsequent events.

3. June 2, 1821–April 28, 1823 — The four months prior to the baptism; then from the baptism to the sending out of the apostles.

4. April 29, 1823–Oct. 21, 1823 — No communication (due to Clemens Brentano's absence).

5. Oct. 22, 1823–Jan. 8, 1824 — Reconstruction of the first eleven weeks of period 4, from the sending out of the apostles onward.

6. Jan. 9, 1824–Feb.9, 1824 — Day-by-day communications concerning the ministry resumed, then discontinued (due to ill health).

The Powell record of the visions of Sister Emmerich has been reviewed for occurrences of the names John and Lazarus. In Table 5 can be found a summary of these occurrences. It should be noted that there are several categories to which these occurrences can be assigned. If the person is part of Sister Emmerich's vision, this is considered a "Genuine" occurrence. If the person is referred to in the vision but not an actual part of the vision, that is considered a "Passing" reference and is not included in the count of the "Genuine" occurrences. In some cases

3. Powell 1996 pp. 48–50.

the "Genuine" occurrences are "Implied"—when, for example, the person is present on the first day of a sequence, not mentioned on the second day, but mentioned again on the third day. For our example, all three days would be considered as "Genuine" occurrences but the second day would be listed as "Implied". Some "Genuine" occurrences are considered "Contested" when additional evidence suggests that Sister Emmerich may not have "seen" the correct person. Fortunately, the latter occurrences are infrequent and may be eliminated by further thoughts (see Chapters 11 & 12). They are nevertheless troublesome from the point of view of the authentication of the visions. See Appendix 2 for details on the validation of the visions.

Quite apart from the subtleties of "Contested" occurrences, the total number of "Genuine" occurrences for John the son of Zebedee, at forty-one, is in marked contrast to the total number of "Genuine" occurrences for Lazarus, which is ninety-five. This provides additional evidence to suggest the importance of Lazarus/Lazarus-John in understanding the Mystery of the Beloved Disciple.

The "Contested" occurrences have been defined above, but they will be reviewed here while there is a focus on the visions of Sister

TABLE 5 : *Summary of Occurrences (for explanation, see text)*

Summary of analysis of Sister Emmerich's visions regarding occurrences of John and Lazarus

Time period: May 31, 29 to April 3, 33 C.E.

Total number of occurrences for John the son of Zebedee: 42

One of these is considered a "Passing" reference, which makes for a total of *forty-one* "Genuine" occurrences; but one of those is "Questionable" and three are "Contested."

Total number of occurrences for Lazarus of Bethany: 132

Of these thirty-seven are considered as "Passing" references, which makes for a total of *ninety-five* "Genuine" occurrences; but seven of these are "Implied," and none are "Contested."

Emmerich. In the same sense that Sister Emmerich was not aware of the Mystery of the Two Jesus Children (see page 19), it can be concluded that she was not aware of the Mystery of the Beloved Disciple. Here, too, there is an explanation for why this might be the case. Dr. König reviewed some materials from various places in Dr. Steiner's lectures to establish the true meaning of the name John.[4] Dr. Steiner not only indicates that "in former times the giving of names was nothing arbitrary" but that "John" means the "forerunner or predecessor." Dr. König goes on to explain that the name "John'" grows from being a proper name into being a symbol of one who is to become the herald of the individuality. Thus, in the first half of John's Gospel there is the testimony of John the Baptizer, the *old* John; whereas in the second half there is the testimony of the *new* John whom Christ Jesus had initiated, for this is the Lazarus-John who was brought back from the dead. This touches on the profound Mystery of Golgotha, the mission of the Christ Being, and the need for the individuality to become an independent identity in each human being. It is understandable that Sister Emmerich did not have the esoteric background more recently provided by Dr. Steiner to begin explaining these substantive and significant spiritual verities.

Finally, for the remainder of this discourse, there needs to be yet another effort at establishing consistent terminology. It is obvious that different names are used in the various sources. In order to avoid confusion surrounding different names and to acknowledge changes in status, the names identified in Table 6 will be used wherever possible. In that same manner, although the initiation of Lazarus by Christ Jesus on July 26, 32 C.E. is also called a raising from the dead and suggests a name change from Lazarus to Lazarus-John for several authors, it will be preferred to refer to it as an initiation and to focus on the breathing by Christ Jesus on Lazarus seven times making him an Apostle approximately one year before Pentecost when that change in status also occurred for John the son of Zebedee.

---

4. König 2000 pp. 156–57.

TABLE 6: *Consistent Nomenclature—John and Lazarus*

Date	John the Son of Zebedee	Lazarus of Bethany
July 26, 32		Initiation–Apostle Lazarus
May 24, 33[5]	Pentecost–Apostle John	
circa 34		Move to France where the Apostle Lazarus becomes the Bishop of Marseille
circa 36	The Apostle John takes Mary-Sophia to Ephesus	
August 15, 44	Death of Mary-Sophia in Ephesus	
circa 50	Death of the Apostle John	
circa 66		Return to Ephesus where the Apostle Lazarus takes on the name Presbyter John[6]
circa 95		Exile to Patmos
circa 100		Death in Ephesus

---

5. This momentous event also brought about a change in the Blessed Virgin Mary such that Mary-Sophia becomes a more appropriate name as well as a means to recognize a new status. See Robert Powell *The Most Holy Trinosophia and the New Revelation of the Divine Feminine* (Great Barrington, MA: Anthroposophic Press, 2000) p. 47.

6. It is acknowledged that Lazarus-John, John the Evangelist, John the Divine, and the Beloved Disciple are name equivalents for Presbyter John.

CHAPTER 11

THE JOHN MYSTERY

(This chapter is contributed by Robert Powell.)

CONTEMPORARY SCHOLARSHIP

IN THIS CHAPTER an attempt is made to shed light on the mystery of "the disciple whom the Lord loved" through a tapestry woven from the visions of the Blessed Anne Catherine Emmerich, one of the most extraordinary saintly seers in the entire history of Christianity. Other sources, notably Rudolf Steiner, are also drawn upon—including several authors who have been inspired by Dr. Steiner's indications, like the writer of this chapter, to contemplate more deeply the Mystery of the Beloved Disciple. In Chapter 9 Karl König's thoughts concerning Lazarus of Bethany and John the son of Zebedee are presented. Dr. König accepted Dr. Steiner's identification of the Apostle Lazarus as the one who wrote John's Gospel. Dr. König assumed, as the Washing of the Feet is described in this gospel [John 13], that the Apostle Lazarus was present at the events described in Chapter 13 and is the one referred to as "the disciple whom [Christ] Jesus loved, [who] was lying close to the breast of Jesus." [John 13:23]

The Reverend Irene Johanson, a priest of the Christian Community, also accepts Dr. Steiner's identification of the Apostle Lazarus as the one who wrote *The Gospel According to John*. However, she indicates that the Apostle Lazarus, having been initiated by Christ Jesus himself, was able to move freely outside of his body, and thus it was not necessary for him to be *physically present* at the Last Supper because he was able to be *spiritually present*. Moreover, in one of her books she indicates that there was a special inner relationship between John the son of Zebedee and the Apostle Lazarus such that the latter, who was able to move around freely outside his body, could be present at the Last Supper ind-welling John the son of Zebedee.[1]

Thus, when John the son of Zebedee laid his head on Christ Jesus' breast and heard the beating of the Lord's heart, the Apostle Lazarus also participated in this intimate scene on a spiritual level and therefore later, in writing John's Gospel, incorporated aspects of the events that took place on the evening of the Last Supper into his gospel, but with-out describing everything—for example, as remarked upon in Chapter 9, he does not describe the sacramental inauguration of the Holy Mass. Dr. König concludes, as described in Chapter 9, that the Apostle "Laz-arus bears witness only of those things in which he himself took part after his raising,"[2] and thus he believes that the Apostle Lazarus only joins the twelve disciples just before the Washing of the Feet begins. According to Irene Johanson, the Apostle Lazarus was *spiritually present* with the twelve disciples at the Last Supper, indwelling John the son of Zebedee:

The Gospels speak of three human beings who bore the name John. They speak of John the [Baptizer], known as the preparer of the way for [the Christ Being]. They speak of a second John, the brother of James and son of Zebedee, who belonged to the circle of the twelve disciples. And they speak of a third John. He wrote [*The Revelation to John*] and the gospel named after him. He is the one who bore the name Lazarus and who was called back to life by Christ [Jesus] after having undergone [several] days of death. For this new life he received a new name. He became the disciple whom the Lord loved, which means that he had reached the perfect condition of discipleship. *The name for someone who could live discipleship perfectly was John.* Lazarus-John had already undergone the experience of death and since then was able to live consciously in two worlds. For him the abyss between this world and the yonder world no longer existed. Christ [Jesus] was able to say of him that he would not taste death and that he would remain independent of the body

---

1. Irene Johanson *Wie die Jünger Christus Erleben* (*How the Disciples Experienced Christ*) (Stuttgart: Urachhaus Verlag, 1992) p. 41.
2. König 2000 pp. 147–148.

until the second coming of [the Christ Being]. Thus there are: John the [Baptizer]; John [the son of] Zebedee, one of the twelve disciples; and [the Apostle] Lazarus, also called John the Evangelist....[3]

The foregoing description of the three Johns by Irene Johanson offers a key to understanding the Mystery of the Beloved Disciple. Now consider this mystery on a deeper level. Accepting her description above, at least as a working hypothesis, "the disciple whom the Lord loved" is actually a composite being made up of all three Johns. At the Last Supper, John the son of Zebedee was *physically present*. This can be confirmed because it is explicitly stated in Matthew's Gospel that after the Last Supper, Christ Jesus and the disciples went to the Mount of Olives and that when they reached the Garden of Gethsemane, Christ Jesus took "with him Peter and the two sons of Zebedee." [Matthew 26:37]

It is also brought out in John's Gospel that "[Christ] Jesus loved Martha and her sister and [the Apostle] Lazarus" [John 11:5], signifying that the expression "the disciple whom the Lord loved" certainly applies to the Apostle Lazarus.

Irene Johanson's indication concerning the spiritual indwelling of the Apostle Lazarus in John the son of Zebedee explains not only the use of this expression at the Last Supper: "One of his disciples, [the one] whom Jesus loved, was lying close to the breast of Jesus" [John 13:23], but also its use in the last chapter of John's Gospel when, "Peter turned and saw following them the disciple whom [Christ] Jesus loved.... This is the disciple who is bearing witness to these things, and who has written these things." [John 21:20, 21:24] As will emerge in the following discussion based on the visions of Sister Emmerich, according to her in each of these two scenes it was John the son of Zebedee who was physically present and not the Apostle Lazarus. But if the Apostle Lazarus was the one "who has written these things," then the Apostle Lazarus must have been *spiritually present* in (or through)

3. Irene Johanson *Die Drei Jünger Johannes* (*The Three Disciples Called John*) (Stuttgart: Urachhaus Verlag, 1997) pp. 9–10; translated by Robert Powell. (For additional translations from this author see Appendix 5.)

John the son of Zebedee. The spiritual presence of the Apostle Lazarus indwelling John the son of Zebedee, as suggested by Irene Johanson, would have been apparent to Christ Jesus, who saw everything both on the physical and on the spiritual level.

For, as discussed in Chapter 9, John the Baptizer united with the Apostle Lazarus when the latter was initiated by Christ Jesus on July 26, 32.[4] This is the deeper esoteric reason why, later, the Apostle Lazarus took on the name of Presbyter John when he wrote *The Revelation to John*, in composing his gospel, and when sending out the *Letters of John*.

THE LAST SUPPER REVISITED

Returning to consider the Last Supper, the presence of the Apostle Lazarus at this event *on a spiritual level* (rather than physically) resolves many problems, especially when we consider that the Apostle Lazarus was under threat of death, "For the chief priests planned to put also [the Apostle] Lazarus to death." [John 12:10] Therefore, as Sister Emmerich describes, the Apostle Lazarus was obliged to keep a low profile, so most of the time he remained hidden at his home in Bethany. "[The Apostle] Lazarus and the Blessed Virgin [Mary] with six of the holy women remained hidden [in Bethany]. They were in the same subterranean apartments in which [the Apostle] Lazarus lay concealed during the persecution that had risen against him [earlier]."[5] Further, Sister Emmerich describes on the morning of the Last Supper how Christ Jesus, having stayed there overnight, took leave of the Apostle Lazarus, the Blessed Virgin Mary, and the holy women in Bethany, when he set out with the disciples to go to Jerusalem. "Jesus took an affecting leave of the holy women, [the Apostle] Lazarus, and His Mother [the Blessed Virgin Mary] in Bethany."[6] For the sacred event that took place that evening she gives a description in minute detail of the seating arrangement of the disciples at the Last Supper, or rather of how the disciples stood prior to being seated: "John [the son of Zebedee], James the Greater, and James the Less stood on [Christ] Jesus' right; then came Bartholomew, … Thomas, and next to him Judas

---

4. When dates are specified in the text, the full account of the vision as provided by Powell can be found in Appendix 4.
5. Emmerich 1954b vol. IV, p. 11.
6. Ibid. p. 55.

Iscariot. On [Christ] Jesus' left were Peter, Andrew, and Thaddeus; then … came Simon … Matthew, and Philip."[7] Knowing that John and James the Greater, the sons of Zebedee, are explicitly mentioned in Matthew's Gospel as having been taken by Christ Jesus, together with Peter, to the Garden of Gethsemane after the Last Supper, clearly—if we take Sister Emmerich's description to be reliable and trustworthy[8]—the Apostle Lazarus was evidently not physically present at the Last Supper. In fact, according to Sister Emmerich, that evening the Apostle Lazarus was together with Nicodemus and Joseph of Arimathea.

> The Mother of the Lord [Blessed Virgin Mary], with [Mary] Magdalene, Martha, Mary Cleophas, Mary Salome, and Salome had gone from the Coenaculum to the house of Mary Mark. Alarmed at the reports that she had heard, [the Blessed Virgin] Mary and her friends went on toward the city to get some news of [Christ] Jesus. Here they were met by [the Apostle] Lazarus, Nicodemus, Joseph of Arimathea, and some relatives from Hebron, who sought to comfort [the Blessed Virgin] Mary in her great anxiety.[9]

According to this account, the Apostle Lazarus had evidently ventured forth to Jerusalem by cover of night and was in the company of Nicodemus and Joseph of Arimathea on that Thursday evening. On a spiritual level, as a great initiate who could travel independently of his physical body, he was according to Irene Johanson *spiritually present* at the Last Supper, indwelling John the son of Zebedee. This ability to be in one place physically and simultaneously in another place spiritually is called in the Christian mystical tradition *bilocation*. Evidently, the Apostle Lazarus had the gift of bilocation.

Taking into account the spiritual union of John the Baptizer with the Apostle Lazarus, a picture emerges at the Last Supper of "The Beloved Disciple" as a composite being comprising:

---

7. Emmerich 1954b vol.iv, pp. 60–61.
8. The reliability and trustworthiness of Sister Emmerich's account is discussed in Appendix 2.
9. Emmerich 1954b vol. IV, p. 87.

John the son of Zebedee, who was physically present;

The Apostle Lazarus, who was spiritually present indwelling him; and

John the Baptizer, who was also spiritually present through his inner union with the Apostle Lazarus.

AT THE SEA OF GALILEE

This image, if true, would apply also to other instances when "The Beloved Disciple" is mentioned in *The Gospel According to John*. For example, in Chapter 21 of this gospel the appearance of the Risen Christ to a group of seven disciples by the Sea of Galilee is depicted: "Simon Peter, Thomas called the Twin, Nathanael of Cana in Galilee, the sons of Zebedee, and two others of his disciples were together." [John 21:2] This group of seven includes John the son of Zebedee and his brother James the Greater. But who were the "two others"? According to Sister Emmerich they were John Mark and Silas.[10] So, if one reads the chapter attentively, it is clear that the Apostle Lazarus was not physically present as one of the seven to whom the Risen Christ appeared. Yet "the [Beloved] Disciple, who had lain close to his breast at the supper" [John 21: 20] *was present* and says of himself at the end of that chapter: "This is the disciple who is bearing witness to these things, and who has written these things." [John 21:24] Now, Dr. Steiner indicates that "the awakened Lazarus is the one who wrote [*The Gospel According to John*],"[11] and thus it is clear that the Apostle Lazarus, by his own testimony as the writer of this gospel, *was present* at this scene by the Sea of Galilee. Since he was not physically present, he must have been *spiritually present*. Here again Irene Johanson's depiction of the Apostle Lazarus indwelling John the son of Zebedee solves the apparent contradiction presented by this scene described in the last chapter of John's Gospel.

---

10. Emmerich 1954b vol. IV, p. 397. The identification of the two others as John Mark and Silas is given in the account of this event by Sister Emmerich. John Mark was the son of Mary Mark, one of the holy women, whose house in Jerusalem was a meeting place for Christ Jesus and the disciples [Acts 12:12]; and Silas was one of the three youths who accompanied Christ Jesus on his journey to Ur and Heliopolis after the initiation of the Apostle Lazarus.

11. Rudolf Steiner *From the History & Contents of the First Section of the Esoteric School, 1904–1914* (Great Barrington, MA: Anthroposophic Press, 1998) p. 220.

A further interesting aspect regarding this scene is brought forth by Sister Emmerich, when she describes in detail what took place when "Peter turned and saw following them [The Beloved Disciple]." [John 21:20] In her own words: "I had at this moment a vision of [the death of] John in Ephesus.[12] I saw him stretch himself out in his grave, address some words to his disciples, and die."[13] These words clearly indicate that the mystery of the Apostle Lazarus indwelling John the son of Zebedee was veiled to her. For it was not John the son of Zebedee who died in Ephesus in this manner. Rather, it was Presbyter John, the writer of *The Gospel According to John,* who (as indicated in the biographical sketch of Lazarus of Bethany in the following chapter) took on the name of Presbyter John when he came to Ephesus and died in Ephesus in the manner described. It can be inferred that while Sister Emmerich beheld the physical figure of John the son of Zebedee, her clairvoyant gaze fell upon the Apostle Lazarus spiritually indwelling John the son of Zebedee, but for all the amazing power of her clairvoyance she did not know this mystery consciously.

FROM THE PERSPECTIVE OF DR. STEINER

This mystery, however, was penetrated in an extraordinary way by Dr. Steiner through his advanced faculty of clairvoyance. It is thanks to Dr. Steiner that we know so much about the Mystery of the Beloved Disciple. Not only did Dr. Steiner identify Lazarus of Bethany as the writer of John's Gospel, but also he indicated something of the profound connection between Lazarus of Bethany and John the son of Zebedee. For, according to Dr. Steiner, "When Lazarus becomes [Lazarus]-John, he takes the place of the one who is Zebedee's son, and as such he is the one who lay on the breast of Jesus at the Last Supper."[14] Did Dr. Steiner see this as a *spiritual union* of Lazarus-John with John the son of Zebedee (Lazarus indwelling John the son of Zebedee) or that Lazarus-John *physically took the place* of John the son of Zebedee at the Last Supper? As noted above, according to John's Gospel, John the

---

12. The Consistent Nomenclature effort would have added [son of Zebedee] after the name John, but Dr. Powell preferred the ambiguity of the original.
13. Emmerich 1954b vol. IV, pp. 401–402.
14. Steiner 1998 p. 220.

son of Zebedee was *physically present* at the Last Supper and accompanied Christ Jesus afterwards to the Garden of Gethsemane. [Matthew 26:37] And from Sister Emmerich's description the Apostle Lazarus was *not one of those physically present* at the Last Supper. The only possible solution here—taking Anne Catherine Emmerich's account together with that of Matthew's Gospel—is the one offered by Irene Johanson, that the Apostle Lazarus was *spiritually present* at the Last Supper, indwelling John the son of Zebedee, who lay on the breast of Jesus, so that the Apostle Lazarus spiritually participated in this event. Since Irene Johanson arrived at her insight through a deep study of Dr. Steiner's various indications concerning the Beloved Disciple, it can be surmised that her interpretation is implicit in Dr. Steiner's words, even if in his speaking out concerning the Mystery of the Beloved Disciple, perhaps for the sake of simplification, he did not elaborate upon this mystery further to the extent of explicitly stating that the Apostle Lazarus spiritually united with John the son of Zebedee. Dr. Steiner's further indications concerning the relationship between the Apostle Lazarus and John the son of Zebedee, which he gave in response to questions during the course of a private conversation, have been recorded as follows:

Question: Is he who is called John in the first three gospels the same as Lazarus?

Answer by Dr. Steiner: The writer of [The Gospel According to John] is Lazarus. He is only called "John" in the same way that many were called "John" in his day. What was the name "John" at that time?

Question: Is Lazarus the same as the son of Zebedee?

Counter question by Dr. Steiner: Do the sons of Zebedee belong anyway to the intimate circle of the Twelve? To the starry circle where [the] Christ [Being] saw himself mirrored? It must be a mistake if it is written thus in the Gospels. We must not be surprised if mistakes do occur, because the Apostles were able to exchange their physical bodies with one another under the prevailing, very different soul conditions of that time. The three disciples in the Garden of Gethsemane belonged, at any rate, to the most intimate circle of the Twelve and Lazarus belonged to it too.

(Recorded conversations of the Christian Community priests Werner Klein and Emil Bock with Rudolf Steiner, February 1924)[15]

There is something of a mystery in Dr. Steiner's words here. On the one hand, he puts the question: "Do the sons of Zebedee belong anyway to the intimate circle of the Twelve?" and answers that "it must be a mistake if it is written thus in the Gospels." On the other hand, he points out that "the three disciples in the Garden of Gethsemane belonged, at any rate, to the most intimate circle of the Twelve and Lazarus belonged to it too." Since two of the three disciples in the Garden of Gethsemane were the sons of Zebedee, Dr. Steiner's words indicate that they "belonged, at any rate, to the most intimate circle of the Twelve." Not only were these three disciples (Peter, James, and John, i.e., Peter and the two sons of Zebedee) present in the Garden of Gethsemane, but also they were present at the Transfiguration on Mt. Tabor [Matthew 17:1], at the raising of the daughter of Jairus from the dead [Mark 5:37], and (as already mentioned) at the appearance of the Risen Christ to the seven disciples by the Sea of Galilee. [John 21:2] These explicit gospel references are unmistakable. There is an inner consistency that whenever something deeply significant takes place, these are the three disciples whom Christ Jesus chooses to take with him. As stated in the gospel, "James and John, sons of Zebedee, were partners with Simon [Peter]" [Luke 5:10], who—together with the brothers Simon [Peter] and Andrew—were the first disciples chosen by Christ Jesus. [Mark 1:16–20] Is it conceivable that John the son of Zebedee, who in the gospels seems inseparable from his brother James and in the Acts of the Apostles (after James left for Spain) inseparable from Peter, would not have been present together with the other disciples at the culminating event of the Last Supper? The closeness of the sons of Zebedee, James and John, is also referred to by Dr. Steiner:

Among the twelve Apostles, Lazarus-John is similarly also represented by another. John the brother of James and the son of Zebedee is not an Apostle in the real sense. James and John are in

15. Steiner 1998 p. 226.

a way a single person.... But when Lazarus becomes John, he takes the place of the one who is Zebedee's son, and as such he is the one who lay on the breast of Jesus at the Last Supper.[16]

Perhaps Dr. Steiner's word "represented" can be interpreted in the light of Irene Johanson's depiction of the Apostle Lazarus as having a special relationship with John the son of Zebedee, who thus "represented" him in the circle of the twelve disciples, and perhaps Dr. Steiner's words "takes the place of" can be interpreted as signifying the profound level of the spiritual indwelling of the Apostle Lazarus in John the son of Zebedee. And Dr. Steiner's remark that "the Apostles were able to exchange their physical bodies with one another" could point in the direction of such an exchange taking place at times between John the son of Zebedee and the Apostle Lazarus, i.e., at times that the latter *spiritually indwelt* the body of John the son of Zebedee.

With regard to the Apostle status of John the son of Zebedee, he is explicitly designated as an Apostle in Acts in Chapter 1 and is named several times together with Peter in Chapters 3 and 4. One reference in Chapter 4 clearly disqualifies an identification of the Apostle John with the writer of John's Gospel: "They saw the boldness of the Apostles Peter and John, and perceived that they were uneducated, common men." [Acts 4:13] They were fishermen from Galilee and were thus "uneducated, common men." On the other hand, the Apostle Lazarus was highly educated and he was extremely wealthy,—hardly an "uneducated, common" man! Thus, as the author of John's Gospel, he displays a knowledge of philosophy and of the Greek language. At any rate, Dr. Steiner's indication quoted above that Lazarus of Bethany, after his initiation by Christ Jesus, belonged to the intimate circle of the Twelve, i.e., that Lazarus was an Apostle, is a significant one. The following outline offers a possibility for grasping the apostleship of Lazarus.

Here it is important to comprehend the deeper meaning of the word "Apostle." It can be understood by way of contrast with the word "disciple." The disciples became Apostles at the time of Pentecost, through the Descent of the Holy Spirit. Up to this point in time they

---

16. Steiner 1998 p. 220.

were disciples, i.e., they were *pupils* of Christ Jesus. Through the Descent of the Holy Spirit they became empowered from above to go out and teach and heal *in the name of Christ Jesus.* This inner empowerment—the birth of the Christ Being within—is what made them Apostles rather than disciples. It should be noted—as described in Acts—that because one of the original twelve, Judas Iscariot, had died in the meantime (not to mention that through his betrayal he had disqualified himself from the circle of twelve), lots were cast "and the lot fell on Matthias, and he was enrolled with the eleven Apostles." [Acts 1:26] However, the Apostle Lazarus was the true "replacement" for Judas, as remarked upon already in Chapter 9 in the quote from Dr. König: "Metaphorically speaking, the Eagle [Lazarus-John] has now taken the place of the Scorpion, Judas." [17] Already prior to the publication of Dr. König's book in the year 2000, attention was drawn to this mystery of Lazarus replacing Judas and how this had taken place far in advance of Judas' betrayal, when Lazarus was initiated by Christ Jesus:

> Jesus raised his eyes to heaven and prayed aloud, calling in a loud voice: "Lazarus, come forth!".... Lazarus knelt before the Lord, who laid his right hand upon Lazarus' head and breathed upon him seven times.... Through being breathed upon seven times, Lazarus received the seven gifts of the Holy Spirit,[18] receiving them before the other Apostles.... Lazarus became an Apostle from this moment onwards by way of receiving the gifts of the Holy Spirit [through the breath of Christ] already, prior to the Descent of the Holy Spirit at Pentecost. It was the Descent of the Holy Spirit at Pentecost which transformed the disciples into Apostles. But as Lazarus received the seven gifts of the Holy Spirit as part of his initiation by Christ, he became an Apostle before the others.... In effect, Lazarus took the place of Judas in the circle of twelve.... Judas left the circle of twelve, but his place had already been filled in advance by Lazarus. Both their destinies stood under the sign of death, the sign of the Scorpion in the circle of the twelve signs of the zodiac, whereby a corre-

---

17. König 2000 p. 149.
18. True Godliness, Wisdom, Counsel, Understanding, Might, Knowledge, and Fear of the Lord; see Isaiah 11:2.

spondence exists between the twelve disciples and the twelve zodiacal signs. Judas' sign was that of the Scorpion.... Lazarus, on the other hand, lived solely for the Light of the spirit. He stood under the sign of the Eagle, and—dying—he ascended like an eagle ever higher into the Kingdom of Light. Called back by Christ Jesus, he came as a messenger of this world of spirit, this Kingdom of Light. Then he stood under the sign of the Dove, which is the symbol of the Holy Spirit. Here we see the metamorphosis of this zodiacal sign: from the Eagle to the Scorpion to the Dove. This is one of the more profound aspects of the raising of Lazarus from the dead.[19]

Thus in Christian iconography the writer of John's Gospel is symbolized by the Eagle.

AT THE CRUCIFIXION

There is still another occurrence of the expression "the Beloved Disciple" in John's Gospel that deserves attention. It occurs in relationship to the scene of the Crucifixion and to words that Christ Jesus spoke, looking down from the Cross: "When [Christ] Jesus saw his mother [the Blessed Virgin Mary] and the Beloved Disciple standing near, he said to his mother [the Blessed Virgin Mary], 'Woman, behold, your son!' Then he said to the disciple, 'Behold, your mother!' And from that hour the disciple took her to his own home." [John 19: 26–27]

According to Dr. Steiner: "The awakened Lazarus is the one who wrote John's Gospel. He is the one who stood beneath the Cross and to whom Christ Jesus spoke from the Cross, indicating the Mother Sophia-Mary: Behold thy mother!"[20] If Irene Johanson's image of the Apostle Lazarus indwelling John the son of Zebedee also applies to this scene beneath the Cross, then it can be understood that Christ Jesus' words applied on two levels: to John the son of Zebedee on the physical level, that he had the task of caring for the Blessed Virgin Mary; and to the Apostle Lazarus on the spiritual level, that his task would be to care for the Divine Feminine, i.e., Sophia. This is borne out by considering

---

19. Powell 1998 pp. 159–163.
20. Steiner 1998 p. 220.

the further destinies of the Apostle Lazarus and John the son of Zebedee after the Mystery of Golgotha (see below).

> About one year after the Crucifixion of Our Lord, Stephen was stoned, though no further persecution of the Apostles took place at that time. The rising settlement of new converts around Jerusalem, however, was dissolved, the Christians dispersed, and some were murdered. A few years later, a new storm arose against them. Then it was that the Blessed Virgin [Mary-Sophia], who until that time had dwelt in the small house near the Coenaculum and in Bethany, allowed herself to be conducted by [the Apostle] John to the region of Ephesus, where the Christians had already made settlements. This happened a short time after the imprisonment of [the Apostle] Lazarus and his sisters by the Jews and their setting out over the sea. [The Apostle] John returned again to Jerusalem, where the other Apostles still were. James the Greater was one of the first of the Apostles who ... left Jerusalem.... He sailed first to Ephesus in order to visit Mary[-Sophia], and thence to Spain. Shortly before his death, he visited Mary[-Sophia] and [his brother the Apostle] John a second time in [her] home at Ephesus. Here Mary[-Sophia] told him that his death would soon take place in Jerusalem. She encouraged and consoled him. James took leave of her and his brother [the Apostle] John....[21]

If Anne Catherine Emmerich's report is to be trusted, it was the Apostle John, the brother of James the Greater, who accompanied Mary-Sophia to Ephesus and helped to take care of her there, signifying that the Apostle John fulfilled the injunction of Christ Jesus' words spoken from the Cross that he should care for the Blessed Virgin Mary as if she were his own mother. Consequently it seems certain that it was indeed John the son of Zebedee who was with Blessed Virgin Mary at the foot of the Cross. As "the Beloved Disciple," however, it was clearly again the Apostle Lazarus who was also present *spiritually indwelling* John the son of Zebedee, just as at the Last Supper. This is confirmed by Dr. Steiner's words that it was "the awakened Lazarus ... who stood

---

21. Emmerich 1954b vol. IV, pp. 448–449.

beneath the Cross," quoted above. A further confirmation is provided by Sister Emmerich's words that "the Mother of God [the Blessed Virgin Mary] lived [after the Mystery of Golgotha] for a time in Bethany at the home of [the Apostle] Lazarus and Martha." [22]

The words from the Gospel "from that hour the disciple took her to his own home" [John 19:27] were fulfilled by the Apostle Lazarus, in whose home she lived, *until* she went with the Apostle John to Ephesus, although Sister Emmerich points out in the above quote that the Blessed Virgin Mary also "dwelt in the small house near the Coenaculum," which probably belonged to the Apostle Lazarus.[23] Again it emerges that "the Beloved Disciple" was really a composite being comprising John the son of Zebedee, the Apostle Lazarus, and also John the Baptizer, who had spiritually united himself with the Apostle Lazarus at the time of his initiation by Christ Jesus.

In the next chapter will be presented more details of the biographies of John the son of Zebedee, who became the Apostle John, and Lazarus of Bethany, who became the Apostle Lazarus, then the Bishop of Marseille, and finally Presbyter John.

---

22. Anne Catherine Emmerich *Das Leben Unseres Herrn und Heilandes Jesu Christi* (3 vols.; Regensburg, 1858-1860) vol. III, p. 612. This is the original German edition of *The Life of Jesus Christ* by Anne Catherine Emmerich, which contains her visions of the later lives and destinies of the Apostles. Unfortunately these most interesting visions have been left out of all subsequent editions.
23. Emmerich 1954b vol. I, p. 396: "The Apostle Lazarus had been for some days at his house in Jerusalem on the west side of Mt. Zion . . . ." This is possibly the house where the Blessed Virgin Mary stayed, alternating between staying in Jerusalem or at the Apostle Lazarus' castle in Bethany.

CHAPTER 12

THE JOHANNINE TRADITION: BIOGRAPHICAL OUTLINES

(This chapter is contributed by Robert Powell.)

EARLY TESTIMONIES CONCERNING JOHN

A CLEAR PICTURE of the deep and profound relationship between John the son of Zebedee and Lazarus of Bethany emerges when we consider their further destinies, even though these destinies initially took them in completely different directions: the Apostle John first to Ephesus and then back to Jerusalem, and the Apostle Lazarus first to France, where he stayed for approximately thirty years, and only then to Ephesus. However, before considering these remarkable destinies in more detail, let us consider the testimony of Papias of Hierapolis (ca. 65–ca. 125) who "distinguished between the Apostle John and Presbyter John."[1] (Hierapolis in Asia Minor is said to be the place where the Apostle Philip died a martyr's death.)

At the start of the second and third of the Letters of John, John refers to himself as "the Presbyter," which usually appears in English translation as "the Elder." (It is interesting to note that the English word "priest" comes via the Latin translation of the Greek word *presbyteros*). It is the same word (in the plural form, *presbyteroi*) that is used by Presbyter John in describing his vision of "the twenty-four Elders" round the Throne of God. [Revelation 4:4] These twenty-four Presbyters (*presbyteroi*) are heavenly Elders. Presbyter John was the Elder of the Christian settlement in Ephesus, and it is how he chose to designate himself in his *Letters of John*. (John the Evangelist and John the Divine

---

1. Gerd-Klaus Kaltenbrunner *Johannes Ist Sein Name* (*John Is His Name*) (Zug, Switzerland: Die Graue Edition, 1993) p. 62.

are later designations given to "the Beloved Disciple," but Presbyter John was the expression that he used himself.)

Papias of Hierapolis distinguished Presbyter John from the Apostle John, who together with his brother the Apostle James and with the Apostle Peter were designated by Paul as the three "pillars" of the Church. [Galatians 2:9] Papias, when he visited Ephesus, came too late to experience the Apostle John, but evidently he did meet Presbyter John there.[2] That the two are to be distinguished from one another is apparent from the following fragment by Papias embedded in the *Historia Ecclesiastica* by the theologian and historian Eusebius of Caesarea (ca. 264–ca. 340 C.E.).

I searched and enquired into the statements of the Presbyter[s] and asked: "What did Andrew say, and Peter, Philip, Thomas or James, and what did John or Matthew or any of the other disciples of the Lord say? And what do the disciples of the Lord, Aristion and Presbyter John, say?"

Eusebius commented upon these words:

What is noteworthy about these words is that Papias lists the name John twice. The first time he counts John together with Peter, James, Matthew and the other Apostles.... The second time, in a new sentence, he counts John to another category, which is different from that of the Apostles. He places Aristion's name before his and expressly designates him as Presbyter. Thereby he confirms the truth of the report that two disciples in Asia had the same name and that two graves were erected in Ephesus which even now both bear the name John....[3]

And from another source:

Papias, whom we have just quoted from, acknowledges receiving the teachings of the Apostles from their pupils and to having heard in person Aristion and Presbyter John.[4]

---

2. Kaltenbrunner 1993 p. 62.
3. Eusebius *Historia Ecclesiastica* vol. III, 39, 3ff. in Kaltenbrunner 1993 pp. 63–64.
4. Eusebius *Historia Ecclesiastica* vol. III, 39, 3 in Johannes Hemleben *Johannes der Evangelist* (John the Evangelist) (Hamburg: Rowohlt Verlag, 1972) p. 14.

As will emerge in the following biographical outlines, John the son of Zebedee is the Apostle John referred to by Eusebius (quoting Papias), and Lazarus of Bethany is Presbyter John, the writer of *The Revelation to John*, *The Gospel According to John*, and the *Letters of John*. Both lived in Ephesus and, according to the tradition still known to Eusebius in the fourth century, both died and were buried in Ephesus,[5] *but Presbyter John obviously at a much later point in time than the Apostle John.* Thus, when Papias came to Ephesus the Apostle John was no longer living, but evidently Presbyter John was still living, since from Papias' testimony for the Apostle John he uses the past tense ("What did John say?") and in relation to Presbyter John he uses the present tense ("What does Presbyter John say?"). Moreover, there is a statement by St. Irenaeus (ca. 130–ca. 202 C.E.), who was Bishop of Lyons from about 177/178 C.E. until the end of his life, that Papias himself had written down that he had "listened to John,"[6] which implies that he heard Presbyter John before the death of this *hagios theologos* ("holy theologian"), as he is known in the Greek Orthodox Church. It is possible that Papias came to Ephesus just before the death of Presbyter John and heard him, and then after his death sought to learn more of the words spoken by "the wise old man from the mountain," as Presbyter John was also known in the Christian tradition stemming from Ephesus.[7]

Generally speaking, however, no distinction is drawn between the Apostle John and Presbyter John (John the Evangelist), as can be seen from the following account:

John, John the Evangelist, John the Divine: One of the twelve apostles of Jesus. He was one of the three who were admitted to closest intimacy with him, preeminently "the disciple whom Jesus loved." He was the son of Zebedee, and originally a fisherman. His brother James and he were designated *"Boanerges"*— sons of thunder. He leaned on the bosom of Jesus at the Last

---

5. Another ancient tradition indicates that the Apostle John "the son of Zebedee was killed by the Jews;" see Hemleben 1972 p. 83. In this case it is probable that the Apostle John died a martyr's death in Jerusalem or somewhere else in Palestine.
6. Irenaeus *Adversus Haereses* V, 33, 4 in Kaltenbrunner 1993 pp. 62–63.
7. Kaltenbrunner 1993 p. 53.

Supper, and was present at the Crucifixion, when Jesus committed his mother to John's special care. He is generally believed to
have been the author of the gospel and the three epistles that
bear his name, and also of the Apocalypse or Revelation, though
the question of the authorship of all these has more or less been a
matter of discussion. Early ecclesiastical traditions tell that, after
an enforced or voluntary exile to the isle of Patmos, he returned
to Ephesus and died there at a great age.[8]

This typical encyclopedia entry concerning "John" does not distinguish at all between the Apostle John and Presbyter John, and thus a
conglomerate biography of "the Beloved Disciple" has arisen. However,
each of these figures has a unique biography.

Now begins an endeavor to trace the destinies of the Apostle John
and Presbyter John—destinies that led them both to the ancient city of
Ephesus. First, note that the designation "Apostle John" is an appropriate one for John the son of Zebedee *after* the event of Pentecost at
which all of the disciples became Apostles. Moreover, as already noted
above, since it is the "common, uneducated"[9] fisherman, John the son
of Zebedee, who is referred to (usually together with the "Prince of the
Apostles," Peter) in the Acts of the Apostles, it is certainly appropriate
to refer to him as the Apostle John. Thus, herewith consider the biography of the Apostle John.

THE APOSTLE JOHN

As indicated in the above quote by Sister Emmerich, see page 108, the
Apostle John accompanied Mary-Sophia to Ephesus. In the period following the Mystery of Golgotha, according to Sister Emmerich, the
Blessed Virgin Mary lived alternately in a small house near the Coenaculum on Mt. Zion[10] and at the home of the Apostle Lazarus in Bethany.

---

8. Entry "John" in the *New Century Cyclopedia Of Names* (3 volumes, edited by C.L. Barnhart; Englewood Cliffs, NJ: Prentice Hall, 1954) vol. 2, p. 2197. Note that *boanerges* is Ara-
maic, and the Greek expression for "sons of thunder" is *hyioi brontes*.
9. Acts of the Apostles 4:13. "Common, uneducated" is the translation of the Greek
"agrammatoi, idiotai."
10. Emmerich 1954b vol. I, p. 396: "Lazarus had been for some days at his house in Jerusalem on the west side of Mt. Zion...."

Further, she relates, concerning the Apostle Lazarus, that "three or four years after Christ's death he and Martha were captured by the Jews, and also Mary Magdalene...."[11] However, in *The Life of the Blessed Virgin Mary*, Sister Emmerich describes the situation more precisely:

> After [the] Ascension [of the Risen Christ, the Blessed Virgin] Mary [who became Mary-Sophia at the time of Pentecost] lived for three years on Mt. Zion, for three years in Bethany, and for nine years in Ephesus, whither [the Apostle] John took her soon after the Jews had set [the Apostle] Lazarus and his sisters adrift upon the sea.[12]

Since the latter event was three or four years after the Mystery of Golgotha in the year 33 C.E., and since the Apostle John took her to Ephesus shortly after the Apostle Lazarus and his sisters had been captured, it is reasonable to suppose that Mary-Sophia traveled with the Apostle John to Ephesus in C.E. 36 or shortly thereafter. In light of the above quote by Sister Emmerich, this would signify that after the Ascension, the Blessed Virgin Mary/Mary-Sophia lived alternately between the house on Mt. Zion and the home of Lazarus in Bethany for about three years. Further, it is highly probable that it was the capture of the Apostle Lazarus and his sisters by the Jews that prompted Mary-Sophia to leave for Ephesus. Since her death took place in Ephesus on August 15, 44 C.E.[13]—in the ninth year since leaving Israel—the statement that she lived for nine years in Ephesus is approximately correct.

> I saw how [the Apostle] John, as long as Mary[-Sophia] lived, was always with her and never left her. I saw how he always gave her the most holy sacrament, prayed with her the Way of the Cross, blessed her and received the blessing from her, and how [the Apostle] John—like a son—was closer to her than everyone else.[14]

11. Emmerich 1885–1860 vol. 3, p. 612.
12. Emmerich 1954a p. 346.
13. Powell 1996 pp. 134–135.
14. Emmerich 1885–1860 vol. 3, p. 558.

Sister Emmerich, as is evident from the continuation of this quotation, must mean that the Apostle John came every day, or as often as possible, to give Mary-Sophia the holy sacrament—not that he lived there in the house he had built for Mary-Sophia.

> [Mary-Sophia] lived here alone, with a younger woman, her maidservant, who fetched what little food they needed. They lived very quietly and in profound peace. There was no man in the house, but sometimes they were visited by an Apostle or disciple on his travels. There was one man whom I saw more often than others going in and out of the house; I always took him to be [the Apostle] John, but neither here nor in Jerusalem did he remain permanently near the Blessed Virgin [Mary-Sophia]. He came and went in the course of his travels.... After three years' sojourn here [near Ephesus] Mary[-Sophia] had a great longing to see Jerusalem again, and was taken there by [the Apostles] John and Peter.... She came to Jerusalem from Ephesus once again, eighteen months before her death, and I saw her again visiting the Holy Places with the Apostles at night.... When the Lord's summons to Ephesus came to the Apostles.... [Peter, Andrew, and Judas Thaddeus] came to Mary [-Sophia]'s house, where they met [the Apostle] John.... [He] had been in Jericho a short time before; he often traveled to the Promised Land. He usually stayed in Ephesus and its neighborhood, and it was here that the summons reached him.... Soon afterwards [after the death and assumption of Mary-Sophia] the Apostles separated to go their different ways.... The others, except [the Apostle] John, who stayed on for a while, went all together to Palestine before separating....[15]

From this account it is possible to understand why the Apostle John is mentioned only in the first few chapters of Acts. After chapter 8, in which the persecution of the Christians instigated by Saul is described, there is no further mention of the Apostle John—presumably because he left for Ephesus not long after the persecutions started, in order to bring Mary-Sophia into safety.

---

15. Emmerich 1954a pp. 350–382.

From Sister Emmerich's description, the Apostle John accompanied Mary-Sophia to Ephesus and built a house for her there, the ruins of which were discovered in 1891 (based on Sister Emmerich's description)—and the house of Mary-Sophia has since been recon-structed (again based on Sister Emmerich's description).[16] Mary-Sophia lived there until August 15, 44 C.E., the date of her death and assumption.[17] After this event, according to Sister Emmerich, the Apostle John "stayed on for a while" in Ephesus. These words imply that the Apostle John left Ephesus after a while. Thus, perhaps shortly after the event of Mary-Sophia's death the Apostle John returned to Jerusalem to rejoin the Apostle James the Lesser (not John's brother James the Greater, who was martyred in 44 C.E. under Herod Agrippa I), since "it is reported that the Apostle John was killed by the Jews."[18]

In Acts it is written that around Easter 44 C.E.: "About that time Herod the king [Herod Agrippa I] laid violent hands upon some who belonged to the church. He killed James the brother of John with the sword." [Acts 12:1-2] Since, as Sister Emmerich describes, the Apostle John was present at the death and assumption of Mary-Sophia, which took place some four and one half months after the murder of James, it is apparent that he did not go to Jerusalem until after Mary-Sophia's death. The same applies to the other Apostles, since they were all present at Mary-Sophia's death in Ephesus, although the Apostle Tho-mas only arrived immediately after she had died.[19] Sister Emmerich goes on to say, "Now James the Greater has come from Spain.... After Mary-Sophia's death he went with some six others to Jerusalem and suf-fered a martyr's death."[20] Later Sister Emmerich corrected this when she described the martyrdom of James the Greater: "He left Spain in order to travel to Jerusalem, as Mary[-Sophia] had commanded him. On this journey he visited Mary[-Sophia] in Ephesus. Here [she] said to him that he would soon die in Jerusalem, and she strengthened and comforted him. James took leave of Mary[-Sophia] and his brother [the

---

16. Powell 1996 p. 135, note 2. (See Appendix 2 of this citation for complete text.)
17. Ibid. pp. 134–135.
18. Hemleben 1972 p. 83.
19. Emmerich 1954a pp. 355–383 describes the summons of the Apostles to Ephesus to be present at Mary-Sophia's death.
20. Ibid. pp. 362-65.

Apostle] John and went to Jerusalem."[21] The editor of the original German edition of Sister Emmerich's visions, Carl E. Schmöger, added the following footnote:

> Here, as in other places, Sister Emmerich spoke out very clearly that James the Greater died before Mary[-Sophia] did and that he was not present at her death in Ephesus, which followed much later. Thus the relevant passages in *The Life of the Blessed Virgin Mary* must be corrected. When she speaks about James at the death of Mary[-Sophia], she means either Joses Barsabas, who was there in place of James as his representative—or she means that James was spiritually present there.

It seems likely that the Apostle John was at the gathering of Apostles, attended also by the Apostle Paul, referred to in Acts, where it says: "The apostles and the elders were gathered together...." [Acts 15:6], although of the Apostles only Peter and James the Lesser are explicitly mentioned as being present at this council, which is thought to have taken place around 50/51 C.E.

Although it is difficult to find out much more about the Apostle John, "According to ancient tradition [he] died a martyr's death like his brother James."[22] If, as mentioned above, he died at the hands of the Jews, it was most likely in Jerusalem, where his brother James the Greater was killed in 44 C.E. and where later, in 62 C.E., James the Lesser (also known as "the brother of the Lord") was murdered. The visions of Sister Emmerich indicate that James the Lesser and James "the brother of the Lord" were one and the same person. James the Lesser—like his brothers Judas Thaddeus and Simon—was the son of Mary Cleophas, who was the daughter of Mary Heli, the elder sister of the Nathan Mary. Mary Heli was about nineteen years older than the Nathan Mary and thus Mary Heli's daughter, Mary Cleophas, was approximately the same age as the Nathan Mary. This means that Mary Cleophas' sons, the three disciples Judas Thaddeus, Simon, and James the Lesser, were in the same age group as Jesus of Nazareth. According to Sister Emmerich, James the Lesser was about eight years younger

---

21. Emmerich 1858–1860 vol. 3, p. 555.
22. Hemleben 1972 p. 17.

than Jesus of Nazareth, and she indicates it was on account of his great similarity in appearance to Christ Jesus that he was called "the brother of the Lord." He was indeed related to Jesus of Nazareth—as the son of the latter's cousin Mary Cleophas (first cousin once removed)—but obviously in this context the expression "brother" was used in the rather loose sense of being a close relative of Jesus of Nazareth. James the Lesser played a leading role among the community of Christians in Jerusalem. In fact, after the Apostle Peter left for Rome, James became the head of the community, the first Bishop of Jerusalem. According to Sister Emmerich, James the Lesser died a martyr's death in Jerusalem "several years" after James the Greater. She says that he was "pushed out of the Temple and stoned to death." [23]

It seems, in fact, that all of the Apostles died a martyr's death—only Presbyter John died a natural death. However, if Eusebius' account is to be believed, the Apostle John's grave was in Ephesus, which would also imply that he *died* in Ephesus—in which case he would most likely have died a natural death. From the present vantage point, and without any further specific indications concerning the Apostle John, who is usually confused with Presbyter John, it is not certain whether the Apostle John died a natural death in Ephesus, as indicated by Eusebius (quoted above), or a martyr's death in Jerusalem or somewhere else in Palestine.

THE APOSTLE LAZARUS

The situation is different with regard to the biography of the Apostle Lazarus, which it is possible to follow in some detail. The beginning of the relationship between Christ Jesus and Lazarus of Bethany goes back to the presentation of the Solomon Mary in the Temple at the age of three. According to Sister Emmerich, "[The Solomon] Mary's teacher and nurse in the Temple was called Noemi, she was the sister of Lazarus' mother and was fifty years old." [24]

The father of Lazarus was named Zarah, or Zerah, and was of noble Egyptian descent. He had dwelt in Syria, on the confines of Arabia, where he held a position under the Syrian king; but

23. Emmerich 1858–1860 vol. 3, pp. 529ff.
24. Emmerich 1954a p. 117.

for services rendered in war, he received from the Roman emperor property near Jerusalem and in Galilee. He was like a prince, and was very rich. He had acquired still greater wealth by his wife Jezabel, a Jewess of the sect of the Pharisees. He became a Jew, and was pious and strict according to the Pharisaical laws. He owned part of the city on Mt. Zion, on the side upon which the brook near the height on which the Temple stands, flows through the ravine. But the greater part of this property he had bequeathed to the Temple, retaining, however, in his family some ancient privilege on its account. This property was on the road by which the Apostles went up to the Coenaculum, but the Coenaculum itself no longer formed a part of it. Zarah's castle in Bethany was very large. It had numerous gardens, terraces, and fountains, and was surrounded by double ditches. The prophecies of Anna and Simeon were known to the family of Zarah, who were waiting for the Messiah. Even in [the Solomon] Jesus' youth, they were acquainted with the [Solomon] Holy Family....

The parents of Lazarus had in all fifteen children, of whom six died young. Of the nine that survived, only four were living at the time of Christ [Jesus]'s teaching. These four were: Lazarus; Martha, about two years younger; [Silent] Mary, looked upon as a simpleton, two years younger than Martha; and Mary Magdalene, five years younger than the simpleton. [Silent Mary] is not named in Scripture, not reckoned among the Lazarus family; but she is known to God. She was always put aside in her family, and lived altogether unknown. [Mary] Magdalene, the youngest child, was very beautiful and, even in her early years, tall and well-developed like a girl of more advanced age. She was full of frivolity and seductive art. Her parents died when she was only seven years old.... In Bethany Jesus [of Nazareth/Christ Jesus] visited Lazarus, who looked much older than [the former]; he appeared to me to be fully eight years his senior. Lazarus had [inherited from his parents] large possessions, landed property, gardens, and many servants; Martha had her own house, and ... [Mary] Magdalene lived in her castle at Magdalum. Lazarus was already long acquainted with the [Solomon] Holy Family. He had at an early period aided the [Solomon] Joseph and the

[Solomon] Mary with large alms and, from first to last, did much for the Community. The purse that Judas carried and all the early expenses, he supplied out of his own wealth.[25]

From this account it is understandable how the friendship between Jesus of Nazareth/Christ Jesus and Lazarus initially developed through the relationship between the Solomon Mary and Noemi, who was Lazarus' aunt. After the death of his parents Lazarus helped the Solomon Holy Family financially, and from the very beginning of the ministry of Christ Jesus, Lazarus was the patron and financial supporter of the Lord and his community of disciples. However, it would be wrong to assume that Lazarus was simply "a do-gooder" supporting Christ Jesus and the disciples, for he was preeminently the *spiritual friend* of the Lord. Nearly always when Christ Jesus came to the region of Jerusalem, he visited Lazarus at his home in Bethany. It was on such a visit—on September 22, 29 C.E.[26]—when also the Solomon Mary was visiting there, that Jesus of Nazareth had the decisive conversation with the Solomon Mary during which he affirmed that now the time had come for him to go to the River Jordan and be baptized by John the Baptizer.[27] He journeyed through the night from Bethany to the place of Baptism, near where the River Jordan flows into the Dead Sea, and he was accompanied on this night walk by Lazarus. Moreover, Lazarus was present at the Wedding at Cana and at many other events in Christ Jesus' life, as can be seen from Appendix 4. The greatest testimony concerning the deep relationship between Christ Jesus and Lazarus is conveyed in the words: "Now [Christ] Jesus loved Martha and her sister and Lazarus." [John 11:5]

If Lazarus was the *spiritual friend* of Christ Jesus, Martha and her sister Mary Magdalene could also be thought of as *companions* of Christ Jesus. In fact, *The Gospel of Philip* speaks of Mary "Magdalene, the one who was called his companion."[28]

In Luke's Gospel something of the relationship between Martha and Mary [Magdalene] is revealed:

25. Emmerich 1954b vol. I, pp. 334–335.
26. See Appendix 4 for the complete text.
27. Powell 1996 p. 199. See also Powell 1998 pp. 59–61.
28. *The Gospel of Philip* II, 3, 59 in *The Nag Hammadi Library* (ed. J.M. Robinson; Leiden-New York: E.J. Brill, 1988) p. 145.

He entered a village [Bethany]; and a woman named Martha received him into her house. And she had a sister called Mary [Magdalene], who sat at the Lord's feet and listened to his teaching. But Martha was distracted with much serving; and she went to him and said, "Lord, do you not care that my sister has left me to serve alone? Tell her then to help me." But the Lord answered her, "Martha, Martha, you are anxious and troubled about many things; one thing is needful. Mary [Magdalene] has chosen the good portion, which shall not be taken away from her." [Luke 10:38–41]

In the third century, the theologian Origen (ca. 185–254 C.E.) wrote of Martha and her sister Mary [Magdalene] as symbolizing the active and contemplative forms of the religious life.[29] Whereas Mary Magdalene in this scene was directed contemplatively toward the soul of Christ Jesus, Martha was attentive to the Lord's physical need for food, to which she attended. She provided active companionship attending to the Lord's physical needs, and Mary Magdalene was his *soul companion*. The expression "[Christ] Jesus loved Martha and her sister and Lazarus" points to *companionship* on the bodily (Martha), soul (Mary Magdalene), and spiritual (Lazarus) level—a companionship that bonded Lazarus and his sisters in a deep and profound way with the Lord. And not only with Christ Jesus, but also with the Solomon Mary, whose teacher and nurse at the Temple had been Noemi, the aunt of Lazarus and his sisters. The fact mentioned above that the Blessed Virgin Mary lived at Bethany after the Mystery of Golgotha further indicates the closeness of the relationship of the Apostle Lazarus and his sisters to the Blessed Virgin Mary.

Against this background, the shock of the arrest of the Apostle Lazarus, Martha and Mary Magdalene for Mary-Sophia must have been very great, and thus the Apostle John was prompted to accompany her to Ephesus in order to prevent a similar fate befalling her.

The Mother of God [Blessed Virgin Mary] lived during the first period [after Christ's Ascension], in Bethany with [the Apostle]

---

29. Susan Haskins *Mary Magdalen: Myth and Metaphor* (New York: Riverhead Books, 1995) p. 20.

Lazarus and Martha. [The Apostle] Lazarus remained hidden most of the time and came out only after nightfall. The Blessed Virgin Mary did not harm a soul. Later she went to Ephesus. [The Apostle] Lazarus was [often] with the disciples. Three or four years after Christ's death he and Martha were taken captive by the Jews; and also [Mary] Magdalene, as she came to visit her brother and sister one night, was captured on the way. With [the Apostle] Lazarus, who was already a priest, was a disciple, Maximin, and also a man, [subsequently Sister Emmerich identifies him as Chelitonius, also known as Sidonius]…who were taken captive, also Marcella…Martha's maidservant, and [Mary] Magdalene's maidservant.[30]

Chelitonius (Sidonius) was the man born blind, who was healed by Christ Jesus and became a disciple. [John 9:1–41] Maximin was one of the seventy disciples—"the Lord appointed seventy others" [Luke 10:1]—and he was close to the Apostle Lazarus, as was the man born blind who had been healed of his blindness. In addition to these three men, there were four women who were captured: Martha and her maidservant Marcella, and Mary Magdalene and her maidservant Sara, who according to tradition was Egyptian and dark-skinned. The group of seven was taken to the coast of Palestine, to the Mediterranean Sea, and set out in a small boat that was towed out to sea and then cut adrift—in the supposition that the group would perish in the waters of the Mediterranean. However, Divine Providence ensured that they survived, and they eventually landed at a small place on the coast of Southern France. This (and the following) is attested to not only by Sister Emmerich but also by the thirteenth-century Archbishop of Genoa, Jacobus de Voragine, in his famous account of the saints, originally written in Latin and titled *Legenda Aurea* (*The Golden Legend*).[31]

The Provence region in the south of France is associated with the lives of the Apostle Lazarus, Martha, Mary Magdalene, and the four others who, a few years after the Mystery of Golgotha, accompanied them in the little boat across the Mediterranean, landing at the place

---

30. Emmerich 1858–1869 vol. 3, pp. 612–613.
31. Jacobus de Voragine *The Golden Legend: Readings on the Saints* (trsl. William Granger Ryan, Princeton: Princeton University Press, 1993) vol. I, p. 376 and vol. II, p. 23.

that is now called St. Maries-de-la-Mer, some fifty miles west of Marseille. There is a shrine in the crypt of the church in St. Maries-de-la-Mer to Mary Magdalene's black Egyptian maid-servant Sara, who is revered as the patron saint of the gypsies.

From St. Maries-de-la-Mer the little group proceeded to Marseille, at that time known as Massilia. According to tradition they lived initially in a subterranean grotto that is now the location of the crypt of St. Victor's basilica in Marseille. There, in the caverns below St. Victor, where now the catacombs are located, the Apostle Lazarus, Martha, and Mary Magdalene are said to have stayed, before Mary Magdalene went to Sainte-Baume and Martha went on her missionary journey first to Aix-en-Provence and then to Tarascon. Many inhabitants of Massilia, deeply impressed with their teaching and way of life, came to the Apostle Lazarus to be baptized, and thus the latter remained as Bishop of Marseille.

Mary Magdalene left to live the life of a hermit in the cave and area known as Sainte-Baume in Provence, about twenty miles east of Marseille. For many centuries Sainte-Baume was a place of pilgrimage to this site associated with Mary Magdalene. It is one of the world's most ancient Christian spiritual sites, made holy by the mystical, contemplative life there of the woman who—on account of having been the first to have beheld the Risen Christ and having guided the Apostles Peter and John to him [John 20:1–18]—bears the title "the Apostle to the Apostles." In this mountainous area there is a majestic mountain range towering up with a smooth cliff face, at the center of which is the cave where Mary Magdalene is said to have lived the last thirty years of her life in mystical contemplation. At the top of the cliff face there is a place (Saint-Pilon) to which, according to tradition, Mary Magdalene was frequently raised up by angels.

According to Sister Emmerich, Mary Magdalene died at Sainte-Baume and her relics became preserved in the crypt of the church built by Maximin. *The Golden Legend* tells how prior to her death she came down from Sainte-Baume to the church in the place where Maximin dwelt, about ten miles to the northeast, in the town now named after him, St. Maximin, and that she received Holy Communion from him there and then died. The basilica of St. Maximin in this town is built upon the site where Mary Magdalene, and also later Maximin himself, died and were buried. Her (and his) relics are said to be preserved in the crypt there. "The tomb of Mary Magdalene at Saint Maximin is the third most important tomb in the world. It ranks immediately after the tombs of our Saviour in Jerusalem and of Saint Peter in Rome," wrote Father Henri Lacordaire in 1860. [32]

Sister Emmerich also gave some details concerning the biography of Mary Magdalene's sister Martha when she left Marseille. Sister Emmerich described Martha's journey with her maidservant Marcella and some other women who had joined her in Massilia to found a community in a place close to the town that is now called Aix-en-Provence, some twenty miles north of Marseille. There Martha was active and taught and converted many. Sometimes Maximin came and visited, and she received Holy Communion from him.[33] According to tradition, in about the year 48 C.E. Martha left Aix-en-Provence and then journeyed to Tarascon, about fifty miles northwest of Marseille, and founded a community there. According to the one-page guide to the church in Tarascon, her remains are said to be preserved in the crypt of that church.

According to Sister Emmerich, "[The Apostle] Lazarus was still in Massilia as bishop. I saw that [Mary] Magdalene died shortly before Martha." [34] In the *The Golden Legend* it is indicated that Martha died just seven or eight days after Mary Magdalene. [35] And from Sister Emmerich's indications we can determine approximately when this was—at which point "[The Apostle] Lazarus was still in Massilia." If the Apostle Lazarus and his sisters left the Holy Land in approximately 36 C.E., then thirty years later, when the death of the two sisters occurred, it was around 66 C.E. The wording of Sister Emmerich's statement that "[The Apostle] Lazarus was still in Massilia" implies that she knew that he left Marseille but that he was still there when his sisters died. However, she does not say anything explicitly about his leaving the Provence region.

Considering the close spiritual bond between the Apostle Lazarus/ Bishop of Marseille and his two sisters, even though they were separated by several miles in terms of their living situations, they were spiritually

---

32. Philippe Decouvoux du Buysson *The Sainte Baume: A Mountain Steeped in Geological and Religious History* (Marseille: Editions PEC, 1995) p. 30.
33. Emmerich 1858–1860 vol. 3, pp. 616–617 provides the primary source of reference for the brief biographies of Martha and Mary Magdalene described here.
34. Ibid. p. 616.
35. de Voragine 1993 vol. II, p. 24.

linked on an inner level with one another, and the Apostle Lazarus—as the elder brother—kept his protective spiritual gaze upon his beloved sisters while fulfilling his task as Bishop of Marseille. After the death of the two sisters, the deeper reason and motivation for his presence there in Provence (as spiritual protector of his two sisters) was gone, and we may conjecture that he then felt the inner call to take up a new life in Ephesus—in the spiritual aura of the place where Mary-Sophia had lived the last few years of her life. As Johannes Hemleben points out, since he left Marseille, one would search in vain for the Apostle Lazarus' grave in the Provence region. "Perhaps he chose the land route back thus coming for the first time to Rome—and from there to Ephesus."[36] There in Ephesus, evidently, he adopted the name John, in honor of the Apostle John, who had come to Ephesus with Mary-Sophia about the same time as the Apostle Lazarus and his sisters had gone to France. His status as one who—like the younger Apostle John before him—had been so close to Christ Jesus earned him the title Presbyter John, meaning "John the Elder." The Apostle John who had been there at Ephesus before him was, metaphorically speaking, the "Younger John"—the one who had been there before and who had already died. Whereas with the arrival of Lazarus-John in Ephesus there was now another John who had also been closely connected with Christ Jesus and who in his old age had come to grace the city with his presence.

However, is there a deeper reason why the Apostle Lazarus adopted the name John when he came to Ephesus? The raising of Lazarus of Bethany from the dead, which was a great initiation and justified his being called an Apostle, had marked a turning point in his life. This event took place on July 26, 32 C.E., perhaps when he was about thirty-three-and a third years old.[37] Here it should be borne in mind that at the Mystery of Golgotha, Christ Jesus was thirty-three-and a third years old, in agreement with Rudolf Steiner's statement:

For all things arise from the grave historically in a metamorphosed form after thirty three years through a force that has to do with what is most holy and most redemptive which humanity has received through the Mystery of Golgotha....

36. Hemleben 1972 pp. 95–96.
37. Powell 1996 pp. 316-317.

And when such a seed which has been planted ripens, then it works on further. A thought seed ripens during one generation of thirty three years to become a seed for deeds. Once ripened, then it further works during sixty-six years in the historical process. One recognizes the intensity of an impulse which the human being implants into the historical process if it takes effect through three generations—through a whole century.[38]

(A whole century is one hundred years, or three times thirty-three and a third years, confirming that Rudolf Steiner meant a rhythm of *thirty-three and a third years* even though he said "thirty-three years" probably for the sake of simplicity in speaking.)

From this point in time onward, John the Baptizer was spiritually united with the Apostle Lazarus. In 66 C.E., some thirty-three and a third years later, an inner ripening resulting from his great initiation (when he had been raised from the dead) took place. Since his initiation he was able to move about outside of his body and was therefore able to be spiritually present at the side of Christ Jesus. This ability was enhanced through his intimate connection with the Apostle John. Through John, as described above, the Apostle Lazarus bore witness to the Last Supper, the Crucifixion, and the Resurrection.

> Mary Magdalene came to the tomb early, while it was still dark, and saw that the stone had been taken away from the tomb. So she ran, and went to Simon Peter and the other [the Beloved] Disciple, and said to them: They have taken the Lord out of the tomb, and we do not know where they have laid him. [John 20:1–2]

As with the Last Supper and the Crucifixion, here again "the Beloved Disciple" is referred to and, together with Peter, was among the first of the disciples to recognize the fact of Christ's Resurrection. Again it is clear from the whole context that it was John the son of Zebedee who was *physically present* together with Peter in this scene described in chapter 20 of John's Gospel, but that, as with the Last Supper and the

---

38. Rudolf Steiner *Mysterienwahrheiten und Weihnachtsimpulse* (*Mystery Truths and Christmas Impulses*) (Dornach, Switzerland: Rudolf Steiner Verlag, 1994) GA 180, lectures of December 23 and December 26, 1917.

Crucifixion, the Apostle Lazarus must have been there *spiritually present* indwelling John the son of Zebedee. In each case, as outlined above, "the Beloved Disciple" consists of the union of the Apostle John, the Apostle Lazarus, and John the Baptizer. [39]

Thus, an outer reason for the Apostle Lazarus to adopt the name John was to honor the Apostle John with whom he had been so deeply connected, who had been his predecessor in the settlement of Christians at Ephesus. An inner reason was the inner resurrection of his initiation ("raising from the dead") through which he was spiritually united with John the Baptizer. By adopting the name John he inaugurated the *Johannine tradition* in Asia Minor, a tradition centered in Ephesus, proceeding from the Apostle John and continued by him as Presbyter John (John the Evangelist).

According to one tradition, John the Evangelist was bishop in Ephesus for about forty years. From *The Revelation to John,* which he wrote in about 95 C.E. while in exile on the island of Patmos, it appears that he was responsible as bishop not only for those Christians who had settled in Ephesus but also for six other Christian settlements in that region of Asia Minor: the communities of Christians in Smyrna, Pergamum, Thyatira, Sardis, Philadelphia, and Laodicea. [Revelation 2 and 3] In the first chapter of *The Revelation to John* he wrote: "I John, your brother, who share with you in [Christ] Jesus the tribulation and the kingdom and the patient endurance, was on the island called Patmos on account of the word of God and the testimony of [Christ] Jesus." [Revelation 1:9] [40] From Patmos he returned to Ephesus, where he was known as Presbyter John ("John the Elder"), which helped to distinguish him from the Apostle John. There he wrote *The Gospel According to John* in Ephesus shortly before his death—according to Sister Emmerich, three years before his death. [41] Judging from the style of the *Letters of John,* these three epistles were written shortly after he wrote

39. Edward Reaugh Smith *The Disciple Whom Jesus Loved* (Great Barrington, MA.: Anthroposophic Press, 2000) offers a penetrating study of "The Beloved Disciple." See also Edward Reaugh Smith *The Burning Bush* (Great Barrington, MA.: Anthroposophic Press, 1997) for a comprehensive Christology.
40. In order not to make this chapter too long, the details concerning the exile of Presbyter John on Patmos and his writing of *The Revelation to John,* although highly interesting, have been omitted, as also have many details concerning the biography of Presbyter John.
41. Emmerich 1858–1860 vol. 3, p. 363.

The Gospel According to John, i.e., they were written in the period immediately before his death. Presbyter John thus became the source of inspiration for the stream of Johannine Christianity, the cornerstone of which is *The Gospel According to John* (together with *The Revelation to John* and the *Letters of John*).

He died at an advanced age, probably at least a hundred years old, and was buried there at Ephesus, his tomb being now located in the ruins of the great basilica of St. John that was later built at this place. According to tradition the aged John, when he addressed his fellow Christians, always spoke the same words: "Children, love one another." [I John 4:7] The *Acts of John* relate that on the day of his death the aged John once again celebrated the Eucharist:

> Afterwards he turned to Brother Verus and said to him: "Take some men with you with spades and two baskets and follow me." They went out through the gate of the city to a place where another brother had been buried. He indicated that here a grave should be dug. He accompanied this work with continuous prayer. Then he removed the outer layer of his clothing and threw it down into the grave for him to lie on. Dressed only in his underclothes, he raised his hands and prayed. When he had spoken the words, "Be with me, Lord Jesus Christ," he laid down in the grave upon his out-spread clothes and said to his brothers: "Peace be with you, my brothers," and joyfully yielded up his spirit.[42]

And from another source:

> I saw him stretch himself out in his grave, address some words to his disciples, and die.[43]

To summarize the life of Lazarus of Bethany who became first the Apostle Lazarus and then Presbyter John: assuming that he lived approximately one hundred years, it can be divided into three periods of thirty-three and a third years. Perhaps it was around the end of the

---

42. Hemleben 1972 p. 136.
43. Emmerich 1954b vol. IV, pp. 401–402.

first period that there took place the raising of Lazarus from the dead—the great initiation Lazarus received from the incarnated Christ Jesus that made him the Apostle Lazarus. The next period of thirty-three and a third years is characterized—after Lazarus was taken prisoner—by the journey to Marseille, France, where he lived until the end of this second period as Bishop of Marseille. The close of this second period was marked by the death of his two sisters. The last period is associated with Ephesus and Patmos, where he called himself Presbyter John. Towards the end of that period, around 95 C.E., he experienced the Risen Christ in the cave on Patmos. This experience was the *octave* of the initiation he had received when he was raised from the dead. Thus there were two great initiations in the life of Lazarus of Bethany: the first by Christ in the flesh, and the second by the Risen Christ (no longer in the flesh). Three periods—the Bethany period (Israel), the Marseille period (Provence, France), and the Ephesus period (Turkey)—constitute the life of Lazarus of Bethany, the continuer of the Johannine tradition from the Apostle John. Indeed, through his writings Lazarus-John who became Presbyter John was actually the *founder* of the Johannine tradition.

PART FOUR

THE
MYSTERY
OF THE
INCARNATION
OF THE
CHRIST BEING

* * *

THIS SECTION is based on two documents: "Selected Entries from 'Chronicle of Christ's Ministry,'" which can be found in Appendix 4, and Chapter 13 which consists of a commentary on the entries selected from Dr. Powell's "Chronicle of Christ's Ministry." Although Appendix 4 is provided primarily as reference material, like its predecessors— Emmerich's *The Life of Jesus Christ and Biblical Revelations* and the complete "Chronicle of Christ's Ministry" in Dr. Powell's *Chronicle of the Living Christ*—it can be used not only to support new inferences but also as a basis for meditation. As is indicated in Chapter 13, Dr. Powell has reduced the presentation of Sister Emmerich's visions considerably. Nevertheless, this material contains many details of the life of Christ Jesus that are not mentioned in the biblical gospels. They are presented here under seven sub-headings: 1) The Messiah Is a Very Devout Jew, 2) The Messiah Is an Intentional Itinerant, 3) The Messiah Is an Engaging Teacher, 4) The Messiah Is a Compassionate Healer, 5) The Messiah Is Unquestionably Prescient, 6) The Messiah Is Capable of the Extraordinary, and 7) The Messiah Is a Tireless Servant. Thus, a new understanding of the Mystery of the Incarnation of the Christ Being emerges from these sources.

CHAPTER 13

FURTHER UNDERSTANDINGS FROM "CHRONICLE OF CHRIST'S MINISTRY"

IN THE LAST VERSE of John's Gospel, which this discourse affirms was written by Lazarus of Bethany at a time when he called himself Presbyter John, it states, "But there are also many other things that [Christ] Jesus did; if every one of them were written down, I suppose that the world itself could not contain the books that would be written."[1] Without doubt, the visions of the Blessed Anne Catherine Emmerich (1774–1824) provide a rich view into that extended world. But the documentation of that view, though incomplete, as has been determined by Dr. Powell, has still been fraught with many difficulties. It has been previously indicated that Clemens Brentano, who lived seventeen years after the death of Sister Emmerich, was unable to bring that extensive mass of material into a reasonable order. So Brentano's literary executor, The Very Reverend Carl E. Schmöger, C.SS.R., arranged and edited the visions as recorded in the journals of Clemens Brentano. By 1881 four German editions had been prepared under his leadership. The last of these is the version that was subsequently translated into English "by an American nun, since deceased, who desired to remain anonymous."[2]

This four-volume compendium runs a total of 2,047 pages. By contrast, the "Chronicle of Christ's Ministry" published by Dr. Powell consists of only 169 pages. These numbers are not strictly comparable for two reasons: 1) the page format of the Emmerich saga is 4x7 inches

---

1. John 21:25.
2. Emmerich 1954b vol. I, p. xi.

whereas the page format of the Powell record is 6x9 inches, but more importantly, 2) the Emmerich version starts with the creation and the Fall, and includes many details of the life of the Blessed Virgin Mary as well as the life of Jesus of Nazareth before the Baptism in the River Jordan, which, as has already been noted, marks the beginning of the Incarnation of the Christ Being. When one corrects for the latter difference, the relevant number of Emmerich pages is reduced to 1,715. Although the page sizes differ, there is more empty space in the Powell pages, so that the difference in the number of words per page is only about fifteen to twenty percent greater in the Powell. Thus, approximately 1,700 pages have been summarized in approximately 200 comparable-sized pages. This is a substantial reduction. Nevertheless, the Powell record contains many details that are totally absent from the canonical gospel accounts, none of which exceeds 50 of those comparable-sized pages. It is these "new" details that permit bringing forward a fresh perspective on the Mystery of the Incarnation of the Christ Being.

Another set of selections from this material has been compiled. Whereas Dr. Powell desired to mention every day of the Ministry, there were two reasons for creating "Selected Entries from Dr. Powell's 'Chronicle of Christ's Ministry.'" [3] The first reason was to record the occurrences of the names Lazarus and John the son of Zebedee, as has already been summarized in Chapter 10. The second reason was to provide documentation for new insights on the nature of the Messiah. These insights are the substance of this chapter; they reveal a personage who is similar to the one known heretofore, yet also wondrously different.

THE MESSIAH IS A VERY DEVOUT JEW

Dr. Powell's "Chronicle of Christ's Ministry" has the advantage of including the actual dates for many of the days of the Messiah's ministry. Any vision in which Sister Emmerich "saw" Christ Jesus going to a synagogue for the opening of the Sabbath had to be a Friday. This fact has become part of the evidence to authenticate the visions, as is indicated in Appendix 2. It may be striking to the modern reader

---

3. See Appendix 4.

how determined both Jesus of Nazareth and then Christ Jesus are to attend synagogue for the opening and closing of the Sabbath. Note on Friday, September 9, 29, because there was no synagogue at Endor, Jesus of Nazareth returns to Chimki, where there was a synagogue and where he had celebrated the Sabbath in the previous week.[4] The next week, when he feels the need to be alone on Friday, September 16, 29, he requests that a scroll be brought from the synagogue to his room at an inn so that he can celebrate the Sabbath. Even on the day of the Baptism, Friday, September 23, 29, Christ Jesus, and the disciples who had witnessed the Incarnation event, make a point of going to a synagogue, at a small village near Ono called Bethel, in order to celebrate the opening of the Sabbath.

An exception to the above generality occurs on Friday, October 21, 29, when Christ Jesus begins his forty-day fast in a cave on Mount Quarantania. Though not actually in a synagogue, Christ Jesus spends the entire Sabbath as well as the following day, October 22, 29, and night in prayer. "So intense was [Christ] Jesus' praying that [Sister Emmerich] saw him sweat blood." After the forty-day period, Christ Jesus continues his habit of celebrating the Sabbath, usually at a synagogue, but elsewhere if none is close at hand.

Another manifestation of the Messiah's status as a devout Jew relates to his intimate knowledge of the Hebrew scriptures of that era. In those days, they were referred to as the Law and the Prophets.[5] The Law consisted of the first five books of the Hebrew scriptures, traditionally ascribed to Moses. The Prophets included: Joshua, Judges, Samuel, Kings, Isaiah, Jeremiah, Ezekiel, each of which was deployed in one or two scrolls, and the twelve so-called Minor Prophets, combined in a single scroll. There is no indication that Jesus of Nazareth had any formal religious training. Nevertheless, the Messiah uses the Hebrew scriptures frequently in his teaching.

Often as he travels through the land, the Messiah arrives at a site where some significant event had occurred. On such occasions, he uses that locale as a basis for retelling the biblical story. Frequently, as on July 20, 29, the old teaching is reinterpreted into a prophetic

4. Where dates are incorporated in the text, the actual entry from Powell's summaries can be found in Appendix 4.
5. Matthew 22:36–40

understanding of the mission of the Messiah. When Christ Jesus crosses the Jabbock River near Manhanaim, on September 5, 30, he tells the story of the patriarch Jacob as found in Genesis 32. When Christ Jesus and his disciples walk along the "Way of David," he touches on: how David had hid himself, as told in 1 Samuel 22; how Abraham had approached the promised land by this route; and how the three holy kings had also traversed this path on their way to Bethlehem. On Friday, September 22, 30, "[Christ] Jesus teaches in the synagogue at Gadara for much of the day. As the Sabbath begins that evening he teaches about the renewal of God's covenant through Moses." [Deuteronomy 29ff.] This selection is also important because it sets the stage for a new covenant that the Messiah will eventually affirm through his own life and sacrifice. On the evening of Friday, July 6, 31, at the synagogue in Thantia, Christ Jesus speaks of Balaam and the star of Jacob from Numbers 24 and the prophecy concerning Bethlehem from Micah 5.

A final example will illustrate the influence of the locale on his teaching. When Christ Jesus and the disciples arrive at Gischala in southern Galilee on November 5, 30, he gives instruction on three "men of zeal" who had been born there. The first is not mentioned in the Holy Bible; regarding the second and third, they had not yet become renown, thus Christ Jesus is foretelling the future. Therefore, in identifying: a) the founder of the Sadducees, who had lived two hundred years before; b) John of Gischala, a Galilean hero who was active after Christ Jesus' death; and c) Saul, who was yet to become the Apostle Paul, Christ Jesus was drawing on revelation. Whether this was direct access to the Akashic record or some other visionary source is not clear.

Josephus, the first-century Jewish historian, identifies Pharisees, Sadducees, and Essenes as three Hebrew sects and distinguishes them on the basis of their belief structures.[6] Other sources suggest that determining the actual name of "the founder of the Sadducees" would not be something easy to do. By contrast, although the heading Gischala is not found in the index of Josephus' collected works, "John, son

6. *The New Complete Works of Josephus* (trsl. William Whiston, Grand Rapids, MI: Kregel Publications, 1999) p. 429.

of Levi" is found.[7] This John is identified as one who rebuilds Gischala, one who is an enemy of Josephus, and one who aims at dominion; the eight citations can be found in *Life of Flavius Josephus* and in *The Jewish War.* This suggests that Christ Jesus not only had access to the Akashic record for the past (and made use of this eternal resource to enliven his teaching) but also that he was aware of what was going to happen in the future. This latter point will be expanded upon in a later section of this chapter.

There are a number of recurring themes: a) the story of Naboth's vineyard (1 Kings 21), b) preaching from one of the ten commandments, c) the story of Joseph who had been sold into slavery (Genesis 37), and d) the sacrifice of Jephtha's daughter (Judges 11). Less specifically, but still of significance, are the occasions when Christ Jesus interprets the scriptures, particularly those passages which relate to the coming of the Messiah.

Another confirmation of the devotion of Christ Jesus to the Hebraic tradition occurs in Gadara, on September 23, 30, where he not only exorcizes a pagan priestess, but also converts a group of pagans, who were worshiping the idol Moloch, to turn to the God of Israel.

A detail that emerges from the visions, once there are better data for actual days, is that the Messiah uses the synagogue as a place to teach, not just on the Sabbath but on all the days of the week. Sometimes he is denied access to a synagogue, but more often his teaching is well received. Certainly there is no sense of inadequacy regarding his authority, either as a rabbi or as a prophet. He even enters, as on April 1, 30, the inner court in the Temple at Jerusalem, a space that is open only to those sanctioned by Temple leaders.

Yet another aspect of the lives of both Jesus of Nazareth and Christ Jesus is attendance and participation in various elements of the Festival of the Passover in Jerusalem. This was an annual obligation for Jews in good standing, and it seems certain that it was adhered to. One of the Festivals occurred during the 313-day gap in Sister Emmerich's vision-based chronicle, so there is no record of it; but one can readily assume that Christ Jesus would have been present then. In fact, on September 6, 29, Jesus of Nazareth tells the Solomon Mary

---

7. Ibid. p. 1129.

that he will go to Jerusalem *four times* to celebrate the Passover, but that the last time will be one of great affliction for her. And Dr. Powell, in his review of the 313-day period for which we have no record of Sister Emmerich's visions, affirms, "Although not mentioned in [John's Gospel], it is almost certain that [Christ] Jesus attended the [Festival] of the Passover in Jerusalem" which took place between April 14, 32 and April 22, 32.[8]

A final subject, emerging from the visions with great clarity, is that Christ Jesus sees his mission as directed to the Hebrew people. He does heal some who are not Jewish, but often this requires persistence on the part of the person desiring to be healed. The healing of the Syrophoenician woman, on February 12, 31, is a case in point. Sister Emmerich clearly sees him saying " ... that it [is] not yet time, that he [wants] to avoid giving offense, and that he [will] not help the pagans before the Jews." Again at Gadara, on September 23, 30, where he deals with pagans and heals many of them, this occurs on the second day of his visit *after* he has healed many Jews. And even before the Incarnation, as in the interval between July 9, 29, and July 19, 29, although he visits pagan places in the region of Sarepta, Jesus of Nazareth admonishes "the Jews not to mix with the pagans."

THE MESSIAH IS AN INTENTIONAL ITINERANT

Prior to starting his "Chronicle of Christ's Ministry," Dr. Powell points out an intriguing relationship. After confirming the divinity of the Christ Being and the humanity of Jesus of Nazareth, the perfect human being who fulfills a "divine archetype," Dr. Powell goes on to say,

> We catch a glimpse of one such divine archetype that is fulfilled by Jesus [of Nazareth] if we consider the figure of Cheiron, the teacher of Jason and the Argonauts, who was represented in classical mythology as half-human, half-horse. Cheiron appears in the heavens in the zodiacal sign of Sagittarius. Also at the birth of [the Nathan] Jesus, as we have seen, the Sun stood in the middle of Sagittarius. Therefore we shall not be surprised

---

8. Powell 1996 p. 309.

to find [the Messiah], like Cheiron, traveling from place to place with untiring energy, *teaching and healing* wherever he went.[9]

It is obvious from the gospel accounts that the Messiah is constantly on the move and that he never settles down at any specific place in spite of encouragement to do so. What the visions of Sister Emmerich make abundantly clear, especially as reinforced by the outstanding maps of Helmut Fahsel (which are included in Dr. Powell's *Chronicle of the Living Christ*), is that the Messiah literally crisscrosses the Holy Land from one end to the other. For example, consider Map 1 (reproduced as Figure 6) where, in a period of approximately three weeks, the Messiah walks a distance of some 120 miles from Capernaum in Galilee to Hebron in Judea, primarily on the west side of the Jordan River; and he returns to Capernaum by walking primarily on the east side of the Jordan River.[10]

In addition, he visits the island of Cyprus from April 26, 31, to May 30, 31, and later makes an "extensive journey" on foot from August 7, 32, to January 7, 33, starting at Cedar, northwest of Great Chorazin (now Syria), to Mozian and Ur (now Iraq), and thence to Heliopolis (now Egypt) before returning to the Holy Land.[11] The latter is said by Sister Emmerich to be absent from the gospel accounts because the Messiah was accompanied only by three young shepherds. Since none of the more recognized disciples was on this journey, it has not been brought forward into the traditional accounts. As has been previously indicated, the gospels are summaries as opposed to being day-to-day accounts.

Now to link this itinerant behavior into the Messiah's mission as he speaks of it himself. In both Matthew's Gospel and Luke's Gospel, Christ Jesus uses colorful language to describe his situation, "Foxes have holes, and birds of the air have nests; but the Son of Man has nowhere to lay his head."[12]

---

9. Powell 1996 p. 182.
10. Ibid. The numbered maps can be found on unnumbered pages starting after p. 373.
11. Ibid. See Map 30 for Cyprus and Map 37 for the "extensive journey."
12. Luke 9:58 and Matthew 8:20.

Journey to the Place Where John the [Baptizer] Grew Up
MAY 29 – JUNE 20, 29 C.E.

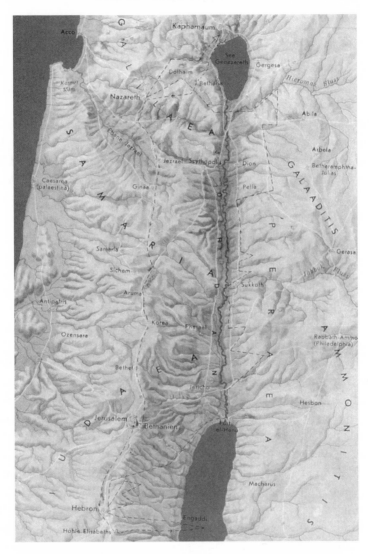

Capernaum—Bethulia—Bethany—Jerusalem—Hebron—Elizabeth's Cave—
Dead Sea—Hebron—Perea—Hieromax—Nazareth—Capernaum

FIGURE 6 : *Map 1 – From Helmut Fahsel* [13]

13. In Powell 1996, unnumbered page after p. 373.

On another occasion, when two disciples of John the Baptizer ask Christ Jesus where he is staying, he replies, "Come and see." They stay with him that night at an inn; one of them becomes not only a disciple but eventually an apostle. It is obvious that it is not because of the luxury of the accommodations.[14]

Finally, it must be acknowledged that much of this seemingly peripatetic behavior is linked to specific visitations of sites that were important in the earlier life of the progenitors of Christ Jesus. Examples of such sites and the dates on which they are visited include: Elizabeth's cave on June 1, 29; the valley of the shepherds near Bethlehem on September 29, 29; Zechariah's house at Juttah on January 8, 31; the tent city of King Mensor and King Theokeno west of Babylonia on September 21, 32; and the home of those who had earlier befriended the Solomon Holy Family in Heliopolis on January 2, 33.

THE MESSIAH IS AN ENGAGING TEACHER

There is much teaching spoken of in the gospel accounts, but there are many examples of more extended sessions that have been compressed in the gospel "summaries." For example, on November 28, 30, Sister Emmerich tells us that Christ Jesus and the disciples go "to a mountain near Bethsaida-Julias where many people [have] gathered to hear [Christ] Jesus preach. Here [begins] the 'Sermon on the Mount' referred to in Matthew 5 and Luke 6." But these gospel accounts suggest that the "Sermon" was delivered in one session. Sister Emmerich acknowledges that on that occasion, "The instruction lasted the whole day." Apparently, on that first day, Christ Jesus spoke only on the first beatitude. But Sister Emmerich affirms that the entire "Sermon" was preached on *fourteen* different days, with the conclusion not being delivered until March 15, 31. In fact, in the Powell summaries of Sister Emmerich's visions, there are sixteen entries that relate to this particular teaching. These have been set forth with some additional details in Table 7 starting on the following page. Note that not all the occasions occurred at the Mount of the Beatitudes—some actually took place in synagogues. Several presentations deal with only one of the beatitudes.

14. John 1:37–39.

The later sessions also include the introduction of the Lord's Prayer. On another occasion, April 18, 31, Christ Jesus starts teaching "at about ten in the morning" and he teaches "without interruption until evening." It takes a charismatic teacher to hold an audience for a long day, more so for a period of several months.

A second measure of the engaging nature of Christ Jesus' teaching is the size of the audience. The story is present in the gospel accounts, but on November 26, 30, the crowd is so large that Christ Jesus and the disciples board a boat moored nearby. "From there, [Christ] Jesus continues to teach the crowds on the shore." Two days later, when he begins his "Sermon on the Mount," it is indicated that "many people were gathered to hear [Christ] Jesus teach." On another occasion, January 28, 31, "a large crowd [has] already assembled on the mountain above Matthew's customs house…. Still more people [come] from the surrounding area…. [Christ] Jesus [dismisses] the crowd saying that he [will] teach next morning on the mountain near Bethsaida-Julias."

THE MESSIAH IS A COMPASSIONATE HEALER

The gospels mention the role of the Messiah as a healer, but there is a substantial difference between the extent of the healing presented in the gospel "summaries" of the Incarnation of the Christ Being and the day-to-day record revealed in the visions of Sister Emmerich. In fact, Sister Emmerich makes a point of saying that on June 4, 29, prior to the Baptism, Jesus of Nazareth visits "…the sick to console and comfort them, *but [does] not heal anyone*" (emphasis added). Similarly, in the interval between June 23, and June 29, 29, her visions indicate: "… everywhere he [goes], Jesus [of Nazareth teaches] in the synagogues and [consoles] the sick *but [does] not perform any healing miracles*" (emphasis added).

TABLE 7 : *Components of the "Sermon on the Mount"*

Session Date	Location	Audience	Subject
1. 11-28-30	Mt of the Beatitudes	Many people	1st Beatitude
2. 11-29-30	Mt of the Beatitudes	Included holy women and disciples	2nd Beatitude

Session	Date	Location	Audience	Subject
3.	11-30-30	Mt of the Beatitudes	Not specified	2nd Beatitude + Teachings of the prophets
4.	12-01-30	Mt of the Beatitudes	Not specified	3rd Beatitude
5.	12-03-30	House in Capernaum	Not specified	Beatitudes
6.	12-04-30	Mt of the Beatitudes	Not specified	4th Beatitude
7.	12-09-30	Capernaum Synagogue	Not specified	1st Beatitude
8.	12-11-30	Hucuca Synagogue	Not specified	Beatitudes + Parables
9.	12-15-30	Galgala Synagogue	Not specified	2nd Beatitude
10.	12-17-30	Carianthaim Synagogue	Not specified	Beatitudes
11.	01-29-31	Mt of the Beatitudes	Five thousand	Beatitudes + Lord's Prayer
12.	01-30-31	Dalmanutha Shore	Not specified	Beatitudes + Lord's Prayer
13.	02-02-31	Road to Bethsaida	Two thousand	Beatitudes + Lord's Prayer
14.	02-03-31	Bethsaida Synagogue	Not specified	Lord's Prayer + 1st Beatitude
15.	03-14-31	Mt northeast of MB	Considerable crowd	8th & 9th Beatitudes
16.	03-15-31	Mt northeast of MB	Four thousand	Conclusion of Sermon on the Mount

It might be imagined that healing was a power only to come with the Incarnation, but in the period from July 2, to July 5, 29, and without any fanfare that this might have been a first occurrence, Sister Emmerich indicates that Jesus of Nazareth casts out a demon from one who was possessed. Later, on August 18, 29, Jesus of Nazareth teaches in a synagogue in Sephoris. "Next to the synagogue [is] a madhouse, and inmates [are] obliged to attend the synagogue, accompanied by custodians. As Jesus [of Nazareth teaches], one or the other of the inmates [begins] to speak out loud: 'This is Jesus of Nazareth, born in Bethlehem, visited by wise men from the east.' 'His mother is with Maraha.' 'He is bringing a new teaching,' and so on. Jesus [of Nazareth speaks] the words: 'The spirit that speaks this is from below and should return there.' At this, all the inmates [become] quiet *and [are] healed*" (emphasis added).

On September 3, 29, after teaching at the synagogue at Chimki, Jesus of Nazareth stays with a poor family and heals "the mistress of the house who was suffering from dropsy." Two days later, in a shepherd village, Jesus of Nazareth heals "two people who had been smitten with leprosy." Thus it can be seen that even before the Incarnation of the Christ Being, Jesus of Nazareth has considerable powers and does not hesitate to heal on the Sabbath!

After the Incarnation, Christ Jesus loses no time in continuing the healing ministry begun by Jesus of Nazareth. On September 26, 29, the third day after the Baptism in the River Jordan, on the way to Luz, Christ Jesus heals "several sick people" as he travels. From here on, the healings become so numerous that note will be taken of the number of occurrences without necessarily specifying the actual day and place where they occurred. During the months of October and November in the year 29, there are only three instances of healing in the visions, but one should recall that this period includes the forty days in the wilderness during which he was tempted by Satan. During the following two months, December of 29, and January of 30, there are fourteen instances of healing, many of which involve several persons being healed on the same day. In the Powell summaries of Sister Emmerich's visions, for the remaining eleven months of the year 30, there are some eighty specific healings identified. During the next six months there are another 80 healings mentioned in the visions. Then there is the 313-day gap. From this time forward there seem to be fewer references to healing activity in the visions; but when they do occur, the number being healed is generally not specific; rather it is often "several" or "many." Without doubt, the healing ministry continues.

THE MESSIAH IS UNQUESTIONABLY PRESCIENT

Even before the Incarnation of the Christ Being, Jesus of Nazareth has an appreciation of what is going to happen in the future. On September 22, 29, while attending a banquet given by Lazarus at his castle in Bethany, "Jesus [of Nazareth] again alludes to the persecutions that lay ahead of him, saying that those who ally themselves with him will suffer with him." After the Baptism, Christ Jesus in Luz on September 25, 29, speaks "of the need to forsake all to follow the Messiah and to have no great concern for one's daily needs." Two weeks later, on October 6, 29, in a farmhouse near Bethlehem, Christ Jesus predicts "that in three and a half years' time they [will] see no more strength and beauty in his appearance, his body [will] become so disfigured as to be unrecognizable." On October 20, 29, even before the Forty Days in the Wilderness, Christ Jesus speaks of "the dangers facing those who follow him." He encourages each disciple, during a period of separation from him, to consider carefully whether he really wants to continue being a disciple.

Although not mentioned in the Powell version of the vision for Wednesday, December 28, 29, at the wedding in Cana, the description in the second chapter of John's Gospel includes Christ Jesus saying, "My hour has not yet come." This did not prevent him from saving the day when they had run out of wine, but it is a phrase that occurs in numerous other places.

On December 16, 30, a Saturday, Christ Jesus is healing in Saphet. Some Pharisees and Sadducees who were visiting "from Jerusalem, [are] scandalized at what they [see]. They [can] not tolerate such a disturbance on the Sabbath and [begin] to dispute with [Christ] Jesus that he [does] not observe the Law. [Christ] Jesus [reduces] them to silence by writing an account of their secret sins and transgressions on a wall in Old Hebrew, which only they [can] read." Then he [offers] them a choice: [do] they prefer to have the writing remain on the wall and become publicly known, or [will] they "allow him to continue his work in peace, in which case they [can] efface the writing. Thoroughly frightened, they [rub] out the writing and [depart leaving Christ Jesus] to continue his work of healing the sick." Not only does the Messiah know the past and the future, he is aware of unvoiced intentions and can also detect the sins and transgressions of those who are in his presence.

An additional example of Christ Jesus' ability to read another's thoughts occurs on November 8, 30, in the town of Gabara. A certain Pharisee named Simon Zabulon has invited Christ Jesus to a banquet. During the meal a woman enters and washes his feet with her tears and dries them with her hair. Sister Emmerich's version differs a bit from the one in Luke 7:36–50. But the important issue is that Simon thinks to himself, "If this man were a prophet, he would have known who and what kind of a woman was touching him—that she is a sinner." [15] Christ Jesus knows exactly what Simon is thinking and uses that knowledge to contrast the Pharisee's hospitality with that of the woman. The Luke version does not mention the woman by name; but Sister Emmerich identifies the woman, who honors Christ Jesus with ointment, as Mary Magdalene. This could well have been the case because, earlier on that selfsame day, Christ Jesus had converted Mary Magdalene, who would have every reason to be grateful. She also performed similar acts of veneration, as described previously on page 81, but those events occurred *some three years later.*

Christ Jesus is able to undertake what appears, to his mother and to his disciples, as very risky behavior because he has a clear sense of the future. He knows that, ultimately, things are not going to go well for him by ordinary human standards; but he also knows that this is not going to happen right away. Another example of his knowledge of future events is described in a vision on January 1, 31, when he tells Peter and John the son of Zebedee "that John the [Baptizer will] soon meet his end, and that he [wants] to go to Hebron to comfort the [Baptizer's] relatives." [16] Again, on February 3, 31, he is very explicit on the subjects of his persecution, of being deserted by even his most faithful disciples, and of being put to death. And on March 16, 31, the subject comes up again: "[Christ] Jesus [teaches] the disciples concerning the persecution and suffering that he [will] endure."

On April 19, 31, the Pharisees, being dismayed by the crowds that have gathered as Christ Jesus develops the various themes of his "Sermon

---

15. Luke 7:39.
16. According to the visions of Sister Emmerich and the dating by Powell, John the Baptizer was killed two days later on January 3, 31.

on the Mount," and considering him as a "disturber of the peace," threaten "to complain to Herod—who [will] certainly put a stop to [Christ] Jesus' activities." But Christ Jesus is not concerned about such accusations and threats. He replies "that he [will] continue to teach and heal, in spite of Herod, *until his mission [is] complete*" (emphasis added). Once again, it is obvious that Christ Jesus' certainty about the future enables him to ward off what would have been significant threats for an ordinary mortal. On the following day, April 20, 31, in Capharoth, where some Pharisees who are well disposed toward him warn that Herod is about to imprison him as he had done with John the Baptizer. Sister Emmerich sees Christ Jesus reaffirm the sentiments in the following manner: "...he [has] nothing to fear from 'the fox' and that he [will] do what his Father [has] sent him to do (Luke 13:31–33)."

Later in Cana on June 20, 31, under similar circumstances, when well-meaning friends warn him "that it [is] becoming more and more dangerous for him to continue his teaching, [Christ] Jesus then [teaches] about his mission. He [says] that he [will] do nothing except follow the will of his Father."

Another example of Christ Jesus' confidence in what he is doing relates to his actions regarding the raising of Lazarus. Details of this event will be presented later in this chapter, but here it is worthwhile to highlight a conversation between Mary Magdalene, the sister of Lazarus, and Christ Jesus. On July 19, 32, Mary Magdalene comes to meet Christ Jesus as he returns from having celebrated the Sabbath at Ginnim. She laments "over the death of Lazarus, saying that if [Christ] Jesus had been there [her brother] would not have died. [Christ] Jesus [replies] *that his time [has] not yet come*" (emphasis added). He uses again the familiar phrase to indicate that he is following a carefully designed plan, presumably originated in the spiritual world.

THE MESSIAH IS CAPABLE OF THE EXTRAORDINARY

Specific examples below are listed in chronological order. According to Sister Emmerich, even before the Incarnation, Jesus of Nazareth has significant powers. He spends eleven days with the venerable Eliud, an elderly Essene widower, between September 5, 29, and September 16, 29. Near the end of this period on September 15, 29, they have been "walking after dark, deep in conversation. Around midnight, Jesus [of

Nazareth says] to Eliud that he [will] reveal himself, and—turning toward heaven—he [prays]. A cloud of light [envelops] them both and Jesus [of Nazareth becomes] radiantly transfigured. Eliud [stands] still, utterly entranced. After a while, the light [melts] away, and Jesus [of Nazareth resumes] his steps, followed by Eliud, who [is] speechless at what he [has] beheld." During the baptism in the River Jordan on Friday, September 23, 29, Jesus of Nazareth again becomes "transparent with radiant light." This time one can surmise that it is because of the descent of the Christ Being (the Incarnation) since it coincides with a heavenly voice saying, "You are my Son, today I have begotten you." [17]

In the forty-day period during which Christ Jesus fasts and is tempted, there are a number of examples of very unusual occurrences, which have not been included in the Powell summaries. Interested readers are encouraged to review that material in Volume II of the English translation.[18] In summary, it can be said that Satan tempts Christ Jesus on each of the forty days and uses many disguises to attempt to fool Christ Jesus, but the latter always knows it is really Satan. At the close of the forty-day period on November 30, 29, Dr. Powell does summarize the "heavenly celebration of [Christ] Jesus' triumphant victory over temptation ... " which includes participation by the twelve angels of those who were to become apostles and the seventy-two angels of those who were to become disciples.

The next momentous occurrence relates to the interchanges between Nathanael Chased and Christ Jesus that have already been described in Chapter 4.[19] That presentation was intended to demonstrate that scriptures have been written in code language; but, from the current perspective, it is also an illustration of Christ Jesus' special powers that make Nathanael Chased, himself an initiate, realize that he is in the presence of the Godhead. This event occurred on Sunday, December 25, 29.

Three days later at the wedding in Cana, Christ Jesus performs his first miracle, the transformation of water into wine. This has been well documented in John's Gospel. However, on December 28, 29, in Sister

---

17. See page 58.
18. Emmerich 1954b vol. II, pp. 1–19.
19. See pages 23–24.

Emmerich's rendition of the event, there are additional insights about the meaning of this miracle. She indicates that all who drink the wine become convinced of Christ Jesus' power and of "the lofty nature of his mission. Faith [enters] their hearts, and they [become] inwardly united as a community." She also suggests that this miracle sets the stage for the final miracle, the Last Supper.

Now comes the first instance of a raising from the dead. This one is *not* recorded in the gospel narratives. It takes place in Cana and involves "a man who [has] died as a consequence of falling from a tower." It is significant in that it occurs on Saturday, December 31, 29, during the celebration of the Sabbath and in the presence of the priests. A second raising from the dead, also *not* acknowledged in the gospel accounts, takes place in Phasael and involves the daughter of an Essene named Jairus. Christ Jesus is in Aruma when the messenger from Jairus comes to him and tells him that Jairus' daughter has died. He leaves his disciples and hastens to Phasael. "When he [arrives] at the home of Jairus, on February 7, 30, the daughter lies bound in sheets and wrappings ready for burial. [Christ] Jesus [orders] the bindings to be loosened. Then he [takes] the girl's hand, commanding her to rise. She [sits] up, and [rises] to stand before him. She [is] about sixteen years old. [Christ] Jesus [warns] those present not to speak about what they [have] witnessed." The entry from Dr. Powell cautions the reader not to confuse this raising from the dead with the one of the daughter of Jairus of Capernaum; that account will follow at the appropriate chronological moment.

A month later on March 13, 30, leaving Nazareth, Christ Jesus sets "off on the same route that the [Solomon] Holy Family had taken on the flight to Egypt. He [passes] first through the little place called Nazara. Here he [performs] a miracle: He [buys] bread and [multiplies] it in his hands and [distributes] it to the poor."

Two months later on May 3, 30, Christ Jesus is at the place of baptism near Ono where he himself had been baptized. "His disciples [are] gathered there, and many people [have come] to hear him. While [Christ] Jesus [is] teaching, a messenger from King Abgara of Edessa [arrives]. The messenger [asks Christ] Jesus to accompany him back to Edessa, or—if not—if he could at least paint a portrait of him. He [produces] a letter from the king in which the king [describes] that he [is] ill, and [believes in Christ] Jesus as God or the Son of God, and [requests] to be healed. [Christ] Jesus [replies] to the king's letter by miraculously causing a perfect likeness of his countenance to be imprinted on the messenger's paper. The sight of this image later effected a deep transformation in the king's life."

Later on July 30, 30, in a village in northern Galilee called Atharot, "a group of Sadducees [try] to trick [Christ] Jesus into raising someone who has already been dead eight days. [Christ] Jesus [exposes] their plot, however...."[20] Once again, extraordinary powers are at work where the Messiah is fully aware of the intentions of those about him as well as a long dead corpse that had been disguised as carefully as humanly possible.

On August 3, 30, in Cana "a messenger from Zorobabel, a high-ranking official of Capernaum, [arrives] with a message that his son [is] dying. There then [occurs], at a distance, the miraculous healing of the boy, as described in John 4:46–54." Sister Emmerich further indicates this is "the second sign that [Christ] Jesus did upon coming from Judea to Galilee...."

In Nazareth, where Christ Jesus frequently was not well received: "At the close of the Sabbath on August 12, 30, when [Christ] Jesus comes out of the synagogue [where he has been teaching, he is] immediately surrounded by about twenty Pharisees. They [begin] to lead him out of the town toward a nearby hill, for they [intend] to cast him down from the brow of the hill. Suddenly, however, [Christ] Jesus [stops, stands] still, and with the help of angelic beings [passes]—as if invisible—through the midst of the crowd to his escape (Luke 4:29–30)." As noted by Dr. Powell, this story is told in Luke's Gospel but there the language is sparse. It says only, "And they rose up and put him out of the city, and led him to the brow of the hill on which their city was built, that they might throw him down headlong. But passing through the midst of them he went away." Contrast this with the words of the English translation of Sister Emmerich's vision. "They [are] not far from the scene of action when [Christ] Jesus, who is being led as a prisoner among them, [stands] still, while they [continue] their way mocking and jeering. At that instant, I saw two tall figures of light near [Christ] Jesus, who [takes] a few steps back through the hotly pursuing crowd, [reaches] the city wall on the

---

20. A more detailed version of this event can be found in Emmerich 1954b, vol. II, pp. 199–200.

mountain ridge of Nazareth, and [follows] it till He [comes] to the gate by which He had entered the evening before." [21] Presumably, the author of Luke's Gospel had access to the Akashic record and "experienced" a scene similar to that of the vision of Sister Emmerich, or perhaps his level of clairvoyance was such that the angelic beings were not obvious to him, or perhaps he chose to make his description more accessible to those who do not regularly "see" angelic beings.

On August 23, 30, in Gadara, Christ Jesus not only raises the child of a pagan priestess from the dead, but he heals "many pagan children, who [are] all suffering because of their parents' worship of Moloch." Then Christ Jesus exorcises the priestess and reveals to the assembled people the nature of their idolatry. "The people [believe; they determine] to renounce the worship of Moloch and turn to the God of Israel."

On October 25, 30, Christ Jesus performs another miracle at a distance. While still in Meroz, he heals the daughters of a widow from Nain called Lais. Her two daughters, Sabia and Athalia, had remained in Nain because they were possessed. Christ "Jesus [exorcises] Lais' daughters from afar and [tells] her to purify herself, saying 'The sins of the parents are on these children.'" The widow and her two daughters are mentioned at more than one point in subsequent visions.

On November 13, 30, Christ "Jesus and the disciples [are] approaching Nain, [when] they [meet] a funeral procession emerging from the city gate." Although Christ Jesus has no relationship with this individual, he has compassion and commands the coffin bearers to stand still and set the coffin down. Now something strange takes place. Dr. Powell's summary indicates that Sister Emmerich sees Christ Jesus raise his eyes toward heaven and speak the words recorded in Matthew 11:25–30 as a prelude to subsequent action.

I thank you, Father, Lord of heaven and earth, because you have hidden these things from the wise and the intelligent and have revealed them to infants; yes, Father, for such was your gracious will. All things have been handed over to me by my Father; and no one knows the Son except the Father, and no one knows the Father except the Son and anyone to whom the Son chooses to reveal him.

21. Emmerich 1954b vol. II, p. 236.

However, as shown above, there is no mention of a raising from the dead. To find that story, one must turn to Luke 7:11–17, but here there is no mention of the preliminary words. This, then, is an example of the greater detail in the visions enabling a story line different from that found in the abbreviated gospel texts. There are other examples of this type of situation.

During the Second Festival of the Passover at the Temple in Jerusalem on March 28, 31, "[Christ] Jesus [goes] up to the great teacher's chair in the court before the sanctuary. A large crowd [gathers] around, including many Pharisees and also the man who had been healed at the pool of Bethesda [on Friday, January 19, 31]. The Pharisees [accuse Christ] Jesus of breaking the Sabbath because he had healed this man on the Sabbath. [Christ] Jesus replies that the Sabbath was made for humanity, not humanity for the Sabbath. [He then recounts] the parable of the [rich] man and poor Lazarus. This so [outrages] the Pharisees that they [press] around and [send] for the Temple guards to take [Christ] Jesus into custody. At the height of the uproar, it suddenly [grows] dark. [Christ] Jesus [looks] up to heaven and [says]: 'Father, render testimony to thy Son!' A loud noise like thunder [resounds] and a heavenly voice [proclaims]: 'This is my beloved son in whom I am well pleased!' [Christ] Jesus' enemies [are] terrified. The disciples then [escort Christ] Jesus from the Temple to safety...."

And now on April 3, 31, the Transfiguration occurs. Dr. Powell provides very few details but cites Matthew 17:1-8. Here in the well-known words we are told,

[Christ] Jesus took with him Peter and James and his brother John [the son of Zebedee] and led them up a high mountain, by themselves. And he was transfigured before them, and his face shone like the sun, and his clothes became dazzling white. Suddenly there appeared to them Moses and Elijah, talking with [Christ Jesus]. Then Peter said to [Christ] Jesus, "Lord, it is good for us to be here; if you wish, I will make three [shrines] here, one for you, one for Moses, and one for Elijah." While he was still speaking, suddenly a bright cloud overshadowed them, and from the cloud a voice said, "This is my Son, the Beloved; with him I am well pleased; listen to him!" When the disciples heard this, they fell to the ground and were overcome by fear.

But [Christ] Jesus came and touched them, saying, "Get up and do not be afraid." And when they looked up, they saw no one except [Christ] Jesus himself alone.

The following day, April 4, 31, is filled with significant events. Dr. Powell's summary contains six citations to the gospels and therefore leaves out a number of details. The important issues are: 1) Christ Jesus' admonition that the three disciples should tell no one about the mountaintop experience "until after the Son of Man has been raised from the dead"; [22] 2) "the healing of the possessed boy whom the disciples had been unable to heal (Mark 9:14–27);" 3) conversations about the roles of Elijah, John the Baptizer, and the Son of Man in the short-term future; 4) explanations about why the disciples had been unable to heal the possessed boy (Matthew 17:19–21); and 5) a dinner for Christ Jesus and the disciples as guests of the Pharisees "who attacked them for breaking the Sabbath…(Matthew 12:2–8)." Interestingly, no single source has a complete story. Even the sequence of these five components varies. The most complete version is from the English translation,[23] but that longer account does not mention the dinner with the Pharisees. (See next section for an analysis of multiple occurrences of such an event.) And only the account in Mark 9:29 acknowledges that prayer and fasting are necessary for the exorcism of the boy's unusual demon.

Another transfiguration-like event occurs when the disciples return from their missionary assignments on June 21, 31. Once again, Christ Jesus leads them to a secluded spot. After a time of sharing their missionary successes, Christ Jesus asks for silence and, looking up to heaven, he creates a vision to help them understand that all they had done was in the name of the Father, as indicated in Luke 10:18–20. Then, to emphasize their unique relationship to him and to his heavenly Father, he closes the experience with these words: "Blessed are the eyes that see what you see! For I tell you that many prophets and kings [desire] to see what you see, but [do] not see it, and to hear what you hear, but [do] not hear it." [24]

---

22. Matthew 17:9–13.
23. Emmerich 1954b vol. III, pp. 300–03.
24. Luke 10:23b–24.

On July 26, 32, Christ Jesus raises Lazarus from the dead. In recognition of this unique event, in this discourse, Lazarus who was raised from the dead will be called Lazarus-John. It has been suggested earlier that this was not just a raising from the dead but that it had elements of an initiation. Clearly, in earlier situations where Christ Jesus raised persons who had been dead, there was a limited time between the death and the raising. Recall that he refused to raise a Pharisee from the dead because he had already been dead eight days. Yet in the case of Lazarus, Christ Jesus made a point of delaying the process, much to the dismay of Lazarus' two sisters, Martha and Mary Magdalene. They had waited four days before burying him, and he had been in the grave for an equal period of time. Nevertheless, Christ Jesus is able to bring him back to life. It seems as if something unique, absent from other raisings from the dead, is being performed. Note how Sister Emmerich emphasizes the special ritual that Christ Jesus undertakes in the midst of the twelve disciples. This included a blessing by Christ Jesus, the latter breathing upon the one raised from the dead seven times. She goes on to indicate "thus he [consecrates] Lazarus[-John] to his service, purifying him of all earthly connections and infusing him with the seven gifts of the Holy Spirit, which the [disciples will] receive only later, at [Pentecost]." The significance of this event is not lost on the Pharisees, who now feel that they want to apprehend Lazarus-John as well as Christ Jesus. In fact, both Lazarus-John and Christ Jesus maintain a low profile for several months after that event.

Some of the elements of a raising from the dead alluded to above are confirmed on September 1, 32, when, east of Sichar, Christ Jesus raises a rich herd owner named Nazor from the dead. It is because "Nazor's soul had not yet passed on to be judged but was still present over the place in the field where he had died," that Christ Jesus is able to return him alive to his wife and children.

Christ Jesus has a special affinity for shepherds. On September 14, 32, during his journey to Chaldea he spends the night with some shepherds. In the course of teaching the shepherds about the creation of the world, the Fall, and the promise of the resurrection of all, "something wonderful happens. [Christ Jesus appears] to catch a sunbeam with his right hand, and he [makes] a luminous globe of light from it. It [hangs] from the palm of his hand on a ray of light. While he [is] talking, the shepherds [can] see all the things he [is] describing in the globe of light. The Holy Trinity itself [appears] there."

At the tent city in Chaldea where Christ Jesus has gone to visit the two surviving kings, after the close of the Sabbath on September 27, 32, Christ

Jesus [goes] into the temple where there [is] an idol of a dragon. As one of the women [casts] herself down before this idol to worship it, [Christ] Jesus [says]: "Why do you cast yourself down before Satan? Your faith has been taken possession of by Satan. Behold whom you worship!" Instantly there [appears] before her, visible to all, a slender, red fox-colored spirit with a hideously pointed countenance. All [are] horrified... [Christ] Jesus says: "Every person also has a good angel." ... All then [see] a radiant figure at the woman's side. At the approach of the good angel, the satanic spirit [withdraws].

On March 20, 33, Christ Jesus is teaching in the Temple at Jerusalem. At one point, "With his hands folded, he [gazes] up to heaven. From a cloud of light, a ray [descends] upon him, and a voice like thunder [resounds]: 'I have glorified him, and I will glorify him again.'" This miraculous occurrence is recorded in John 12:20–26.

Obviously, the resurrected Christ also has extraordinary powers, but these are well recorded in the New Testament; and there are no visions from Sister Emmerich, in the Powell summaries for that period, to give us additional details.

THE MESSIAH IS A TIRELESS SERVANT

In this final section, it is appropriate to document events that are mentioned in the canonical gospels, but not in the same detail as found in the visions of Sister Emmerich. This is especially the case where multiple events have been compressed into a single episode. The way in which the "Sermon on the Mount" was developed has already been mentioned—not a single event, but one that lasted several months.

The Messiah and the Money Changers—Another example is Christ Jesus' desire not to have the money changers in the forecourt of the Temple. This issue first surfaces in the days preceding the Festival of the Passover in the year 30 C.E. This is called the First Passover by Dr. Powell since it was one of the four that Christ Jesus would attend. On April 3, 30, Christ Jesus finds "...vendors ranged around the court selling their wares. He [admonishes] them in a friendly manner and [bids] them retire with their goods to the court of the Gentiles. He and the disciples [help] them move their tables." The next day when Christ Jesus and the disciples return to the Temple, they find the vendors once more in the forecourts. "[Christ] Jesus [admonishes] them more severely this time, and [sets] about forcibly removing their tables to the outer court." Some pious Jews approve of his action. The Pharisees, put to shame by Christ Jesus' action, are angered by the crowd's response. On April 6, 30, "Vendors [have] again erected tables to sell their wares, and [Christ] Jesus [demands] that they withdraw. When they [refuse], [Christ] Jesus [draws] a cord of twisted reeds from the folds of his robe. With this in hand, he [overturns] their tables and [drives] the vendors back, assisted by the disciples. [Christ] Jesus [says], "Take these things away; you shall not make my Father's house a house of trade."

This third episode sounds very much like the version present in the synoptic gospels. However, there are some problems here: the gospel versions do not include the build-up of the previous days when Christ Jesus was trying to be pleasant about having the vendors leave; and the gospel version occurs *after* the triumphal entry into Jerusalem, which takes place *three years later*. It can be assumed that a confrontation of this sort occurred at each of the Festivals of the Passover that Christ Jesus attended. However, although there were confrontations with the Pharisees during the Second Festival of the Passover occurring in March 27/28 of 31, there is no mention of a dispute with the vendors. The Third Festival of the Passover took place during the 313-day gap on April 14/15 of 32, and thus there is no record from Sister Emmerich to confirm the likelihood that there was a concern over the vendors at that time. The occurrence described in Matthew's Gospel took place on March 20, 33.

The Raising of Jairus' Daughter from the Dead — In Capernaum on November 18, 30, Christ Jesus is approached by Jairus, the chief of the synagogue. "Jairus [pleads] with [Christ] Jesus to come and heal his daughter, Salome, who [is] on the point of death." This story is told in the fifth chapter of Mark's Gospel. It is a convoluted tale in which, as Christ Jesus and Jairus walk toward the latter's home, there is, first, an interruption by an extraneous healing—that of the woman with a long-standing issue of blood who touches him in the midst of the crowd and is healed; second, a messenger who comes to relate the news that Salome is already dead; and third, "[Christ] Jesus, in his mercy, [performs] the miracle of raising Salome from the dead." In Sister Emmerich's version there is no mention of the intervening healing on that first date, but an insight is presented regarding the real cause of Salome's death—an imitation of her parents' negative attitude toward Christ Jesus. This is born out by the fact that, since the condition that caused her original illness did not change, by December 1, 30, she becomes ill once more. On this second occasion, Jairus pleads once again with Christ Jesus to come and heal his daughter. "[Christ] Jesus [agrees] to go. On their way, the message of Salome's death reaches them, but they continue on. Then occurs the healing of the widow Enue from Caesarea Philippi, who had been suffering from a flow of blood for twelve years (Matthew 9:20–22, Mark 5:25–34, and Luke 8:43–48). Reaching Jairus' home [Christ] Jesus repeats the raising of Salome from the dead...." The following day, December 2, 30, [Christ] Jesus returns to Jairus' house and cautions "Salome to follow the word of God." Although all three synoptic gospels carry the story of the second raising as if it were the first and only one, none makes it clear what the cause of the illness was. This is finally elucidated in a subsequent vision on December 9, 30, mentioned in Powell only as a visit to Jairus' home. But, in the English translation, a more complete story is presented.[25]

> The next day [Christ] Jesus, accompanied by some of His disciples, [visits] Jairus' family whom He [consoles and exhorts] to the practice of good. They [are] very humble and entirely changed. They [have] divided their wealth into three parts, one for the poor, one for the Community, and the third for themselves. Jairus's old mother [is] especially touched and thoroughly converted to good. The daughter [does] not make her appearance until called, and then [comes] forward veiled, her whole deportment breathing humility. She [has] grown taller. She [holds] herself erect, and [presents] the appearance of one in perfect health.

A later visit to Jairus' house occurred on January 26, 31; nothing more is said about Salome. There is confirmation, however, that Jairus

---

25. Emmerich 1954b vol. III, p. 93.

has now "committed himself wholly to the service of [Christ] Jesus." This story documents substantial repentance and change. It makes clear how tirelessly the Messiah entered into the lives of others.

The Messiah and the Sea of Galilee — In the gospels there is an account of Christ Jesus sleeping through a storm on a boat upon the Sea of Galilee. "A great windstorm arises, and the waves beat into the boat, so that the boat [is] already being swamped. But [Christ Jesus is] in the stern asleep on the cushion; [the disciples wake] him up saying, 'Teacher, do you not care that we are perishing?' He [wakes] up and [rebukes] the wind, and [says] to the sea, 'Peace! Be still!' Then the wind [ceases] and there [is] a dead calm." [26]

This is not the only occasion in which Christ Jesus subdues a storm on the Sea of Galilee. On March 4, 30, Sister Emmerich indicates, "That night a great storm [arises. Christ] Jesus [prays] with out-stretched arms that danger might be averted. Thus, he [protects] the ships on the Sea of Galilee from afar." Similarly, on the night of the following day, "... another storm arose, and [Christ] Jesus — through prayer — again ... [averts] the danger threatening the people aboard ships on the Sea of Galilee." Both Nazareth and Sephoris, where he was on those two nights, are at least fifteen miles from the seashore.

On December 7, 30, after teaching and healing much of the day, Christ Jesus "instructs the disciples to sail back to Bethsaida, while he withdraws into the hill alone to pray. That night, the disciples [see Christ] Jesus walking across the water toward them." Dr. Powell informs us that this was not the walking on water described in Matthew 14:22–33, which took place on January 29, 31, but he does not give any details. In the English translation of the record of the visions, " ... Peter [cries] out: 'Lord, if it be thou, bid me come to Thee upon the waters.' And [Christ] Jesus [says]: 'Come!'" [27] There follows a scenario that is similar to the one recorded for the second walking on the water, that took place on January 29, 31.

On that second occasion, which took place on the same day as the feeding of the five thousand, once again Christ Jesus withdraws "alone (Matthew 14:22–23), while the apostles [sail] on Peter's ship back

---

26. See Mark 4:35–41 for the complete context and Luke 8:22–25 for another version.
27. Emmerich 1954b vol. III, pp. 88–89.

toward Bethsaida. A great storm [arises] on the Sea of Galilee, and there [takes] place the second miracle of Christ Jesus' walking on the water (Matthew 14:25–33)...." This, the only version in the canonical gospels, is the one in which Peter attempts to join Christ Jesus walking on the water but, because the storm frightened him, he is unable to remain on the surface of the water and begins to sink. In the vision record the event, though similar, does in fact happen twice, some eight weeks apart. Sister Emmerich even comments on how Peter has more faith on the second occasion but still not enough to reach where Christ Jesus is walking on the water.[28]

The Messiah and Accusations about his Disciples — Previously, there was mention of a dinner with the Pharisees on April 4, 31, at which time Christ Jesus is attacked because his disciples plucked ears of corn on the Sabbath. [Matthew 12:2–8] (This probably did happen more than once.) On March 31, 31, this activity of the disciples is described and there is an indication that it led to an attack by the Pharisees on April 5, 31. That, too, is recorded on that actual day, which is the day after it is mentioned in the Powell summaries as happening on April 4, 31. This discrepancy may have arisen because of differences between facsimiles of the handwritten notes of Clemens Brentano as a source, which Dr. Powell used, and the English translation from the fourth German edition developed by Schmöger.

Jesus of Nazareth/Christ Jesus and Prayer—Frequently in the Powell summaries of Sister Emmerich's visions, there are occasions when either Jesus of Nazareth or Christ Jesus sets off alone to pray. The first instance occurs in the interval between July 9, and July 19, 29, in the town of Sarepta, where it is said, Jesus of Nazareth spends "much time, too, alone in prayer in the forests around the town." Later, but still before the Baptism, in the village of Gur on September 16, 29, Jesus of Nazareth not only celebrates the opening of the Sabbath alone at an inn; but, as has already been indicated, he requests "a roll of the Scriptures to be brought to him from the synagogue." On the following day, "the last Sabbath prior to his baptism, Jesus [of Nazareth spends] the whole day in his room alone in prayer." After the baptism the practice

28. Emmerich 1954b vol. III, pp. 217–20.

continues; on October 2, 29, Christ Jesus takes "leave of the shepherds and of his disciples, saying he now [wants] to be alone for a while...." The next week on October 11, 29, after a banquet in his honor in the town of Dibon, Christ Jesus arranges a meeting place with the disciples on the following morning. Then Christ Jesus leaves "the inn where they were staying and [goes] to pray alone on the mountain."

The forty days of the temptation, began on Friday, October 21, 29. "As the Sabbath [begins, Christ Jesus climbs] a mountain—Mount Quarantania—about one hour's distance from Jericho. Here he [starts] his forty-day fast and [spends] the night in prayer in a cave." In her vision, Sister Emmerich sees Christ Jesus kneeling with out-stretched arms and praying to his heavenly Father for "strength and courage in all the trials that [await] him." For the whole of that Sabbath and the following night, October 22, 29, Christ Jesus remains in prayer. "A vast cloud of light [descends] upon him, and he [receives] consolation from on high...." On the next day, October 23, 29, Christ Jesus descends from that mountain before sunrise. He crosses the Jordan River and journeys east of the town of Bethabara into the wilderness beyond the Dead Sea. "Eventually, he [reaches] a very wild mountain range east of Callirrhoe where he [ascends] the forbidding Mount Attarus. This savage, desolate mountain lies about nine hours from Jericho. Here he [continues] to pray and fast, spending the night in a narrow cave near the summit of the mountain." Powell's summaries have only one entry for the period between October 24, 29, and November 30, 29. It starts as follows: "Throughout this period [Christ] Jesus [stays] at the mountain cave on Mount Attarus, praying and fasting. Here he [is] tempted." (A more detailed account is available from the English translation found in the first nineteen pages of volume II.)

Now there is a an interval of some eight months in which solitary prayer by Christ Jesus is not mentioned in the Powell summaries of Sister Emmerich's visions. Such prayer instances are noted for three successive days during the month of July in 30 C.E. On the night of Friday, July 21, 30, Christ Jesus and many of his friends and supporters [are] at Lazarus' castle in Bethany. "After eating together, they [celebrate] the start of the Sabbath. That night, when all was still in the castle, [Christ] Jesus [goes] to the Mount of Olives, to the cave in the Garden of Gethsemane.... Now he [prays] to his heavenly Father for strength to fulfill his mission. He [returns] to Lazarus's castle before daybreak." On the following evening, "... he [prays] again alone on the Mount of Olives." And on the next evening, July 23, 30, Christ "Jesus [retires] to pray alone on the Mount of Olives." Later on August 1, 30, after speaking at the synagogue in Engannim and healing many sick people, Christ Jesus "... [slips] away from the crowd and [withdraws] to pray alone in the hills." And on August 19, 30, which is the Sabbath, Christ Jesus goes to the synagogue in Capernaum and teaches. Later, after healing many people and teaching again in the synagogue, Christ "Jesus [withdraws] to a lonely place where he [spends] the night in prayer."

The next all-night prayer vigil occurred on November 17, 30, in Capernaum after the Sabbath where Christ Jesus had taught in the synagogue. On leaving the synagogue, he heals two lepers by saying, "Your sins are forgiven!" This produces indignation on the part of some Pharisees, who protest "loudly because he [heals] on the Sabbath and question by what right he is able to forgive sins. Without uttering a word, [Christ] Jesus [passes] through their midst. He [goes] to his mother's house. After consoling his mother and the other women there, [Christ] Jesus [leaves] and [spends] the night in prayer. On December 7, 30, Christ "Jesus [teaches] and [heals] for much of the day. Then he [instructs] the disciples to sail back to Bethsaida, while he [withdraws] into the hills alone to pray...."

In the following month, on January 18, 31, "That evening [Christ] Jesus and his friends and disciples [share] a meal in Bethany. After everyone had gone to bed, [Christ] Jesus [goes] alone to pray on the Mount of Olives." After a two month break, there is another occurrence; on March 18, 31, Christ "Jesus and the disciples [leave] Bethsiada-Julias and [journey] to Sogane, where he [teaches] and [heals] until late afternoon.... That night, [Christ] Jesus [withdraws] alone to pray."

The last two occurrences of all-night prayer vigils before the 313-day gap in Sister Emmerich's visions took place on the Island of Cyprus. On May 16, 31, "The Feast of Weeks [begins] that evening. There [is] a torchlight prayer-procession, which [Christ] Jesus [joins]. Afterwards, he [retires] alone to pray." On the evening of May 18, 31, "with the beginning of the Sabbath, [Christ] Jesus [speaks] in the synagogue with tremendous power and earnestness. He [speaks] of the breaking of the commandments and of adultery. Afterward, he [prays] alone all night."

The final occasion when Christ Jesus was reported by Sister Emmerich to go away and pray alone, occurs on the day of the crucifixion, April 3, 33. His experiences in the Garden of Gethsemane are reported only in outline form in the Powell summary. Turning to Matthew's Gospel the familiar story is told.

> Then Jesus went with them to a place called Gethsemane; and he said to his disciples, "Sit here while I go over there and pray." He took with him Peter and the two sons of Zebedee, and began to be grieved and agitated. Then he said to them, "I am deeply grieved, even to death; remain here, and stay awake with me." And going a little farther, he threw himself on the ground and prayed, "My Father, if it is possible, let this cup pass from me; yet not what I want but what you want." Then he came to the disciples and found them sleeping; and he said to Peter, "So, could you not stay awake with me one hour? Stay awake and pray that you may not come into the time of trial; the spirit indeed is willing, but the flesh is weak." Again he went away for the second time and prayed, "My Father, if this cannot pass unless I drink it, your will be done." Again he came and found them sleeping, for their eyes were heavy. So leaving them again, he went away and prayed for the third time, saying the same words. Then he came to the disciples and said to them, "Are you still sleeping and taking your rest? See, the hour is at hand, and the Son of Man is betrayed into the hands of sinners.[29]

But, as has already been developed, some of this language can be interpreted in more than one way. Dr. Steiner denies that Christ Jesus is concerned about the crucifixion; rather he is trying to help his chosen leadership to sustain a higher level of consciousness. Even after three attempts, "the specially chosen ones could not keep themselves sufficiently awake." [30]

---

29. Matthew 26:36–45.
30. See pages 84–85.

It remains now to integrate the meaning of these episodes of prayer. First, as should be obvious, there are probably more indications of Jesus of Nazareth/Christ Jesus undertaking serious prayer in the original vision texts than the ones that have been found in the Powell summaries, but there are sufficient examples present, as reviewed, to make it clear that prayer was an important part of the Messiah's life. From a spiritual point of view, the Messiah was an incarnation of the Godhead; this is what gave him his awesome powers. But the Messiah was also human. It is a testament to the humanity of the Messiah that he spent so much time in prayer to draw his sustenance from the spiritual world. If it was essential for the Godhead periodically to reestablish a relationship with his primary source by prayer, how much more so is it necessary for us, as ordinary mortals, to follow the Messiah's example?

* * *

Seven surveys have been taken through the Powell summaries of the visions of Sister Emmerich. Each has emphasized a different facet of the nature of the Messiah. In Appendix 4 can be found "Selected Entries from 'Chronicle of Christ's Ministry.'" These entries, 243 in number, are the data on which the preceding surveys are based. Some of these entries represent only one of the facets, while others represent more than one facet.

It is not easy to summarize the totality that these seven focused reviews reveal. In general, the visions do not contradict what is contained in the canonical gospels; rather, they enhance and expand what has been condensed in those summary biographies. The critical element is the time line. Once the data have been organized on a day-by-day basis, which is the master work that Dr. Powell has contributed, it should then be possible to create a single narrative that contains all the important items in the Mystery of the Incarnation in the correct sequence. One of the challenges involved in doing this is to select the "best" segments of the traditional gospels to weave into the comprehensive, composite account.

In any case, much about the Incarnation of the divine Christ Being in human form remains in the domain of mystery. That is as it should be, so that each person who reads this record may assimilate all of it, parts of it, or none of it, as is appropriate for the reader's evolving spirituality.

AFTERWORD

ON THE INTRODUCTORY page of this treatise two quotations were set forth. The first by Dr. Steiner suggested that the revelations of the evangelists "... will be understood more and more as humanity progresses." In the second quotation, Professor Pagels asserts " ... Most of us, sooner or later, find that at critical points in our lives, we must strike out on our own to make a path where none exists." She goes on to affirm, in the words of Christ Jesus, " ... search, and you will find; ... "[1]

Next, add the bidding of The Reverend Canon Michael Wyatt, in a recent sermon preached at Washington National Cathedral, "So now, dear sisters and brothers, sit next to Luke, go through the accounts of [Christ] Jesus' life, set them in order and rebuild them as the story of God's activity in your day, conformed by God's trajectory in Scripture. Tell your story as the story of salvation, with the message of your particular sinfulness and gracefulness that God has given to you alone for the salvation of the world." [2]

If I am to tell my story in its simplest form, it comes as a response to the current emphasis in today's culture on the *humanity* of Jesus Christ. What is needed is a countervailing proclamation of the *divinity* of Christ Jesus. This is why I have taken care to reverse the customary Jesus Christ into Christ Jesus. It is a reminder that the Christ Jesus described on these pages represents the descent of the Godhead from the spiritual world to the material world for the salvation of humanity. That process begins with developing an understanding of how carefully the spiritual world prepared the way for the Incarnation of the Christ Being in human form.

---

1. Elaine Pagels *Beyond Belief: The Secret Gospel of Thomas* (New York: Random House, 2003) pp. 184–85. The final quotation is from Matthew 7:7 NRSV.
2. Michael Wyatt *Advent 2* (a sermon preached at Washington National Cathedral on December 7, 2003).

Thus, it is time to recapitulate, to set out what was attempted, and to pull together the seemingly disparate parts of the present discourse. Without Part One it would not have been possible to appreciate the restricted context in which further unveiling of these three Christian mysteries was to take place. Even for anthroposophists, it is worth the effort to restate the fundamentals that underlie the development of the themes in this book. However, for those without that background, it is not just "worth the effort," it is essential. It is the only way they can appreciate that there are, literally, centuries of serious thought that provide the underpinning for the concepts set forth in this book.

In Part Two, starting with a careful reading of the New Testament texts and discovering that artists of the Middle Ages seemed to be familiar with the idea of two holy families, the stage is set for the revelations of Rudolf Steiner regarding why it was necessary to have two Jesus children. First, there was a need for participation from major religious streams: Zoroastrianism (Persia), Buddhism (India), and, within the context of Judaism, the highly evolved individuality that started life as the Solomon Jesus. To this must be added the sister soul of Adam, who had never been incarnated before and thus was not tainted by the Fall, as the individuality for the Nathan Jesus. This leads to two mergers that have not been widely circulated: one that brings about Jesus of Nazareth, a new creature that the birth parents of the Nathan Jesus could not recognize when they encountered him in the Temple at Jerusalem, and another that brings together two families after the deaths of the Solomon Joseph and the Nathan Mary. The final chapter of Part Two sets out differences between the injunctions of orthodoxy and the broadened perspective of the new understandings.

In Part Three the complexities relating to the Mystery of the Beloved Disciple are put forward. The raising of Lazarus from the dead is the most significant miracle that Christ Jesus accomplished in his entire ministry. Unlike other raisings from the dead performed by Christ Jesus, as Dr. Steiner and others have suggested, there was an element of an initiation in this process. Beyond that, from the datings provided by Dr. Powell, it can be said that Lazarus had been dead a long time; his sisters kept him at home four days in the hope that Christ Jesus would come and bring him back from the dead; then he was in the tomb another four days as suggested in John's Gospel. Valentin Tomberg provides the most picturesque description of these events using "the rainbow of the Holy Spirit" as a metaphor for the threshold between life and death:

> There stood the rainbow of the Holy Spirit over the dark cleft of the grave, on which a stone was laid. At [Christ Jesus'] word the stone was taken away.
>
> Thereupon the Son-made-flesh lifted up his eyes to the heavenly Father and thanked him that he had heard him. Then he cried with a loud voice, which condensed the rainbow of Spirit into lightning, bearing within it the rolling thunder of the Father:
>
> "Lazarus, come forth!"
>
> And he that was dead came forth, his hands and feet bound with bandages, and his face wrapped with a cloth. [Christ] Jesus said to them: "Unbind him and let him go!"
>
> Thus it happened that the [individuality] of Lazarus, called out of the bosom of the Father by the Word of the Son, turned back through the portal of the rainbow of the Holy Spirit into the realm of earthly life. In Christ he had died, out of the Father he had been born, and through the Holy Spirit he was brought to new life.[3]

The operative words here are "new life." Just as Dr. Steiner has indicated, see page 78, what would be the point of having Lazarus undergo this fantastic experience, which seems to be a return from the spiritual world rather than merely a raising from the dead or even an advanced initiation, if he were not destined to make important additional contributions? With the new research by Dr. Robert Powell, based on his mastery of German language texts, a contemporaneous explanation of the role of Lazarus of Bethany has been set forth. The Beloved Disciple emerges as a tripartite being consisting of the outward appearance of John the son of Zebedee with an indwelling of the individuality of the Apostle Lazarus and a further indwelling of the individuality of John the Baptizer. Similarly, the visions of the Blessed Anne Catherine

---

3. Valentin Tomberg *Covenant of the Heart: Meditations of a Christian Hermeticist on the Mysteries of Tradition* (trsl. Robert Powell and James Morgante, Rockport, MA: Element, 1992) pp. 78–79.

Emmerich have made it possible to delineate two biographies that eliminate some of the confusion between John the son of Zebedee and Lazarus of Bethany. The former of these two important pillars of the Christian church became the Apostle John at Pentecost but lived only until approximately the middle of the first century C.E. By contrast, Lazarus of Bethany lived a much longer life. He became the Apostle Lazarus when, in his early thirties, he was brought back from the spiritual world by Christ Jesus; then, after being set adrift in the waters of the Mediterranean, he spent some thirty years in France as the Bishop of Marseille, and finally another thirty years in Ephesus as Presbyter John. It is toward the end of this latter period, on the island of Patmos, that he received and set down *The Revelation to John*. Later, presumably back in Ephesus, he wrote *The Gospel According to John* and, only after that, did he write the three *Letters of John*.

Part Four is the climax of the volume. By making seven surveys through the summaries of the visions of Sister Emmerich, as published in *Chronicle of the Living Christ* by Dr. Robert Powell, much new descriptive material has been brought forth. It is not so much that the visions alter the portrait of the Messiah that can be found in the four Gospels; rather, they enhance the portrayal and affirm through additional details some facets that were less evident in the restricted biographical sketches found in the New Testament. The Messiah's roles as a devout Jew, an intentional itinerant, an engaging teacher, and a compassionate healer are reinforced. But there is something new in acknowledging his prescience, the extent of his ability to accomplish the extraordinary, and his tireless servanthood reinforced by expanding the several occasions when biblical versions have been compressed into single occurrences. Most importantly, as presented in Chapter 13, this enhanced portrayal confirms the divinity of Christ Jesus and fulfills the original prophecies concerning the Messiah.

Now it can be affirmed that these three Christian mysteries are not only related but can be said to be *interlocked*. A full understanding of the events that occurred two thousand years ago requires more detail than is communicated in the New Testament. One can argue as to whether every item set forth in the visions of Sister Emmerich is equally valid. Similarly, the *tour de force* that Dr. Powell has accomplished by dating this material can be questioned, but it seems to be on a sound footing and is therefore less susceptible to challenge. This does not deny that it is, for most individuals, a new approach to understanding the early days of Christianity. These fundamentals, reinforced by the clairvoyance of Dr. Steiner and the scholarship of the Rev. Irene Johanson, do provide the basis for a revised view of the Incarnation of the Christ Being and a better appreciation of why Jesus of Nazareth, at the baptism in the River Jordan, became Christ Jesus, the long-sought Messiah of the Hebraic tradition and the salvation of humanity in the Earth planetary cycle of evolution.

BIOGRAPHICAL MATERIAL

(in chronological order by date of birth)

BIRGITTA PERSSON was born early in January 1303, at Finsta in Uppland, Sweden. Her father, Sir Birger, was a lawmaker and the ruler of Uppland. Under him the pagan custom law was replaced by a code of laws based on Christian understandings. In medieval Sweden, the Persson family was one of the most powerful. Being a child of privilege, Birgitta received considerable education: in theology, philosophy, church history, and Latin. At fourteen she married Prince Ulf Gudmarsson of Nericia. Birgitta was the mother of eight children; the best known among them was her daughter Catherine, who not only testified in favor of her mother's becoming a saint but also became the first Abbess of the monastery of nuns and monks founded by her mother at Vadstena, which survives to this day. Catherine herself became a saint as well.

Birgitta was an enthusiast of pilgrimages. Her first was from Stockholm to the shrine of Saint Olaf of Norway in Trondheim. This thirty-five-day march over the mountains was an exercise in spiritual endurance. She managed well, but her husband, Prince Ulf, tired. Subsequently, they undertook another arduous pilgrimage to the shrine of Saint James at Compostela in Spain. On their return, Prince Ulf developed a fever in Arras, France. In a vision, Birgitta was informed that her husband would survive this episode and return to Sweden. This transpired as indicated, and Prince Ulf entered the monastery at Alvastra as he had vowed. At peace with God and himself, a few months later he died.

The young widow spent some time at Alvastra, but, being guided in a vision, she returned to the court of King Magnus in Stockholm as an advisor. In time she was encouraged by another vision to go to Rome and strive for a return of the Papacy, which was at that time in Avignon, France. Although she did not live long enough to actually see that happen, she was influential in bringing it about. Late in her life, she made a final pilgrimage to Jerusalem, where she had visions of the Nativity and also the Passion. She died in Rome on July 23, 1373. By some standards her becoming a saint in 1391 occurred relatively soon after her death. However, she was one of the first female saints who had not been a martyr, and there was controversy about her canonization.

Also, several Popes were involved in the process at a time when the Papacy was being moved to Rome, and the selection of Popes was complicated by the politics of the time.[1]

*   *   *   *   *

ANNE CATHERINE EMMERICH was born September 8, 1774, at Flamske, not far from Coesfeld, in Westpahlia, Germany. Although of simple education, she had perfect consciousness of her earliest childhood and could understand liturgical Latin from her first time at Mass. On November 13, 1803, at the age of twenty-nine, she became a nun of the Augustinian Order in the convent of Agnetenberg at Dülmen (also in Westphalia). On December 29, 1812, she received the *stigmata*, a manifesting of the wounds suffered on the Cross, and the highest outward sign of union with the Christ Being. She died on February 9, 1824.[2]

From early childhood, Sister Emmerich was blessed with the gift of spiritual sight (clairvoyance) and lived almost constantly in inner vision of scenes related to the Holy Bible. As a child her visions were predominantly of pre-Christian material, but these became less frequent with the passing years, and by the time she became a nun her visions had become concerned primarily with the life of Christ Jesus. Because of difficult circumstances brought about by the invasion of Germany by Napoleon, her convent was disbanded on December 3, 1811, and one by one the nuns in residence were obliged to leave. Sister Emmerich—already bedridden—withdrew to a small room in a house in Dülmen. As news spread that she bore the stigmata (which bled on Fridays), more and more people came to see her.

As Dr. Robert Powell (see biography below) put it:

---

1. A scholarly biography is present in Morris 1999; elements of the above have also been taken from Butkovich 1972.
2. A short biography is present in Emmerich 1954b, at the start of each of the four volumes. A biography of intermediate length is present in Powell 1996, pp. 13–15. A definitive biography is also available: Carl E. Schmöger *The Life of Anne Catherine Emmerich* (trsl. Michael Palaivet, Rockford, IL: TAN Books, 1986, in two volumes).

For us, the most significant of these was the poet Clemens Brentano (see biography below) who visited her on the morning of Thursday, September 24, 1818. He was so impressed with the radiance of her being that he decided to move nearby in order to record her visions. [Sister Emmerich] had already had a presentiment that someone—whom she called the "pilgrim"—would come to preserve her revelations. The moment Clemen Brentano entered her room, she recognized him as this "pilgrim."[3]

On July 29, 1820, Sister Emmerich began to communicate visions concerning the *day-to-day* life of Christ Jesus that she had witnessed each preceding day. She was able to describe in extraordinary detail the places that Christ Jesus visited, the people he interacted with, and with "astonishing concreteness" provided many biographical details. As Dr. Powell has clarified, although this was not clear to either Brentano or his later editor, The Very Reverend Carl E. Schmöger, there was a 313-day gap in the record of the visions, which were not recorded in complete continuity (see Table 4). It was only after that gap was discovered and reconciled that it was possible for Dr. Powell to establish the *actual dates* for a chronicle of Christ Jesus' ministry.

* * * * *

CLEMENS BRENTANO was born on September 9, 1778, in Ehrenbreitstein, near Coblenz, Germany. Brentano was a poet, novelist, and dramatist; he was one of the founders of the Heidelberg Romantic School, the second phase of German Romanticism, which placed its emphasis on German folklore and history. He died in Aschaffenburg, Bavaria, on July 28, 1842.[4]

Through his mother and his sister, Brentano was aware of Goethe. As a student in Jena, Brentano became acquainted with the leaders of the early phase of German Romanticism. Settling temporarily in Heidelberg, he met Achim von Armin, with whom he published the collection of German folk songs called *Des Knaben Wunderhorn* (*The Boy's Magic Horn*), which became an important inspiration to later German lyric poets. Later he lived in Berlin. It was from there, after meeting Sister Emmerich, that he settled his affairs and moved to Dülmen early in 1819. With the exception

---

3. Robert Powell *Chronicle of the Living Christ: The Life and Ministry of Jesus Christ: Foundations of Christianity* (Hudson, NY: Anthroposophic Press, 1996) p. 14.
4. *Encyclopedia Britannica* 2003 (CD version).

of a six-month business trip and the gaps previously mentioned above, he was for some five years at Sister Emmerich's bedside recording her visions until her death in 1824. Although he lived for some seventeen years longer, he was not able to produce much material in published form before he died. Most of this was left to his brother and to The Very Reverend Carl E. Schmöger, as has previously been mentioned.[5]

* * * * *

RUDOLF STEINER was born on February 25, 1861, at Kraljevec, just south of Austria. His father was an employee of the Southern Austrian Railway. He entered the Oberrealschule (technical high school) in Wiener-Neustadt (southwest of Vienna) in 1872 and graduated in 1879. He then enrolled at the Technische Hochshule (polytechnic college) in Vienna, where he studied natural history, mathematics, and chemistry. In addition, he did extensive reading in philosophy and attended lectures in philosophy at the University of Vienna by Professor Karl Julius Schröer. This association led to editorial work on the natural scientific writings of Goethe which culminated in his move in 1890 to Weimar, Germany, to become a collaborating editor of the *Natural Scientific Writings of Goethe* for the Sophia Weimar Edition of Goethe's Works. In 1891 he obtained a doctorate in philosophy from the University of Rostock in northern Germany. In 1897, he moved to Berlin as an editor, writer, and critic. In 1902, he founded the German section of the Theosophical Society and was active in the work of that society for almost a decade. Eventually, in 1912, he parted from this organization and established the Anthroposophical Society. The latter was originally founded in Berlin, but it was moved to Dornach, Switzerland (not far from Basel), where Dr. Steiner spent more than five years in the design and construction of the Goetheanum, a substantial building with many sculpted wooden forms that suggested the concept of metamorphosis pioneered by Goethe, and unusual stained glass windows. The building housed a theater, laboratories, classrooms, and headquarters for the growing Anthroposophical Society. (For details of Dr. Steiner's voluminous writing and lectures, see the references in the footnote below.) On New Year's Eve 1922 and New Year's Day 1923, the Goetheanum building, a largely wooden structure, burned to the ground. In the ensuing

---

5. There is a conflict between dates mentioned by Dr. Powell when Brentano was in Dülmen (between 1819 and 1824) and the Britannica biography, which suggests that he spent six years in a monastery after a severe depression in 1817. If that latter date were closer to 1827, it would be consistent with his inability to convert his handwritten notes into a formal publication.

years a concrete replacement was built that remains to this day. Dr. Steiner died in his studio at Dornach on March 30, 1925.[6]

* * * * *

ROBERT POWELL, PH.D. was born in 1947 in Reading, England. He studied mathematics at the University of Sussex, graduating with a master's degree. At the same time, he developed an interest in astronomy, and this in turn led him to explore the roots of astrology, the ancient science of the connections between the stars and human beings.

While researching the history of the zodiac in the mid 1970s at the British Museum in London, Dr. Powell discovered the Rudolf Steiner Bookshop and Library on Museum Street. From that moment on, Dr. Steiner's (see biography above) anthroposophy (spiritual science) became the esoteric or spiritual context in which he was to work: a path and a guide. Dr. Steiner's many works provided the epistemological, cosmological, and Christological foundations he sought to continue his work. Through Dr. Steiner, he was also led to the work of the German-born astrosopher Willi Sucher (1902–1985) and the Russian-born anthroposophist and hermetic sophiologist Valentin Tomberg (1900–1973).

From 1978 to 1982, Dr. Powell, while continuing his research, was in Dornach, Switzerland, at the Goetheanum, where he completed eurythmy training. Since graduating from eurythmy school, still continuing to study, to undertake research, and to lecture on themes arising from the practice of esoteric Christianity and astrology, Dr. Powell has lived and worked as a eurythmist and movement therapist at the Sophia Foundation in Kinsau, Germany. As founder of the School of Cosmic and Sacred Dance, he now gives courses on these subjects in Europe and North America. In 1995, Dr. Powell co-founded the Sophia Foundation of North America. In 2004, he received the Ph.D. degree from the Institute for the History of Science of the Polish Academy of Science in Warsaw. Dr. Powell has been published in various fields: astronomy, astrology, and anthroposophy. A recent title is *The Most Holy Trinosophia and the New Revelations of the Divine Feminine* (Great Barrington, MA: Anthroposophic Press, 2000).[7]

---

6. The previous details were abstracted from a Chronology published in *The Essential Steiner* (edited and introduced by Robert A. McDermott, San Francisco: Harper, 1984) pp. 25–33. A biography of Dr. Steiner that is related to the visions of Sister Emmerich can be found in Powell 1996 pp. 15ff. The definitive life of Dr. Steiner, although not complete, is found in Rudolf Steiner *Autobiography: Chapters in the Course of My Life: 1861–1907* (trsl. Rita Stebbings and edit. Paul M. Allen, Hudson, NY: Anthroposophic Press, 1999).
7. Excerpted from Powell 1996 p. 496 and Powell 2000 p. 159.

APPENDIX 2

AUTHENTICITY OF SISTER EMMERICH'S VISIONS

In his Introduction to *Chronicle of the Living Christ*, Dr. Powell says, "Rudolf Steiner...led me to Anne Catherine Emmerich and what he called her 'exceptionally accurate account.' It was given to [Sister] Emmerich to be so attuned to the life of Christ [Jesus] as a mystical reality that her comprehensive vision encompassed even minute details of time and place—testable 'coordinates,' in fact."[1]

He went on to say, "My first encounter with [Sister] Emmerich's work raised the question: How is it possible that this woman, who never left the area in which she was born (Germany), could describe in such detail the geography and topography of Palestine and the customs and the habits of the people living there? To answer this, I undertook an exhaustive analysis of her work, gradually penetrating the historical reality underlying Christ [Jesus'] life...."

The next paragraph leads off with Dr. Powell's statement, "I am not the first person who has traveled this road." There follow extensive details describing the independent discovery by a French priest, Abbot Julien Gouyet of Paris, in 1881, and several years later by two Lazarist missionaries, of the *Panaya Kapulu,* the house of Mary-Sophia,[2] where she had lived near the Turkish city of Izmir until her death. These discoveries were made possible by Sister Emmerich's detailed descriptions. The house has since been restored and is a place of pilgrimage. The authenticity of the discovery was confirmed by Archbishop Bernardini, who made this statement. "Dear brothers and sisters, all our bishops agree that Mary[-Sophia] died here...." Dr. Powell continues, "This remarkable example demonstrates the authenticity of Anne Catherine Emmerich's visions. That her visions

---

1. Powell 1996 pp. 11–13.
2. See Table 6 n. 5 for the basis to change the name from the Blessed Virgin Mary to Mary-Sophia as the result of a change in her status on the day of Pentecost (May 24, 33 C.E.)

provided spiritual nourishment had long been the experience of many spiritual seekers, but the discovery of Panaya Kapulu confirmed that her visions were objectively authentic and accessible, (at least in part) to corroboration along conventional lines of research."

Conversion of Visions into Dates

In Appendix III of the *Chronicle of the Living Christ*, Dr. Powell describes the complexity of the Hebrew calendar and then shows how the detail in Sister Emmerich's visions made it possible to convert her indications into actual dates.[3] He states categorically that her references to the Sabbath and the Hebrew festivals made it possible to reconstruct the calendar with great certainty. Almost all calendar references given by [Sister Emmerich] during this period are mutually supporting, so there can be little doubt of their authenticity. "*It would be virtually impossible to concoct such a set of consistent and mutually supporting calendar references and communicate them over a period of almost twenty-two months—Sister Emmerich was a simple woman of humble peasant origin with no knowledge of the intricacies of the Hebrew calender* (emphasis added)."[4]

In a later paragraph, Dr. Powell actually calculates the probability of making accurate calendar indications for the extended period of time that is under consideration. The chances of doing this correctly are one in over 50 trillion![5] More recently, and after the 1996 publication of his masterpiece in English, Dr. Powell has revisited the calculation in preparation for the publication of the German and Italian translations. A mistake which has been corrected reduces this probability to one in 440 billion. Dr. Powell considers his statistical validation of the correctness of Sister Emmerich's dates as a very important point and goes on to say, "No one has really grasped the true significance of this extraordinary fact."[6]

And in the Historical Overview Dr. Powell affirms, "From the standpoint of probability theory, it is clear that, at least with respect to dates, she was speaking the truth (leaving aside the intriguing question of *how* this was possible)." Dr. Powell's final conclusion is: "It is upon this scientifically verifiable foundation that the chronicle of the life of Christ [Jesus] presented in this book is based."[7]

---

3. Powell 1996 pp. 447ff.
4. Ibid. p. 450.
5. Ibid. p. 455.
6. Robert Powell (Personal communication dated September 1, 2002).
7. Powell 1996 p. 52.

Comparison of Two Visions

In Part Two of this discourse a similarity was shown between a vision of the birth of the Nathan Jesus by Saint Birgitta of Sweden and a vision of that same moment by Sister Emmerich. It can be suggested that such similarities, occurring across a period of some 350 years, provide a measure of authentication for both visionaries. The following two excerpts from visions about the crucifixion are a second example of this phenomenon. Saint Birgitta saw it this way.

> He extended His arm, not forced, but voluntarily, and opening His right hand, He laid it upon the Cross, and His cruel torturers barbarously crucified it, driving the nail through the part where the bone was most solid. Then violently drawing His left hand by a rope, they affixed it in similar manner. Then stretching His body beyond all bounds, they fastened His joined feet to the Cross with two nails, and violently extended those glorious limbs on the Cross so that almost all His nerves and veins were broken. This done they replaced on His head the crown of thorns, which they had taken off while affixing him to the Cross, and fastened it on His most sacred head. [8]

Sister Emmerich's vision of these events is as follows.

> [Christ] Jesus was now stretched on the cross by the executioners. He had lain Himself upon it; but they pushed Him lower down into the hollow places, rudely drew His right hand to the hole for the nail in the right arm of the cross, and tied His wrist fast. One knelt on His sacred breast and held the closing hand flat; another placed the long, thick nail, which had been filed to a sharp point, upon the palm of His sacred hand, and struck furious blows with the iron hammer.... After nailing Our Lord's right hand, the crucifiers found that His left, which also was fastened to the crosspiece, did not reach to the hole made for the nail, for they had bored a good two inches from the fingertips. They consequently unbound [Christ] Jesus' arm from the cross, wound cords around it and, with their feet firmly planted against the cross, pulled it forward until the hand reached the hole. Now, kneeling on the arm and breast of the Lord, they fastened the arm again on the beam, and hammered the

---

8. Anthony Butkovich *Revelations: Saint Birgitta of Sweden* (Los Angeles, CA: Ecumenical Foundation of America, 1972) p. 41.

second nail through the left hand....The whole body of our Blessed Redeemer had been contracted by the violent stretching of the arms to the holes for the nails, and His knees were forcibly drawn up.... Then they tied ropes around the right leg and, and with horrible violence to [Christ] Jesus pulled the foot down to the block and fastened it with cords.... With similar violence the left foot was drawn and fastened tightly with cords over the right;... The nailing of the feet was the most horrible of all, on account of the distention of the body.[9]

Yes, there are differences in the two accounts. In one, the actual raising of the cross is done empty and a platform is built to accomplish the crucifixion; in the other, the crucifixion is done on the ground. In one, four nails are used; in the other only three. But details of the terrible stretching, not mentioned in the gospel accounts, are common to the two sets of visions.

Contribution of the Cartographer Helmut Fahsel

In the Historical Overview of the *Chronicle of the Living Christ*, Dr. Powell introduces the monumental work of Helmut Fahsel called *Der Wandel Jesu in der Welt* (*The Travels of Jesus in the World*) published in 1942 by Ilionverlag of Basel, Switzerland.[10] The latter took the visions of Sister Emmerich literally and through the use of thirty-nine detailed maps of the Holy Land traced the actual path of the travels of Christ Jesus throughout the final years of his ministry. Dr. Powell provides plates of each of these maps carefully integrated with the reconstructed sequence of the visions. In addition, since the maps are labeled in German, Dr. Powell has included an alphabetical index that correlates the German, Arabic, and English versions of these place names.[11]

It should be added that part of Fahsel's contribution was to take into consideration how long it would take to walk these distances. He concluded that they were all feasible, although he acknowledged that Christ Jesus must have been an accomplished hiker to have covered these great distances in such relatively short periods of time. This also correlates with the visions of Sister Emmerich which indicate that often Christ Jesus and his companions would walk the entire night.

---

9. Emmerich 1986 vol. IV, pp. 268-71.
10. Powell 1996 pp. 53–54.
11. Ibid. pp. 353–73.

Appendix 3

The Bare Bones Story

Date	Event	Comment
Sept. 7, 21 B.C.E.	Birth of Solomon Mary	
Dec.–18 B.C.E.	Solomon Mary took vow to become a Temple virgin	
July 17, 17 B.C.E.	Birth of Nathan Mary	
March 5, 6 B.C.E.	Birth of Solomon Jesus	The Solomon Mary was 14 and 1/2years old
April 17, 6 B.C.E.	Presentation of the Solomon Jesus to the Temple	
Dec. 26, 6 B.C.E.	Adoration of the Magi as described by St. Matthew	This took place 9 1/2 months after the birth
Feb. 29, 5 B.C.E.	Flight into Egypt	
Sept. 15, 5 B.C.E.	Slaughter of the Innocents	Occurred when the Solomon Jesus would have been 1 1/2 yrs. old
March 30, 2 B.C.E.	Visit of Nathan Mary to her cousin Elizabeth	
June 3, 2 B.C.E.	Birth of John the Baptizer	
Dec. 6, 2 B.C.E.	Birth of the Nathan Jesus Adoration of the Shepherds as described by St. Luke	Occurred 4 years and 9 months after the birth of the Solomon Jesus
Jan. 1, B.C.E.	Presentation of the Nathan Jesus to the Temple	
Jan. 28, 1 B.C.E.	Death of Herod the Great	
Sept.–2 C.E.	Return of the Solomon Jesus from Egypt	Return to Nazareth rather than Bethlehem
Before Passover of 12 C.E.	Death of the Solomon Joseph	

Date	Event	Comment
April 3, 12 C.E.	Transfer of Zarathustra individuality from the Solomon Jesus to the Nathan Jesus	The name of Jesus of Nazareth is used to recognize this change
June 4, 12 C.E.	Death of the Solomon Jesus	The Solomon Jesus lived only 17 years
August 4, 12 C.E.	Death of the Nathan Mary	The Nathan Mary lived only 28 years
Date for this event not available but occurred not long after the death of the Nathan Mary	Merger of two families	Nathan Joseph, Nathan Jesus, Solomon Mary, and her 6 children born after the Solomon Jesus (James, Joseph Simon, Judas, and 2 sisters
Before Passover. of 29 C.E	Death of the Nathan Joseph	
Sept. 23, 29 C.E.	Departure of Zarathustra individuality; Baptism of Jesus of Nazareth by John the Baptizer; Incarnation of Christ Being; and transfer of Nathan Mary individuality to Solomon Mary	Now called Christ Jesus Now called Blessed Virgin Mary
April 8, 30 C.E.	Conversation with Nicodemus	Beheading of John the Baptizer
April 3, 31 C.E.	The Transfiguration	
July 26, 32 C.E.	Raising of Lazarus from the Dead	Now called Lazarus-John
March 19, 33 C.E.	Triumphant Entry into Jerusalem	
April 3, 33 C.E.	Crucifixion of Christ Jesus	
April 5, 33 C.E.	The Resurrection	
April 6, 33 C.E.	Appearance to the two disciples: Emmaus	
April 15, 33 C.E.	Appearance to the seven disciples: Sea of Galilee	
May 14, 33 C.E.	The Ascension	
May 24, 33 C.E.	Pentecost	Disciples became Apostles: BVM becomes Mary-Sophia
Aug. 15, 44 C.E.	Death of Mary-Sophia	In Ephesus at age 65

APPENDIX 4

SELECTED ENTRIES FROM "CHRONICLE OF CHRIST'S MINISTRY"

Excerpted from *Chronicle of the Living Christ* by Robert Powell, Ph.D.

Abbreviations used in this appendix:
[ ] indicates editorial emendations by CST.
... indicates omissions from the original text.
Dates in ( ) are derived by context.
Most entries in ( ) are part of the original text. Other entries in ( ) consist of Passing References where either Lazarus of Bethany or John the son of Zebedee is mentioned by name but is not a part of the vision. By contrast, when either **Lazarus** or **John** [**the son of Zebedee**] is shown in boldface, this means that these persons were a part of Sister Emmerich's vision.
Page numbers in {} refer to Powell {183–352}. Biblical citations from Powell are taken from the Revised Standard Version of the *Holy Bible*.
In Table 3 (page 55) and Table 6 (page 95) can be found the basis for the Consistent Nomenclature effort used in these Selected Entries.

Sunday, May 29, 29 [The Powell "Chronicle" starts with Jesus of Nazareth in Capernaum.] {184}

Tuesday, May 31, 29 (Today, they [Jesus of Nazareth, Parmenus, and Jonadab] arrived at Lazarus' castle in Bethany.) After talking with **Lazarus**, Jesus [of Nazareth] and his two friends visited the Temple in Jerusalem.... {185}

Wednesday, June 1, 29 In Hebron, Jesus [of Nazareth], saying he wanted to visit a friend, parted company with Parmenas and Jonadab.... Jesus [of Nazareth] then went into the desert region south of Hebron and found his way to the cave ("Elizabeth's cave") where the young John the [Baptizer] had stayed, having been brought there by his mother Elizabeth. {185}

Friday, June 3, 29… [Jesus of Nazareth] then made his way to Hebron for the Sabbath. That evening he visited the synagogue for the evening Sabbath celebration. {185}

Saturday, June 4, 29 After the morning service at the synagogue, Jesus [of Nazareth] visited the sick to console and help them, but he did not heal anyone. Wherever he went, he evoked wonder and amazement, for he appeared to all as a wonderful and benevolent person. Even those possessed grew quiet in his presence.… {185}

Friday, June17, 29 Today, Jesus [of Nazareth] was in Nazareth.… He wanted to attend the evening Sabbath in the synagogue to teach there, but he was turned away.… {186}

Thursday, June 23, to Wednesday, June 29, 29… Everywhere he went, Jesus [of Nazareth] taught in the synagogues and consoled the sick but did not perform any healing miracles.… {187}

Wednesday, June 29, 29 Today, Jesus [of Nazareth] was in Cana,… (Mary Salome was married to Zebedee—their children, James and John [the son of Zebedee], afterward became [disciples][1]….) {188}

Saturday, July 2, to Tuesday, July 5, 29 During this period, Jesus [of Nazareth] made his way through Galilee in the direction of Capernaum. Here and there, in the region on the west side of the Sea of Galilee, he taught about the Messiah. From time to time, too, one of the possessed would call out after him. He cast out a demon from one of them.… Kolaja and Eustachus accompanied Jesus [of Nazareth] along the way, speaking to him of John [the Baptizer], Lazarus and his sisters.… {188}

Wednesday, July 6, 29 Unaccompanied, Jesus [of Nazareth] went through a fence enclosing a fishery on the Sea of Galilee.… James and **John [the son of Zebedee]**, together with their father Zebedee and several other fishermen, were on the boats.… {189}

Friday, July 8, 29… That evening [at Sidon] the Sabbath began. Jesus [of Nazareth] taught in the synagogue of the Jewish community. He spoke of the coming of the Messiah and the downfall of idolatry. Leaving his com-

---

1. Sister Emmerich used the name apostle for the first twelve disciples. Since the conversion from disciple to apostle did not occur until Pentecost, which takes place after these selected entries, the language has been adjusted to preserve that distinction.

panions behind, Jesus [of Nazareth] left the city, proceeding southward to the town of Sarepta, where he stayed overnight in a dwelling built into the city walls.... {189}

Saturday, July 9, to Tuesday, July 19, 29 Jesus [of Nazareth] decided to remain in Sarepta for several days. He stayed with the pious old Jews living [within] the city walls who revered Elijah and were occupied with interpreting the prophecies concerning the Messiah. Jesus [of Nazareth] also visited the synagogue and taught the children. He spent much time, too, alone in prayer in the forest around the town. Sometimes he remained there all night. He also visited some of the surrounding pagan places and admonished the Jews not to mix with the pagans.... {189}

Wednesday, July 20, 29 Around this time, Jesus [of Nazareth] left Sarepta and went north to a place not far from a battlefield where in a vision Ezekiel had beheld the bones of the dead that were gathered together and restored to life (Ezekiel 37). Jesus [of Nazareth] taught and consoled the people living there, teaching them that Ezekiel's vision was about to be fulfilled (meaning that the breathing of new life into the dead was a vision referring to the sending of the Holy Spirit). {190}

Friday, July 22, 29 Jesus [of Nazareth] taught and celebrated the Sabbath in Sarepta.... {190}

Friday, July 29, 29 ... [Jesus of Nazareth] taught [in Samaria near Sychar] celebrating the Sabbath in the neighborhood. {191}

Monday, August 1, 29 ... Jesus [of Nazareth] taught in the synagogue [at Nazareth], and the holy women attended. {191}

Thursday August 18, 29 Today, Jesus [of Nazareth] taught at the synagogue of the Sadducees in Sephoris. Next to the synagogue was a madhouse, and inmates were obliged to attend the synagogue, accompanied by custodians. As Jesus [of Nazareth] taught, one or the other of the inmates began to speak out loud, "This is Jesus of Nazareth born in Bethlehem, visited by wise men from the east." "His mother is with Maraha." "He is bringing a new teaching," and so on. Jesus [of Nazareth] spoke the words: "The spirit that speaks this is from below and should return there." At this, all the inmates became quiet and were healed .... {193}

Saturday, August 20, 29 That morning, and also at the close of the Sabbath, Jesus [of Nazareth] taught in the synagogue at Bethulia. Many people came from the surrounding area and he was well received. {193}

Friday, September 2, 29 After leaving Kisloth, Jesus [of Nazareth] passed through the Edron valley, accompanied by some followers. He came to the shepherd village of Chimki. That evening, he celebrated the Sabbath and taught in the synagogue there. {195}

Saturday, September 3, 29 Jesus [of Nazareth] again taught in the synagogue, expounding several parables which the Pharisees mocked as childish. That night, Jesus [of Nazareth] stayed with a poor family and healed the mistress of the house who was suffering from dropsy. {195}

Monday, September 5, 29 Jesus [of Nazareth] and his traveling companions went to a shepherd village between the Edron valley and Nazareth. There they ate with some shepherds. Jesus [of Nazareth] healed two people who had been smitten with leprosy. ... {195}

Tuesday, September 6, 29 ... In the course of conversation with the [Nathan Mary], Jesus [of Nazareth] told her that he would go to Jerusalem four times for [the Feast of the Passover], but that the last time would be one of great affliction for her. {196}

Friday, September 9, 29 ... There was no synagogue in Endor, so, for the Sabbath [Jesus of Nazareth and the venerable Eliud, an elderly Essene widower,] returned to the synagogue at [Chimki] where they had been the previous day. {196}

Thursday, September 15, 29 ... Around midnight, Jesus [of Nazareth] said to Eliud that he would reveal himself, and—turning toward heaven—he prayed. A cloud of light enveloped them both and Jesus [of Nazareth] became radiantly transfigured. Eliud stood still, utterly entranced. After a while, the light melted away, and Jesus [of Nazareth] resumed his steps, followed by Eliud, who was speechless at what he had beheld. {197–98}

Friday, September 16, 29 ... [Jesus of Nazareth in the mountain village of Gur.] He celebrated the Sabbath there alone in his room at an inn, having requested a roll of the Scriptures to be brought to him from the synagogue. {198}

Saturday, September 17, 29 On this day, the last Sabbath prior to his baptism, Jesus [of Nazareth] spent the whole day in his room alone in prayer. {198}

Wednesday, September 21, 29 ... ([Jesus of Nazareth arrived] that night at Lazarus' castle in Bethany.) He was greeted not only by **Lazarus** but also by Nicodemus, John Mark, and the aged Obed (a relative of the prophetess

Anna), who were (guests of Lazarus in Bethany). Among the women gathered there (as guests of [Lazarus' sister] Martha) were Veronica, Mary Mark, and Susanna of Jerusalem. Jesus [of Nazareth] greeted them all and they took a meal together before retiring for the night. {199}

Thursday, September 22, 29 During the morning, Jesus [of Nazareth] walked about in the courtyards and gardens of the castle, teaching those who were present. Then Martha took Jesus [of Nazareth] to visit her sister Mary, known as Silent Mary, who lived by herself like a hermit in a part of the castle. Jesus [of Nazareth] was left alone to talk with Silent Mary, who lived in a continuous vision of heavenly things. Normally silent in the presence of other people, [Silent] Mary began to speak of the mysteries of [Christ] Jesus' incarnation, passion and death. After saying some prayers, Jesus [of Nazareth] returned to talk with Martha, who expressed her deep concern about her other sister, Mary Magdalene. At about half-past one, the [Solomon] Mary arrived, accompanied by Mary Chuza, the widow Lea, Mary Salome, and Mary Cleophas. After a light meal, Jesus [of Nazareth] and [the Solomon Mary], retired to talk with one another. In this conversation, [he] told [the Solomon] Mary that he was now going to be baptized and that his real mission would begin with this event. He said that they would meet again briefly in Samaria after the baptism, but that he would then go into the desert for forty days. [The Solomon] Mary was much troubled when she heard this, but Jesus [of Nazareth] answered by saying that he must now fulfill his mission and that she should renounce all personal claim on him. That evening, **Lazarus** gave a feast for all who were present. During the meal, Jesus [of Nazareth] again alluded to the persecutions that lay ahead of him, saying that those who allied themselves with him would suffer with him. The same night, Jesus [of Nazareth] accompanied by **Lazarus** set off in the direction of Jericho. {199}

Friday, September 23, 29 Jesus [of Nazareth] went on ahead of **Lazarus** and arrived at the place of baptism (on the west side of the Jordan River south of Ono) some two hours ahead of him.... John [the Baptizer] felt Jesus [of Nazareth's] presence among the crowd. [John the Baptizer] was fired with zeal and preached with great animation concerning the nearness of the Messiah. Then, he started baptizing. By ten o'clock he had already baptized many people. Jesus [of Nazareth] now came down to the baptizing pool where John [the Baptizer] was being helped by Andrew, later the [disciple], and by Saturnin, a young Greek of royal blood from the city of Patras, who later was one of [Christ] Jesus' closest disciples. At the moment of baptism, a voice of thunder spoke the words, ["You are my son, today I have begotten you." Luke 3:22] and Jesus of Nazareth became transparent with radiant light [as the result of the Incarnation of the Christ Being].[2] Meanwhile, Nicodemus, Obed, John Mark, and Joseph of Arimathea had also arrived to join **Lazarus** in witnessing the baptism. John [the Baptizer] then told Andrew to announce the baptism of the Messiah throughout Galilee.... [Christ] Jesus and his disciples then celebrated the Sabbath in [a small village called] Bethel (not the same as the Bethel north of Jerusalem). {200}

Saturday, September 24, 29 After the close of the Sabbath, Andrew took leave of [Christ] Jesus and departed for Galilee, to proclaim the baptism of the Messiah there. [Christ] Jesus and those with him then went with him to the town of Luz.[3] {200}

Sunday, September 25, 29 In the synagogue at Luz, [Christ] Jesus held a lengthy discourse, interpreting many things from the Old Testament. He also spoke of the need to forsake all to follow the Messiah and to have no great concern for one's daily needs. **Lazarus**, who had accompanied [Christ] Jesus thus far, now parted company with him and returned to Bethany. {200}

Monday, September 26, 29 Accompanied by twelve disciples, [Christ] Jesus traveled southward from Luz, healing several sick people on the way.... {200}

Thursday, September 29, 29 As the sun was rising, [Christ] Jesus and his disciples made their way down to the valley of the shepherds near Bethlehem. He was seen from afar by some of the shepherds, who beheld him in the glory of the light of the rising sun. They quickly summoned more shepherds, who came to greet [Christ] Jesus and praise him with a verse from the Psalms. [Christ] Jesus told them he had come to visit them because of the homage the shepherds had paid to him as an infant in the crib.... {201-02}

Sunday, October 2, 29 [Christ] Jesus took leave of the shepherds and of his disciples, saying that he wanted to be alone for a while, and would visit some people by himself. He arranged to meet with his disciples in a valley on Mount Ephraim in two days' time. He then set off alone, southward. {202}

---

2. This fundamental alteration in status is acknowledged here by changing references to this individual from Jesus of Nazareth to Christ Jesus.
3. "those with him" includes Lazarus, as is obvious from the next day's entry.

Monday, October 3, 29 Passing through a wild region, [Christ] Jesus came to an inn belonging to a man called Reuben, who had been there at the time of the [Solomon] Holy Family's flight into Egypt. [Christ] Jesus greeted and blessed Reuben, and then healed Reuben's grandchildren, some of whom were sick with leprosy, some of whom were lame. {202}

Tuesday, October 4, 29 The disciples met [Christ] Jesus in a valley on Mount Ephraim, some five miles east of Hebron. He conducted them to a nearby cave, where they spent the night. The disciples lit a fire, and [Christ] Jesus recounted all that had taken place in the cave: that David had been there before his fight with Goliath, and that the [Solomon] Holy Family had spent a night there on the way to Egypt. {202}

Thursday, October 6, 29 [Christ] Jesus and his disciples traveled on a couple of hours eastward until they reached a farmhouse, which had been one of the last stopping places of the [Nathan] Holy Family on their way to Bethlehem. The lady of the house, who had been a young woman at the time of [the Nathan] Joseph and [the Nathan] Mary's visit thirty years before, was now blind and almost bent double. She confessed her sins to [Christ] Jesus, who instructed her to bathe in some water he had just used. As she did so, she recovered her sight, was healed, and became upright. The people of the place … remarked on [Christ] Jesus' strong and handsome appearance. [Christ] Jesus answered them that in three-and-a-half years' time they would see no more strength and beauty in his appearance; his body would become so disfigured as to be unrecognizable. {203}

Saturday, October 8, 29 [Christ] Jesus remained for the Sabbath in Gilgal. **Lazarus,** Joseph of Arimathea and some other friends arrived from Jerusalem to hear him preach. The mood was joyful, and as [Christ] Jesus was leaving the synagogue the crowd shouted, "The covenant is fulfilled!" {203–04}

Tuesday, October 11, 29 After teaching in the synagogue [at Dibon, Christ] Jesus found that some sick people had been brought there into the open court. They cried out: "Lord, thou art a prophet! Thou hast been sent from God! Thou canst help us! Help us, Lord!" He healed many of them. That evening he was received at a banquet in his honor. Afterward, [Christ] Jesus arranged with the disciples to meet him on the following morning at a place outside the town. Then [Christ] Jesus left the inn where they were staying and went to pray alone on the mountain. {204}

Thursday, October 20, 29 Toward evening, [Christ Jesus] and his disciples arrived at a hostel near Bethany (that had been put at their disposal by

Lazarus). **Lazarus** came to greet them. Talking with the disciples, [Christ] Jesus spoke of the dangers facing those who follow him. He said that each [disciple] should consider carefully—during the coming period of separation from him—whether he really wanted to continue being a disciple. [Christ] Jesus then took leave of [the disciples] (and made his way to Lazarus' castle at Bethany), accompanied by **Lazarus** and the two nephews of Joseph of Arimathea, Aram and Themini. Here many friends from Jerusalem were expecting him. {206}

Friday, October 21, 29 [Christ] Jesus interpreted various passages from the scriptures to the friends gathered together. Later, he had a conversation with Silent Mary, whom he blessed. He then set off in the direction of Jericho. For the first part of the journey, [Christ] Jesus was accompanied by **Lazarus**. **Lazarus** went with [Christ] Jesus as far as a hostel (that he owned) close to the wilderness. Here they parted company, and [Christ] Jesus continued on his way alone and barefoot. As the Sabbath began, he climbed a mountain—Mount Quarantania—about one hour's distance from Jericho. Here he started his forty-day fast and spent the night in a cave. [Christ] Jesus knelt with outstretched arms and prayed to his heavenly Father for strength and courage in all the trials that awaited him. {206}

Saturday, October 22, 29 For the whole of the Sabbath and the following night, [Christ] Jesus remained in prayer [on Mount Quarantania]. A vast cloud of light descended upon him, and he received consolation from on high. [Christ] Jesus offered up to the Father all his future labors and sufferings so that these fruits should benefit his faithful followers in all ages to come. So intense was [Christ] Jesus' praying that [Sister Emmerich] saw him sweat blood. {206}

Sunday, October 23, 29 [Christ] Jesus descended from the mountain (Mount Quarantania) before sunrise. He walked toward the Jordan [River], which he crossed on a beam of wood, and journeyed east of the town of Bethabara into the wilderness beyond the Dead Sea. Eventually, he reached a very wild mountain range east of Callirrhoe where he ascended the forbidding Mount Attarus. This savage, desolate mountain lay about nine hours' distance from Jericho. Here [Christ Jesus] continued to pray and fast, spending the night in a narrow cave near the summit of the mountain. {206–07}

Monday, October 24, to Wednesday, November 30, 29 Throughout this period [Christ] Jesus stayed at the mountain cave on Mount Attarus, praying and fasting. Here he was tempted.... Throughout the whole period, however, [Sister Emmerich] beheld how [Christ] Jesus was daily submitted to temptation that then culminated in the three temptations described in the Gospels.... {207}[4]

Sunday, December 11, 29 Today, [Christ] Jesus journeyed about three hours from Eleale to Bethjesimoth, a small place on the east side of a mountain. On the way, he was joined by Andrew and Saturnin. In Bethjesimoth, he healed some of those who were possessed. He caused chains in which they were fettered to fall miraculously to the ground. Afterward, he visited and cured many of the sick in their homes. {209}

Monday, December 12, 29 [Christ] Jesus stayed in Bethjesimoth all day teaching, and healing. {209}

Friday, December 16, 29 This morning, Andrew, Saturnin, Aram, and Themini took leave of [Christ] Jesus and set off for Galilee.... [Christ] Jesus and the remaining disciples journeyed to Kibzaim for the Sabbath. There they met **Lazarus** and his servant, together with Martha, Joanna Chuza, and Simeon's son, who were all on their way to the wedding at Cana. {210}

Saturday, December 17, 29 After the Sabbath morning service, [Christ] Jesus healed by word of command several people who had been carried to a place in front of the synagogue. He was invited to a meal at the home of a distinguished Levite. At the close of the Sabbath, [Christ] Jesus went to Sichem (Sychar) where he stayed the night at an inn. {210}

Sunday, December 18, 29 Early this morning, [Christ] Jesus left Sychar and traveled to Thebez. As he entered the town, those possessed cried out: "Here comes the prophet of Galilee! He has power over us! He will cast us out!" [Christ] Jesus commanded them to be quiet and they became silent. He taught in the synagogue, healing many.... {210}

Monday, December 19, 29 Before daybreak, [Christ] Jesus left Thebez and traveled north toward Galilee.... On the road leading to Tarichea, Christ Jesus encountered Andrew, Simon Peter, and **John [the son of Zebedee]**.... To **John [the son of Zebedee]**, [Christ Jesus] said something about seeing him again another time. Peter and **John [the son of Zebedee]** then journeyed on to Gennabris while [Christ] Jesus, together with his disciples (including Andrew), continued on their way to Tarichea.... {211}

---

4. For those interested in additional details, consult Emmerich 1954b vol. II, pp. 1–19.

Tuesday, December 20, 29 [Christ] Jesus and his traveling companions did not go into Tarichea, but stayed at an inn just outside the town. [Christ] Jesus was visited there by **Lazarus**, Saturnin, Simeon's son, and the bridegroom Nathanael, who was to be married at the wedding at Cana. Nathanael invited [Christ] Jesus and everyone else to attend his wedding.... {211}

Sunday, December 25, 29 The [Blessed Virgin Mary] and her companions set off along the road to Cana.[5] [Christ] Jesus and his disciples went a more circuitous route. They traveled through Gennabris, where [Christ Jesus] taught in the synagogue. While he did so, Philip sought out Nathanael Chased who worked in Gennabris as a clerk.... Philip and Nathanael then set off along the road to Cana and soon caught up with [Christ] Jesus....[6] Everyone then went on to Cana, where [Christ] Jesus was received by the bridegroom, Nathanael, and by the bride's father, Israel, by her mother, and [by] the [Blessed Virgin Mary].[7] {212}

Monday, December 26, 29 In Cana, [Christ] Jesus stayed at a house belonging to one of [the Blessed Virgin] Mary's cousins. This cousin was the daughter of Anne's sister Sobe and was also an aunt of Nathanael the bridegroom. Today, [Christ] Jesus spent much time walking and talking with those disciples who later became his apostles. {213}

Tuesday, December 27, 29 About a hundred guests had gathered in Cana to attend the wedding.[8] That evening, [Christ] Jesus taught in the synagogue concerning the significance of marriage, husbands and wives, continence, chastity, and spiritual union. Later, [Christ] Jesus addressed the bridal pair. {213}

Wednesday, December 28, 29 Today,... the marriage ceremony took place at about nine o'clock in the morning. Afterward, the guests left the synagogue and assembled for the wedding banquet.[9] [Christ] Jesus had taken the responsibility for arranging the banquet. However, when [the Blessed Virgin] Mary saw that there was no wine, she said to [Christ Jesus], "They have no wine." Then there followed the sequence of events that culminated

---

5. In consequence of changes occurring in the Solomon Mary on the evening before the Baptism (see pages 57–58) the name Blessed Virgin Mary is used in this discourse from this time forward.

6. For a discussion of the conversion of Nathanael, see pages 23–24.

7. "... Everyone then went on to Cana," includes **Lazarus**.

8. "... About a hundred guests" includes **Lazarus**.

9. "... the guests left the synagogue and assembled for the ... banquet." includes **Lazarus**.

in the miracle of the transformation of water into wine (John 2:4–11).[10] This miracle gave interior strength to all those present who drank the wine. All became convinced of [Christ] Jesus's power and of the lofty nature of his mission. Faith entered their hearts, and they became inwardly united as a community. Here, for the first time, [Christ] Jesus was in the midst of his community. He wrought this miracle on their behalf. After the banquet, Nathanael the bridegroom had a private conversation with [Christ] Jesus in which he expressed his desire to lead a life of continence. His bride came to [Christ] Jesus with the same wish. Kneeling before [Christ] Jesus, they took a vow to live as brother and sister for a period of three years. [Christ Jesus] bestowed his blessing upon them. {213}

Thursday, December 29, 29 [Christ] Jesus taught in the house where the wedding banquet had taken place. Several guests, including **Lazarus** and Martha, departed from Cana. That evening, in a festive procession, the bride and bridegroom were conducted to their house. {213}

Saturday, December 31, 29 [In Cana, Christ] Jesus taught morning and afternoon in the synagogue. When he came out of the synagogue, in the presence of the priests, he healed six people and raised from the dead a man who had died as a consequence of falling from a tower.... {214}

Friday, January 6, 30 In Bethanat, [Christ] Jesus and his three disciples were joined by five disciples of John [the Baptizer]. Together, they walked southward in the direction of Capernaum. Pausing on a hill about a half hour from the Sea of Galilee, they could see Peter, James, and **John [the son of Zebedee]** in their fishing boats. [Christ] Jesus indicated that these three fisherman would also join him. After paying a brief visit to [the Blessed Virgin] Mary in her house between Bethsaida and Capernaum, [Christ] Jesus went to the synagogue in Capernaum to celebrate the start of the Sabbath. {215}

Friday, January 20, 30 [Christ Jesus at Bethabara.] Andrew and five disciples had come from [Ono,] the place of baptizing. Also **Lazarus**, Joseph of Arimathea, and some others had come from Jerusalem to hear [Christ] Jesus teach in the synagogue on the Sabbath. The people of Bethabara were well disposed toward [Christ] Jesus. {217}

Saturday, January 21, 30 At the close of the Sabbath, [Christ] Jesus set off to return to [Ono] the place of baptizing. On the way, he passed through

---

10. In John 2:4 Christ Jesus says to the Blessed Virgin Mary, "... My hour has not yet come."

Bethagla. Meanwhile, **Lazarus** and Joseph of Arimathea traveled to Jerusalem. {217}

Monday, January 23, 30 Because of the New Moon festival, there was no baptizing today, but to prepare those who were going to be baptized [Christ] Jesus taught at the place of baptism. In the evening, at the start of the second day of the month of Shebat, a feast was celebrated to commemorate the death of the wicked king Alexander Jannaeus. **Lazarus** and Obed arrived. {217}

Tuesday, January 24, 30 [Christ Jesus at Ono.] Early this morning, Andrew and Saturnin began baptizing. [Christ] Jesus set off with **Lazarus** and Obed in the direction of Bethlehem. **Lazarus** told [Christ] Jesus of the reports concerning him that were circulating in Jerusalem. They spent the night with some shepherds. {217}

Wednesday, January 25, 30 [Christ] Jesus, **Lazarus**, and Obed started out in the direction of Ono. **Lazarus** and Obed left [Christ] Jesus on the way and returned to Jerusalem. [Christ] Jesus went on, visiting and healing some sick people on the way. He reached the place of baptism, Ono, around three o'clock that afternoon. {217}

Tuesday, February 7, 30 When [Christ] Jesus arrived at Aruma, a messenger came to him from Phasael sent by Jairus, the Essene. The messenger told [Christ] Jesus that Jairus' daughter had died. [Christ] Jesus left his disciples, arranging to meet them in two days' time in Jezrael, and went with the messenger to Phasael. When he arrived at the home of Jairus, the daughter lay bound in sheets and wrappings ready for burial. [Christ] Jesus ordered the bindings to be loosened. Then he took the girl's hand, commanding her to rise. She sat up, and rose to stand before him. She was about sixteen years old. [Christ] Jesus warned those present not to speak of what they had witnessed. (This miracle is not to be confused with the raising from the dead of the daughter of Jairus of Capernaum reported in Mark 5:35–43—see [November 18, 30 and December 16,] 30). {219}

Thursday, February 9, 30 [Today, Sister Emmerich saw Christ Jesus in] Jezrael, where one month before he had publicly healed the sick, [Christ] Jesus now taught and performed a number of miracles. A large crowd assembled, including his disciples from Galilee: Nathanael Chasen, Nathanael the bridegroom, Peter, James, **John** [**the son of Zebedee**] and the sons of Mary Cleophas. **Lazarus**, Martha, Veronica, and Joanna Chuza came from Jerusalem. The women had persuaded Mary Magdalene also to come with them to see [Christ] Jesus. She came, although she was still leading a dissolute life. As she stood at the window of the inn where she was staying, she saw [Christ] Jesus walking by with his disciples. He glanced in her direction, and his look penetrated to the depths of her soul. Overwhelmed by her own misery, Mary Magdalene rushed to a leper house to take refuge. She felt deeply moved by the soul-searching glance [Christ] Jesus had cast upon her. Martha and **Lazarus** came to fetch her. They calmed her and then traveled back to Magdalum, where they celebrated the Sabbath together. {219–20}

Sunday, February 12, 30 So many people flocked to hear him that [Christ] Jesus left Capernaum early in the morning, accompanied by some disciples. [Christ] Jesus withdrew to pray alone in the hills.... That evening, [Christ] Jesus returned to [the Blessed Virgin] Mary's house between Capernaum and Bethsaida. There he met **Lazarus** and Martha, who had traveled from Magdalum to say goodbye to [Christ] Jesus before their return to Jerusalem. {220}

Monday, February 13, 30 [Christ] Jesus went to the synagogue in Capernaum and taught there. Some Pharisees objected to his teaching, saying that the whole land was unsettled and in a state of commotion on his account. [Christ] Jesus rebuked them severely. That night, [Christ] Jesus went to an inn in Gennabris (Nathanael Chased's hometown), accompanied by Nathanael Chased and seven future [disciples]: Andrew, Peter, the brothers James and **John [the son of Zebedee]**, and the sons of Mary Cleophas (Judas Thaddeus, Simon, and James the Lesser). {220}

Saturday, March 4, 30 [Christ] Jesus taught again in the synagogue in Sephoris and visited various homes—mostly of Essene families—to offer encouragement and support to his followers. He spoke with great affection, his words full of love. That night a great storm arose. [Christ] Jesus prayed with outstretched arms that danger might be averted. Thus, he protected the ships on the Sea of Galilee from afar. {223-34}

Sunday, March 5, 30 [Christ] Jesus and his disciples made their way to Nazareth. In the evening, [Christ] Jesus taught at the synagogue. It was the start of the fast day (Adar 13) commemorating Esther. That night another storm arose, and [Christ] Jesus—through prayer—again helped to avert the danger threatening the people aboard ships on the Sea of Galilee. {224}

Monday, March 13, 30 This morning [Christ] Jesus and his disciples left Nazareth.... [Christ] Jesus set off on the same route that the [Solomon]

Holy Family had taken on the flight to Egypt. He passed first through the little place of Nazara. Here he performed a miracle. He bought bread and multiplied it in his hands and distributed it to the poor. (Then he made his way to Lazarus' villa near Ginnim.) He was met by **Lazarus**, John Mark, Obed, and four other disciples. (Together they stayed overnight at Lazarus' villa.) {224-25}

Friday, March 17, 30... At the beginning of the Sabbath, [Christ Jesus and the disciples] arrived at the shepherd's inn where [the Blessed Virgin] Mary and the holy women had stayed (prior to [the] baptism) on their way to Bethany. [Christ] Jesus celebrated the Sabbath there [at the inn]. {225}

Saturday, March 18, 30 [Christ] Jesus and the disciples remained at the inn, where they had celebrated the Sabbath. After the close of the Sabbath, they continued on their way to Bethany. (That night [Christ] Jesus stayed at Lazarus' castle.)[11] {225}

Sunday, March 19, 30 This morning [Christ] Jesus and **Lazarus** went to Jerusalem. By midday the holy women and friends of [Christ] Jesus from Jerusalem were gathered at the house of Mary Mark. They ate a meal together with [Christ] Jesus, who spoke of the nearness of the kingdom of heaven. That evening, [Christ] Jesus and **Lazarus** returned to Bethany. {226}

Monday, March 20, 30 [Christ] Jesus went to Jerusalem again. He visited Obed, the son of Simeon, and ate a meal there. After eating, [Christ Jesus] walked the streets of Jerusalem. That evening, he returned to Bethany, where Saturnin and some of John [the Baptizer's] disciples came to him. Nicodemus also came from Jerusalem to hear [Christ] Jesus.[12] {226}

Wednesday, March 22, 30 Accompanied by **Lazarus** and Saturnin, [Christ] Jesus visited the homes of the sick in Bethany and healed a number of people. That evening the New Moon festival was celebrated in the synagogue. {226}

Thursday, March 23, 30 Together with **Lazarus**, Saturnin, Obed, and several other disciples, [Christ] Jesus was present at the service in the Temple

---

11. Although not mentioned by name, in the Powell summary of Sister Emmerich's visions between March 14 and March 18, it would seem as if **Lazarus** was one of the disciples for that entire period.

12. Although not mentioned by name, in the Powell summary of Sister Emmerich's visions on either March 20 or March 21, since Christ Jesus was staying at Lazarus' castle for that period, it would seem that **Lazarus** would have been a part of the visions on those days.

at Jerusalem. [Christ] Jesus' presence evoked mixed emotions in the people there, ranging from deep sympathy to hatred. {226}

Friday, March 24, 30 ([Christ] Jesus taught his disciple in the great hall of Lazarus' castle [in Bethany]). He spoke about his youth. Among other things, he said: "It is now eighteen years since a *bachir* (youth) in the Temple argued most eloquently with the doctors of the law, who were filled with wrath against him." [Christ] Jesus then related what the *bachir* had taught. That evening he celebrated the Sabbath in the synagogue at Bethany. {226}

Saturday, March 25, 30 This morning [Christ] Jesus went to celebrate the Sabbath in the Temple at Jerusalem. He wore a white woven robe with a cincture and a white mantel. He chanted and sang in turn with the others. Around two o'clock in the afternoon, he and his disciples ate a meal together at a place adjoining the Temple. [Christ] Jesus remained at the Temple for the rest of the day, returning to Bethany at about nine o'clock in the evening. {226}

Sunday, March 26, 30 [Christ] Jesus was in the Temple again this morning, accompanied by about twenty disciples. Afterward, he taught in the house of John Mark. Then he returned to Bethany, where he and **Lazarus** shared a meal with Simon the Pharisee. {227}

Saturday, April 1, 30 [Christ] Jesus went to the Temple for the Sabbath. Together with Obed, he entered the inner court, where the priests and Levites were holding a discourse concerning the Passover festival. The whole assembly was thrown into consternation by the appearance of [Christ] Jesus, who started to put questions that they could not answer. Although it was forbidden [for] ordinary people to come into this part of the Temple, [Christ] Jesus had entered it in his capacity as a prophet. (That evening after the close of the Sabbath, [Christ] Jesus returned to Bethany and talked with Lazarus' sister, Silent Mary, about the nearness of the kingdom of God.) He blessed her, for she was close to death. {227}

Monday, April 3, 30 [Christ] Jesus and his disciple went to the Temple. There [Christ] Jesus found vendors ranged around the court selling their wares. He admonished them in a friendly manner and bade them retire to the court of the Gentiles. He and the disciples helped them move their tables. Today, for the first time [Christ] Jesus healed the sick in Jerusalem. {228}

Tuesday, April 4, 30 A great multitude of people were gathered in Jerusalem. Arriving at the Temple, [Christ] Jesus and his disciples again found the vendors there. [Christ] Jesus admonished them more severely this time, and set about forcibly removing their tables to the outer court. Some pious Jews approved of his action and called out, "The prophet of Nazareth!" The Pharisees, put to shame by [Christ] Jesus's action, were angered by the crowd's response. Later, as [Christ] Jesus left the Temple, he healed a cripple. All was quiet on the streets of Jerusalem that evening, for people were busy in their homes cleansing out the leaven and preparing the unleavened bread. {228}

Wednesday, April 5, 30 [Christ] Jesus remained in Bethany today, the day of preparation for the Passover. In the Temple, the vendors gathered again. In the afternoon, the paschal lambs were slaughtered. **Lazarus**, Obed, and Saturnin slaughtered the three lambs that [Christ] Jesus and the disciples were to eat. (The Passover meal took place in the great hall at Lazarus' castle.) [Christ] Jesus taught, and they sang and prayed together until late in the night. {228}

Thursday, April 6, 30 Having prayed for much of the night on Mt. Zion, at daybreak [Christ] Jesus and his disciples went to the Temple. [Christ] Jesus taught in the forecourts. Vendors had again erected tables to sell their wares, and [Christ] Jesus demanded that they withdraw. When they refused, [Christ] Jesus drew a cord of twisted reeds from the folds of his robe. With this in hand, he overturned their tables and drove the vendors back, assisted by the disciples. [Christ] Jesus said, "Take these things away; you shall not make my Father's house a house of trade."[13] They replied, "What sign can you show us for doing this?" [Christ] Jesus answered them, "Destroy this temple, and in three days I will raise it up." They said, "It has taken forty-six years to build this Temple, and you will raise it up in three days?" But he spoke of the temple of his body. All this occurred between seven and eight o'clock in the morning. {229}

Friday, April 7, 30 This afternoon, [Christ] Jesus healed about ten people—some crippled, some dumb—in the forecourt of the Temple, giving rise to much excitement and jubilation. Summoned to answer for his action, [Christ] Jesus rebuked his interrogators severely. He then returned to Bethany, where he celebrated the Sabbath. {229}

Saturday, April 8, 30 ([Christ] Jesus remained for the whole day at Lazarus' castle.) At the close of the Sabbath, some Pharisees went to the home of

---

13. It is tempting to use the synoptic versions of Christ Jesus' words relating to this event. There is a problem with this. Those words occur in the synoptic gospels *after* the triumphant entry into Jerusalem which took place *three years later* in March of 33 C.E.

Mary Mark, thinking to find [Christ] Jesus there. They wished to take him into custody. However, they found only [the Blessed Virgin] Mary, and the holy women. After addressing the women sharply and telling them to leave the city, the Pharisees went away. The women then hurried to Bethany, where they found Martha together with Silent Mary. The latter died just a few hours later, in the presence of the [Blessed Virgin Mary]. That same night, Nicodemus came to Bethany and talked with [Christ] Jesus through the night. {229}

Sunday, April 9, 30 (Before daybreak, [Christ] Jesus and Nicodemus went to Jerusalem to Lazarus' house on Mount Zion.) Joseph of Arimathea joined them there. Later, a whole group of about thirty disciples came. [Christ] Jesus gave instructions about what the disciples should do during the coming period. {230}

Wednesday, April 26, 30 [Christ] Jesus returned to Bethany after a visit to Galilee. (He remained concealed in Lazarus' castle, where he was visited again by both Nicodemus and Joseph of Arimathea.) {230}

Wednesday, May 3, 30 Around this time (about three weeks after the Passover festival), [Christ] Jesus went to the place of baptism where he himself had been baptized.... His disciples had gathered there, and many people came to hear him. While [Christ] Jesus was teaching, a messenger from King Abgara of Edessa arrived. The messenger asked [Christ] Jesus to accompany him back to Edessa, or—if not—if he could at least paint a portrait of him. He produced a letter from the king in which the king described that he was ill, and believed in [Christ] Jesus as God or the Son of God, and requested to be healed. [Christ] Jesus replied to the king's letter by miraculously causing a perfect likeness of his countenance to be imprinted on the messenger's paper. The sight of this image later effected a deep transformation in the king's life. {230}

Tuesday, July 18, 30 After visiting some shepherd places, [Christ] Jesus, Saturnin, and the other disciple arrived at Gatthepher. Here [Christ] Jesus continued his healing work. Then he traveled to Capernaum, arriving at [the Blessed Virgin Mary]'s house that evening. There [the Blessed Virgin] Mary and about seven holy women, together with **Lazarus**, Obed, Aram, Themeni, Nathanael the bridegroom, and several other disciples awaited him. They discussed John the [Baptizer]'s imprisonment. [Christ] Jesus spoke of it as a sign for the beginning of his public work, the next step of which would be his going to Bethany. {236}

Wednesday, July 19, 30 This morning, [Christ] Jesus comforted [the Blessed Virgin] Mary and told her not to be downcast about his coming journey to Judea. Around midday, he set off with **Lazarus** and about five other disciples. They passed by Bethulia and continued on their way southward. At dusk, the New Moon festival was celebrated at synagogues throughout the land, indicating the start of the month of Ab. [Christ] Jesus and his companions walked through the night. {236}

Thursday, July 20, 30 (Early this morning, [Christ] Jesus and his disciples arrived at an inn, east of Jezrael, belonging to Lazarus.)[14] … Later in the day, they passed by Salem and, further south, crossed the Jordan. That night, they slept at a shepherd's place not far from the river, more or less west of Dibon. {236}

Friday, July 21, 30 [Christ] Jesus and **Lazarus** re-crossed the Jordan before the sun rose. Proceeding onward, they reached Bethany late that afternoon. (The entire group of [Christ] Jesus's friends and supporters were gathered at Lazarus' castle, expectantly awaiting their arrival.) After eating together, they celebrated the start of the Sabbath. That night, when all was still in the castle, [Christ] Jesus went to the Mount of Olives … and prayed to his heavenly Father for strength to fulfill his mission. (He returned to Lazarus' castle before daybreak.) {237}

Saturday, July 22, 30 ([Christ] Jesus and his disciples remained for the Sabbath and the following evening at Lazarus' castle.)[15] [Christ] Jesus spoke of his experiences in Adama. He also related the parable of the good Samaritan. That night [Christ] Jesus prayed again alone on the Mount of Olives. {237}

Sunday, July 23, 30 Today, as [Christ] Jesus explained his intention to teach throughout the land, **Lazarus** and the women made plans how best to help [Christ] Jesus in his mission…. After eating a meal together, everyone gathered in the castle's subterranean hall. Here [Christ] Jesus spoke of how God in his mercy had sent to his people one prophet after another, but each had been disowned and mistreated. Now, however, the people would reject the supreme grace: [Christ] Jesus predicted what would befall them. He summarized this teaching in the parable of the vineyard owner and the evil tenants (Matthew 21:33–43). Later he told the parable of the lost coin and also hinted at Mary Magdalene as he referred to the "joy before the

---

14. "and his disciples" includes **Lazarus**.
15. "and his disciples" includes **Lazarus**.

angels of God over one sinner who repents" (Luke 15:8–15). [Christ] Jesus then retired to pray alone again at the Mount of Olives. He returned shortly before midnight and—with **Lazarus** and Saturnin—set off for Bethoron, where he was expected to teach the following day. {237}

Monday, July 24, 30 Early this morning, on the outskirts of Bethoron, [Christ Jesus, **Lazarus**, and Saturnin] met up with Peter, Andrew, James the Greater, **John [the son Zebedee]**, Judas Thaddeus, James the Lesser, and Philip. Around eight o'clock, [Christ] Jesus and his disciples came to the synagogue. It was already full of people waiting in expectation to hear him. He spoke of the persecution of the prophets and the imprisonment of John the [Baptizer]. He spoke too of his own future persecution and the judgment and woe that would come upon Jerusalem. After healing various people in the town, [Christ] Jesus and his disciples left Bethoron and journeyed to Kibzaim. That night, they stayed at a large house belonging to a shepherd. {237–38}

Wednesday, July 26, 30 While the other disciples were otherwise engaged, [Christ] Jesus went to Jacob's well accompanied by Andrew, James the Greater, and Saturnin. Toward midday, they arrived at the hill on which the well-house was situated. [Christ] Jesus sent the three disciples into Sychar to buy provision and sat down near the well. Then there took place the encounter with the Samaritan woman—named Dina—as described in the Gospel of Saint John 4:1–42. {238}

Thursday, July 27, 30 [Christ] Jesus taught at Sychar for the whole day, expounding again upon the theme of the persecution of the prophets that is summarized in the parable of the vineyard owner and the evil tenants (see July 23, 30). Dina, the Samaritan woman, spoke to [Christ] Jesus concerning her future, for she had resolved to dedicate herself to his work, to help [Christ] Jesus and the disciples in whatever way she could. {238}

Friday, July 28, 30 This morning, having stayed the night at an inn outside Sychar, [Christ] Jesus taught at the inn and later on the surrounding hills. In the afternoon, he journeyed to Ginnim accompanied by his disciples. The Sabbath had already begun when they arrived, so they went straight to the synagogue. (After the service, they made their way to a place belonging to Lazarus situated some three quarters of an hour south of Ginnim.) They stayed overnight there. {238}

Sunday, July 30, 30 (As [Christ] Jesus taught this morning, many children were gathered in a park close to the place belonging to Lazarus where

[Christ] Jesus was staying.) Around mid-day, he set off together with three disciples to Atharot, where a group of Sadducees tried to trick [Christ] Jesus into raising from the dead someone who had been dead already eight days. [Christ] Jesus exposed their plot, however. He then traveled to a place on a hill near Engannim, where he stayed overnight. {239}

Tuesday, August 1, 30 Many came to hear [Christ] Jesus speak as he taught in the synagogue [at Engannim]. He spoke of the deeds of Elijah, and mentioned the three holy kings who had come from the East. When he had finished speaking, he healed many sick people. Later, he slipped away from the crowd and withdrew to pray alone in the hills. {239}

Thursday, August 3, 30 This morning [Christ] Jesus arrived at Cana. He stayed near the synagogue with a doctor of the law. While he was teaching those who had gathered in the forecourt of the house where he was staying, a messenger from Zorobabel, a high ranking official of Capernaum, arrived with a message saying his son was dying. There then occurred, at a distance, the miraculous healing of the boy as described in John 4:46–54.... {239}

Saturday, August 12, 30 [Christ] Jesus taught again in the synagogue at Nazareth and sharply reproached the Pharisees for their misinterpretation of the law. At midday, he dined with an Essene family. He then returned to teach at the synagogue again (Luke 4:23–28). At the close of the Sabbath, when [Christ] Jesus came out of the synagogue, he was immediately surrounded by about twenty Pharisees. They began to lead him out of the town toward a nearby hill, for they intended to cast him down from the brow of the hill. Suddenly, however, [Christ] Jesus stopped, stood still, and with the help of angelic beings passed—as if invisible—through the midst of the crowd to his escape (Luke 4:29–30). {241}

Wednesday, August 16, 30 After teaching some unbelievers on a mountainside near Gerasa, [Christ] Jesus journeyed to a place on the northeast side of the Sea of Galilee, where a boat sent by Peter and Andrew was waiting to collect him. He traveled across the lake and landed near Bethsaida. Peter, Andrew, **John [the son of Zebedee]**, James the Greater, James the Lesser, and Philip met him there. They all went with him to Peter's house, where the [Blessed Virgin Mary] and some of the holy women were waiting. All expressed their concern about the vehemence of the Pharisees directed toward [Christ] Jesus, and said it would be better for him not to teach in Capernaum, where fifteen Pharisees had been sent to investigate the new prophet. [Christ] Jesus, however, dismissed their worries with a few words. {241}

Saturday, August 19, 30 [Christ] Jesus went again to the synagogue in Capernaum to teach. And there took place the scene, described in Mark 1:23–27 and Luke 4:31–36, where [Christ] Jesus healed a man who was possessed. After further healings, around midday, [Christ] Jesus went to Peter's house in Bethsaida where he healed Peter's mother-in-law, who had a raging fever.... Later, after teaching again in the synagogue, [Christ] Jesus withdrew to a lonely place where he spent the night in prayer. {242}

Tuesday, August 22, 30 This morning, [Christ] Jesus taught and healed in Bethulia. And in the afternoon he and the disciples went to the nearby town of Jotopata. Here there were many Herodians. (The Herodians were a secret brotherhood opposed to Roman rule; they had the support of Herod Antipas.) [Christ] Jesus taught in the synagogue. The Herodians tried to trap him into saying that he was the Messiah, but [Christ] Jesus exposed them, and proclaimed their secrets to the assembled people. {242–43}

Friday, August 25, 30 Andrew, James, and **John [the son of Zebedee]** came to [Christ] Jesus to conduct him to Gennabris. They arrived at Gennabris at the start of the Sabbath. [Christ] Jesus taught in the synagogue, which was very full. Afterward he was invited to a meal by a Pharisee. {243}

Saturday, August 26, 30 [In Gennabris Christ] Jesus taught again this morning in the synagogue. Herod Antipas had sent some spies to Galilee to hear what [Christ] Jesus was preaching. [He] referred to them in these words: "When they come, you may tell the foxes (spies) to take back the word to that other fox (Herod) not to trouble himself about me. He may continue his wicked course and fulfill his designs with regard to John the [Baptizer]. For the rest, I shall not be constrained by him. I shall continue to teach wherever I am sent in every region, and even in Jerusalem itself when the time comes. I shall fulfill my mission and account for it to my Father in heaven." ... {243}

Friday, September 1, 30 Many disciples from Ainon and Jerusalem [including **Lazarus**] met up with [Christ] Jesus in Bezech. Altogether about thirty disciples were present. In the morning, [Christ] Jesus taught on a hill in the middle of Bezech and, later in the day, he healed many people. That evening he taught in the synagogue as the Sabbath began. {244}

Tuesday, September 5, 30 [Christ] Jesus instructed Andrew, James and **John [the son of Zebedee]** and some other disciples to remain at Ainon to baptize those who came there for baptism. Meanwhile, accompanied by about twelve disciples, [Christ] Jesus went on to Kamon. Here he taught and healed. Then he crossed the Jabbok where the patriarch Jacob had once been (Genesis 32:2), and entered the town of Mahanaim. Here he held a discourse on Jacob. Afterward, he went on to Ramoth-Galaad where, that evening, he taught in the synagogue on commemorating the sacrifice of Jephtha's daughter (Judges 11:29–40). {245}

Friday, September 8, 30 [Christ] Jesus taught in the synagogue at Arga today and again this evening at the beginning of the Sabbath. He spoke of the slaying of Zimri and the Midianite woman by Phineas the grandson of Aaron (Numbers 25: 6–15). {245}

Friday, September 15, 30... Here, in Betharamphtha, [Christ] Jesus too was received hospitably by the people. That evening, with the onset of the Sabbath, he taught in the synagogue. {246}

Friday, September 22, 30 [Christ] Jesus taught in the synagogue at Gadara for much of the day. As the Sabbath began that evening, he taught about the renewal of God's covenant through Moses (Deuteronomy 29ff.). {247}

Saturday, September 23, 30 This morning, after healing the sick, [Christ] Jesus taught again in the synagogue [at Gadara]. In the afternoon, at the request of a pagan priestess whose child had just died, he went to her house in the pagan quarter of the town and raised the child from the dead. Then he healed many other pagan children, who were all suffering because of their parents' worship of Moloch. [Christ] Jesus exorcised the priestess and then revealed to the assembled people the nature of their idolatry. The people believed; they determined to renounce the worship of Moloch and turn to the God of Israel.... {248}

Friday, September 29, 30 [Christ] Jesus and his disciples proceeded from Succoth to Ainon, where Mara the Suphanite, whom he had healed on [September 4, 30], had prepared a festive welcome for him. After conversing with Mara in her home, [Christ] Jesus went to the place of baptism and met with Andrew, James, and **John [the son of Zebedee]**, who had stayed there baptizing since [September 5, 30]. [Christ] Jesus addressed the assembled people. Among those present were **Lazarus**, Joseph of Arimathea, and some other disciples from Jerusalem who had traveled there for the special Sabbath preceding the Feast of Tabernacles. That evening, as the Sabbath began, [Christ] Jesus taught in the synagogue at Ainon. Afterward, there was a banquet at the public hall arranged by Mara the Suphanite in honor of [Christ] Jesus. {249}

Sunday, October 1, 30 After teaching and healing this morning in Ainon, [Christ] Jesus and the disciples made their way slowly to Succoth, arriving there around five in the afternoon. In the large synagogue at Succoth an adulteress pressed through the crowd listening to [Christ] Jesus and begged for mercy. She confessed her shame. [Christ] Jesus said: "Your sins are forgiven! Arise, child of God!" Then he reconciled her with her husband. {249}

Monday, October 9, 30 In the synagogue [at Ophra Christ] Jesus spoke about Adam and Joshua. He taught concerning worldly cares and referred to the lilies of the field (Matthew 6:25–34). Then he spoke of Daniel and Job. That evening, he received a visit from a messenger of the pagan Cyrinus of Cyprus inviting [Christ] Jesus to Cyprus. {250}

Sunday, October 15, 30 This morning, [Christ] Jesus [still at Aruma], exchanged words with the Pharisees, who defended their adherence to outer customs and forms. [Christ] Jesus pointed out to them that this was of no use because they had in fact lost the inner spirit of their religion. (He and the disciples then proceeded to an inn near Thanat-Silo, which Lazarus had put at their disposal.) {251}

Monday, October 23, 30 This morning [Christ] Jesus left Aser-Michmethat, accompanied by five disciples. Teaching as he walked, [Christ] Jesus arrived at Meroz during the afternoon. In the evening, he taught in the synagogue. (Afterward, he and the disciples went to an inn belonging to Lazarus outside—to the east—of the town.) There he was visited by Bartholomew, Simon, Judas Thaddeus, and Philip. They stayed the night with him. Bartholomew and Simon recommended that [Christ] Jesus accept Judas Iscariot as a disciple, whereupon [Christ] Jesus sighed and appeared to be troubled. {252–53}

Wednesday, October 25, 30 Today [Christ] Jesus continued his teaching from the mountain [between Meroz and Atharot]. Disputing with the Pharisees, he referred to the two commandments: Love of God and love of neighbor (Matthew 22: 36-40). Later in the day, while healing the sick, [Christ] Jesus was approached by a rich pagan widow from Nain, called Lais. She sought [Christ] Jesus' aid on behalf of her two daughters, Sabia and Athalia, both of whom had stayed in Nain because they were possessed. [Christ] Jesus exorcised Lais' daughters from afar and told her to purify herself, saying: "The sins of the parents are on these children." (After this healing, Manahem, the blind youth whose sight [Christ] Jesus had restored in Korea, returned from delivering a message to Lazarus in

Bethany and came to [Christ] Jesus.) Manahem was accompanied by the nephews of Joseph of Arimathea, Aram and Themani. {253}

Sunday, November 5, 30 [Christ] Jesus and the disciples went to Gischala, a stronghold garrisoned by Roman soldiers, whom Herod had to pay for. [Christ] Jesus gave instruction to his disciples in which he mentioned three "men of zeal" from Gischala. The first was the founder of the Sadducees, who had lived over two hundred years before Christ [Jesus]. The second was John of Gischala, who subsequently fomented an uprising in Galilee and actively resisted the Romans at the siege of Jerusalem. The third was Saul, who later became the [A]postle Paul, now living with his parents at Tarsus, but who had been born in Gischala. {255}

Wednesday, November 8, 30 Around ten o'clock [Christ] Jesus arrived at the mountain [beyond Gabara], where there was a teacher's chair. He delivered a powerful discourse, culminating in the words: "Come! Come to me, all who are weary and laden with guilt! Come to me, O sinners! Do penance, believe, and share the kingdom with me!" At these words, Mary Magdalene was deeply moved inwardly, and [Christ] Jesus, perceiving her agitation, addressed his hearers with some words of consolation—words actually meant for Mary Magdalene—and she was converted. That evening [in Gabara], a Pharisee named Simon Zabulon invited [Christ] Jesus to a banquet. During the meal, Mary Magdalene entered the room carrying a flask of ointment, with which she anointed [Christ] Jesus' head. (This scene and the ensuing dispute with Simon Zabulon is described in Luke 7: 36–50). {256}

Monday, November 13, 30 At around nine in the morning, as [Christ] Jesus and the disciples were approaching Nain, they met a funeral procession emerging from the city gate. [Christ] Jesus commanded the coffin bearers to stand still and set the coffin down. He raised his eyes to heaven and spoke the words recorded in Matthew 11:25–30. There then occurred the miraculous raising from the dead of the youth of Nain—the twelve-year-old Martialis, son of the widow Maroni—described in Luke 7:11–17. {257}

Friday, November 17, 30 [In the vicinity of Mount Tabor, t]his morning [Christ] Jesus went to the home of a leper, whom he healed. Then [Christ] Jesus and his disciples walked toward Capernaum, arriving there shortly after the beginning of the Sabbath. They went to the synagogue, where [Christ] Jesus taught. As he was leaving the synagogue, two lepers came to him and—trembling—sank down on their knees before him. [Christ] Jesus laid his hands upon them, breathed upon the face of each, and said:

"Your sins are forgiven!" The Pharisees protested loudly because he had healed on the Sabbath and questioned by what right he was able to forgive sins. Without uttering a word, [Christ] Jesus passed through their midst. He went to his mother's house. After consoling his mother and the other women there, [Christ] Jesus went out and spent the night in prayer. {258}

Saturday, November 18, 30... [Christ] Jesus went to the synagogue in Capernaum and healed a number of sick people who were waiting outside. Here he was approached by Jairus, the chief of the synagogue. Jairus pleaded with [Christ] Jesus to come and heal his daughter, Salome, who was on the point of death (Mark 5:21-24). [Christ] Jesus agreed to go with Jairus, but on the way a messenger came to relate the news that Salome was already dead. [Christ] Jesus, in his mercy, performed the miracle of raising her from the dead. Because of her parents' attitude toward [Christ] Jesus, which the girl imitated, this led again to her illness and death on [December 1, 30] (See second raising of Salome from the dead on that date). {258}

Tuesday, November 21, 30 This morning, from the shore of the Sea of Galilee, [Christ] Jesus called to Peter and Andrew, who were casting a net into the lake, "Come and follow me, I will make you fishers of men." A little further down the shore he called also to the brothers James and **John [the son of Zebedee]** (Matthew 4:18–22). Peter and Andrew baptized today, and also Saturnin. That evening, as crowds thronged around him, [Christ] Jesus and the future twelve [disciples] boarded Peter's boat, and [Christ] Jesus gave instructions to go over to the other side of the lake in the direction of Tiberius (Matthew 8:18). In the middle of the lake a great storm arose, which [Christ] Jesus calmed (Matthew 8:23–27; Luke 8:22–25). Then he commanded the disciples to sail back in the direction in which they had come, toward Chorazin.... {259}

Sunday, November 26, 30 [In Capernaum, after Christ Jesus] and his disciples had distributed gifts and alms to the poor, [Christ Jesus] taught on the shore of the lake. As the crowd grew very large, he and the disciples boarded a boat moored close by. From there [Christ] Jesus continued to teach the crowds on the shore.... As evening approached, [Christ] Jesus instructed Peter to row his boat out onto the lake and to cast the nets. A great shoal of fish filled them (Luke 5:4–5) so that it was not until the early hours of the following morning, between three and four o'clock, that Peter and his helpers were able to land the fish.... {260}

Tuesday, November 28, 30 [Christ] Jesus and the disciples sailed across the Sea of Galilee. After disembarking, they went to a mountain near

Bethsaida-Julias, where many people were gathered to hear [Christ] Jesus teach. [This site is subsequently referred to as the Mount of the Beatitudes.] Here began the "Sermon on the Mount" referred to in Matthew 5 and Luke 6. This sermon lasted some fourteen days, but its conclusion was not delivered until three months later, on [March 15, 31]. To begin with, [Christ] Jesus spoke of the first beatitude (Matthew 5:3). The instruction lasted the whole day. {260}

Wednesday, November 29, 30 Today[, at the Mount of Beatitudes, Christ] Jesus began to teach concerning the second beatitude (Matthew 5:4). Five holy women were present, including the [Blessed] Virgin Mary, Mary Cleophas, and Maroni of Nain, and also the twelve disciples [eleven of whom] later became apostles. After the sermon, [Christ] Jesus taught the disciples as indicated in Matthew 5:14–20. {260–61}

Thursday, November 30, 30 [At the Mount of Beatitudes, Christ] Jesus continued to teach the second beatitude. He also explained many of the teachings of the prophets. {261}

Friday, December 1, 30 [At the Mount of Beatitudes, Christ] Jesus preached today concerning the third beatitude [Matthew 5:5]. But because the Sabbath was approaching, he broke off early and sailed back toward Capernaum. There he taught near the south gate, in a house that Peter had rented. It was here that the healing of the paralytic described in Mark 2:1–2, Luke 5:17–26, and Matthew 9:1–9 occurred. After this, [Christ] Jesus went to the synagogue, where he taught—this time without disruption. Jairus, whose daughter (Salome) [Christ] Jesus had raised from the dead on [December 1, 30], was there. As [Christ] Jesus left, Jairus approached him to ask help for Salome, who was again close to death. [Christ] Jesus agreed to go. On their way, the message of Salome's death reached them. But they continued on. Then occurred the healing of the widow Enue from Caesarea Philippi, who had been suffering from a flow of blood for twelve years (Matthew 9:20–22, Mark 5:25–34, and Luke 8:43–48). Reaching Jairus' home [Christ] Jesus then repeated the raising of Salome from the dead (Matthew 9:23, Mark 5:35–43, and Luke 8:49–56). Afterward, [Christ] Jesus left the house. On his way through the streets of Capernaum he was approached by two blind men, whom he healed (Matthew 9:27–30). Following this, [Christ] Jesus healed Joas the Pharisee, who was possessed (Matthew 9:32–34). {261}

Saturday, December 2, 30 Today[, in Capernaum, Christ] Jesus visited the centurion Cornelius. Then he went to Jairus' house and cautioned Salome to follow the word of God. At the close of the Sabbath, he taught in the synagogue. The Pharisees left early, and [Christ] Jesus continued teaching the disciples, as indicated in Matthew 5:27–37. The Pharisees then returned with a man whose hand was withered, whom [Christ] Jesus healed. {261}

Sunday, December 3, 30 [Christ] Jesus taught again in the house near the south gate of Capernaum and spoke of the beatitudes. Among the hearers was Lea, the sister-in-law of Enue, [the widow from Caesarea-Philippi] whom he had healed two days before. As [Christ] Jesus was saying the sixth beatitude, "Blessed are the pure in heart, for they shall see God," [the Blessed Virgin] Mary and four holy women entered the room. Lea called out: "Blessed is the womb that bore you, and the breasts that you sucked!" [Christ] Jesus replied: "Blessed rather are those who hear the word of God and keep it!" (Luke 11:27–28).… {261-62}

Monday, December 4, 30 Today [Christ] Jesus continued the Sermon on the Mount [of the Beatitudes] near Bethsaida-Julias. He spoke on the fourth beatitude. Afterward, he went with the twelve to a place on the east shore of the lake. There he gave the twelve authority to cast out unclean spirits (Matthew 10:1–4). [Christ] Jesus then sailed with the twelve and about five other disciples to Magdala, where he exorcised some people who were possessed. Peter, Andrew, James, and **John [the son of Zebedee]** also cast out unclean spirits. [Christ] Jesus and the disciples then spent the night on the boat. {262}

Thursday, December 7, 30 [Christ] Jesus taught and healed for much of the day. Then he instructed the disciples to sail back to Bethsaida, while he withdrew into the hills alone to pray. That night the disciples saw [Christ] Jesus walking across the water toward them. (This was not the walking on the water described in Matthew 14: 22–23, which took place later on [January 29, 31]). {262}

Saturday, December 9, 30 [At Capernaum, while Christ] Jesus visited the home of Jairus, Cornelius, and Zorobabel, the disciples baptized at Peter's house.… Before the Sabbath ended, [Christ] Jesus again taught the [first] beatitude: "Blessed are the poor in spirit." At the end of the Sabbath, [Christ] Jesus returned to the synagogue, inveighing against the Pharisees' teaching that he drove out devils with the help of devils (Matthew 12:31–37). {263}

Sunday, December 10, 30 Today there occurred—for the first time—the sending out of the disciples. At about ten o'clock in the morning, with the twelve and about thirty other disciples, [Christ] Jesus left Capernaum and went north in the direction of Saphet and Hanathon, accompanied by a large crowd. Around three in the afternoon, they approached Hanathon. Here [Christ] Jesus and the disciples climbed a mountain used in former times by the prophets. [Christ] Jesus had taught there less than one year ago on [January 5, 30]. This time, however, the crowd did not go up the mountain. On the mountain, Christ Jesus addressed the disciples, giving them instruction and sending them out into the world with the words found in Matthew 9:36–10:16. Each of the twelve had a small flask of oil, and [Christ] Jesus taught them how to use it for anointing and also healing. Afterward, the disciples knelt in a circle around [Christ] Jesus, and he prayed and laid his hands upon the head of each of the twelve. Then he blessed the remaining disciples. After embracing one another, the disciples set off, having received indications from [Christ] Jesus as to where they should go and when they should return to him. Peter, James the Lesser, **John [the son of Zebedee]**, Philip, Thomas, Judas and twelve other disciples remained with him. They all came down the mountain together. At the bottom they met up with the crowd of people returning home from Capernaum. That night [Christ] Jesus stayed in Bethanat (Matthew 11:1). {263}

Monday, December 11, 30 [Christ] Jesus and the disciples who were with him journeyed to a place called Hucuca. Not far from there was a well, where [Christ] Jesus healed a blind man and also several people who were lame. Afterward he taught in the synagogue at Hucuca, speaking of the beatitudes and telling several parables. [Christ] Jesus and the disciples then stayed the night with the chief elder of the synagogue. {263–64}

Friday, December 15, 30 This morning [Christ] Jesus spoke in the synagogue [at Galgala] about the second beatitude. In the afternoon, he taught again, and some Pharisees from Saphet came to hear him. They invited him to Saphet for the Sabbath, and [Christ] Jesus accepted their invitation. He was received with much ceremony, and went straightaway to the synagogue, where a great crowd had assembled. It was not only the start of the Sabbath but also the close of the Feast of Lights; at the same time it was the New Moon Festival denoting the beginning of the [Hebrew] month of Tebeth. {264–65}

Saturday, December 16, 30 This morning [Christ] Jesus healed the sick, the deaf, the blind, the palsied, and the lame. Some Pharisees and Sadducees, visiting Saphet from Jerusalem, were scandalized at what they saw. They could not tolerate such a disturbance on the Sabbath and therefore began to dispute with [Christ] Jesus, saying that he did not observe the Law. [Christ] Jesus reduced them to silence by writing an account of their secret sins and transgressions on a wall in Old Hebrew, which only they could read. Then he asked them whether they wanted the writing to remain on the wall and to be known publicly, or whether they would allow him to continue his work in peace, in which case they could efface the writing. Thoroughly frightened, they rubbed out the writing and went away to leave him to continue his work of healing the sick. {265}

Sunday, December 17, 30 About midday, after healing people on the outskirts of Saphet, [Christ] Jesus went on to Carianthaim. Before entering the town, he blessed a group of children. Then he made his way to the synagogue, healing the sick in the way. In the synagogue [Christ] Jesus again taught the beatitudes and—addressing the Levites—interpreted a passage from [2 Samuel 6:6–7]. {265}

Wednesday, December 20, 30 This morning the steward of the inn [located outside of Abram] laid a dispute before [Christ] Jesus and begged him for a decision. The dispute concerned a well, used by cattle of two different tribes. At issue was the question as to which tribe was really entitled to use the well. [Christ] Jesus replied that each side should set an equal number of cattle free, and from whichever side the greater number went to the well of their own accord, this side should have the greater right to use of the well. He then employed this as an analogy for the living water that the Son of Man would give—that it would belong to those who most earnestly desired it. Then, around ten o'clock, [Christ] Jesus went into Abram. On the way to the synagogue in Abram, [Christ] Jesus cured many of the sick and crippled who were lying in the street. Reaching the synagogue, he taught there, but only in the Pharisees' synagogue, not in the Sadducees' synagogue. That evening, he went to an inn at the southern end of the town. (This inn had been placed at the disposal of Christ Jesus and the disciples by Lazarus.) {266}

Sunday, December 24, 30 [Christ] Jesus went to Dothaim. Arriving at the outskirts of town, he was met by a group of people, including some Pharisees. On the whole, however he received a cool reception. (That night he stayed at an inn put at his disposal by Lazarus.) {267}

Monday, December 25, 30 At the inn at Dothaim, [Christ] Jesus met Martha and **Lazarus** and some other women and disciples from Jerusalem. Martha went from Dothaim to Magdalum, to try and persuade her sister

Mary Magdalene to come and hear [Christ] Jesus speak the next day on a hill near Azanoth. {267}

Tuesday, December 26, 30 [Christ] Jesus made his way to the hill near Azanoth, where he had announced he would teach. On the way, he met [the Blessed Virgin] Mary and some of the holy women—among them were Anna Cleophas, Susanna Alpheus, Susanna of Jerusalem, Veronica, Joanna Chuza, Mary Mark, Maroni, Mara the Suphanite, and Dina the Samaritan. Martha had succeeded in persuading Mary Magdalene to come—it had taken great patience—and she arrived with great pomp and ceremony at the hill. After healing many sick people, [Christ] Jesus spoke of the woe that would befall the towns of Chorazin, Bethsaida, and Capernaum (Matthew 11: 20). Many children who were present then began calling out: "Jesus of Nazareth! Most holy prophet! Son of David! Son of God!" Many listeners, including Mary Magdalene, were deeply moved by this. [Christ] Jesus then spoke the words recorded in Matthew 12:43. [Mary] Magdalene was truly shocked. Turning to different parts of the crowd, [Christ] Jesus commanded the devils to depart from all those who sought freedom from their possession. As the devils departed, many, including Mary Magdalene, sank to the ground. Three times in all, as she took in Christ Jesus' powerful words, Mary Magdalene fell unconscious to the ground. Coming to after the third occasion, she wept bitterly and asked Martha to bring her to join the holy women. **Lazarus** and Martha then brought her to the inn where the holy women were staying. Meanwhile [Christ] Jesus, came down to Azanoth and went into the synagogue to teach. Mary Magdalene came too. He spoke again in her direction. As he looked at her, she fell unconscious again and another devil departed from her. Later, she cast herself at his feet, begging for salvation. [Christ] Jesus comforted her, saying that she should repent with all her heart, and that she should have faith and hope. {267}

Sunday, December 31, 30 [Christ] Jesus left Nazareth around one o'clock in the morning. He went toward Mount Tabor. On the way, around dawn, he healed a number of lepers. Reaching Mount Tabor, he went up to the prophet's teaching chair and, after healing the sick, spoke of the first four beatitudes and recounted some parables. Around midday [Christ] Jesus gathered the twelve and all the other disciples together. After giving them instructions, he sent them out in pairs (Matthew 9:36–38; 10:5–16) Peter and **John** [**the son of Zebedee**] and a few other disciples remained with him. Together, they made their way to Sunem. They got there around sunset. Here [Christ] Jesus healed a dumb, lame, epileptic boy. That evening, in Sunem, [Christ] Jesus spoke alone with the boy's father, for it was his sin that led to his son's condition. [Christ] Jesus said that he should repent. {269}

Monday, January 1, 31 [At Sunem this] morning, Christ Jesus healed the brother and two sisters of the child whom he had cured on the previous day. All three were feeble-minded. Laying his hands upon them, he restored them to normalcy. The three children were astounded, awaking as if from a dream. They had always believed that people wanted to kill them and they were particularly afraid of fire. [Christ] Jesus then taught on the street, and blessed and healed many children. Afterward, accompanied by Peter and **John [the son of Zebedee]**, he set off toward Samaria. They traveled quickly for the rest of the day and on through the whole night. On the way, [Christ] Jesus told them that John the [Baptizer] would soon meet his end, and that he wanted to go to Hebron to comfort the [Baptizer's] relatives. {269}

Wednesday, January 3, 31 This morning [Christ] Jesus taught in the synagogue [at Thanat–Silo]. Afterward, some people from Jerusalem told him of the sudden collapse of a wall and tower in Jerusalem two days before. As a result, a crowd of laborers, including eighteen master workers sent by Herod, had been buried in the falling debris (Luke 13:4). Herod's workmen had engineered the accident to stir up the people against Pontius Pilate. But their plan had backfired, resulting in their own deaths. [Christ] Jesus expressed his compassion for the innocent laborers, but added that the sin of the master workers was not greater than that of the Pharisees, Sadducees, and others who labored against the Kingdom of God.... That night, during the festivities to celebrate Herod's birthday at Machaerus, John the [Baptizer] was beheaded at the request of Herodias' daughter, Salome.... {269–70}

Friday, January 5, 31 [Christ] Jesus journeyed on from Ozensara to Bethoron, where he had already taught on [July 24, 30]. This evening at the start of the Sabbath, he taught in the synagogue. Afterward he healed the sick, but the Pharisees objected to his healing on the Sabbath, saying that the Sabbath belonged to God. [Christ] Jesus replied: "I have no other time and no other measure than the will of the Father in heaven." Afterward, when [Christ] Jesus ate a meal with the Pharisees, they reproached him for allowing women of bad repute to follow him. They meant Mary Magdalene, Dina the Samaritan, and Mara the Suphanite (Luke 8:1–3). [Christ] Jesus answered: "If you knew me, you would speak differently. I have come out of compassion for sinners." {270}

Monday, January 8, 31 [Christ] Jesus left Bethany and crossed the Mount of Olives. Weeping, he turned to those with him and said: "If this city (Jerusalem) does not accept salvation, its Temple will be destroyed like this building that has tumbled down. A great number will be buried in the ruins." He referred, [as he had done on January 3, 31], to the recent catastrophe of the collapsing building as an example that should serve as a warning to the people. He visited the laborers' hospital at the foot of the Mount of Olives, healing the sick there and also those who had been wounded in the catastrophe. Then he went to Bethlehem and visited an inn, not far from the city gate, frequented by Essenes and other holy people. Afterward, he set off in the direction of Hebron, making his way to Zecharias' house at Juttah. Since Elizabeth and Zecharias had died, a cousin of John the [Baptizer] lived in the house. Here [Christ] Jesus met up with [the Blessed Virgin] Mary, the holy women, and others from Jerusalem who had traveled on ahead.[16] They exchanged greetings. [Christ] Jesus then went to the synagogue in Juttah, where he spoke about David, who had been born in Hebron. {271}

Tuesday, January 9, 31 [Christ] Jesus and his disciples spent the day in and around Juttah, teaching and healing. That evening, after the other women had retired, [Christ] Jesus and [the Blessed Virgin] Mary, accompanied by Peter, **John [the son of Zebedee]** and the three sons of Mary Heli (who had been disciples of the [Baptizer]), went into the room where John the [Baptizer] had been born. Kneeling together with the others, on a large rug, [the Blessed Virgin] Mary recounted events from the [Baptizer's] life. Then [Christ] Jesus told them that John [the Baptizer] had been put to death by Herod. Stricken with grief, they shed tears of lamentation on the rug. [Christ] Jesus consoled them with earnest words. He said that silence should be maintained, at least for the time being. For, with the exception of the murderers, apart from them, none knew of John the [Baptizer's] death. {271–72}

Tuesday, January 16, 31 Today [Christ] Jesus went from Libnah to Bethzur, where he was well received. **Lazarus** and some friends from Jerusalem were already waiting for [Christ Jesus] at an inn near the synagogue. {273}

Thursday, January 18, 31 Martha, Mary Magdalene, and the widow Mary Salome, who was living in Bethany as a guest of Martha, came to meet [Christ] Jesus on his way to Bethany. That evening [Christ] Jesus and his

---

16. "others from Jerusalem" includes **Lazarus**.

friends and disciples shared a meal in Bethany. After everyone had gone to bed, [Christ] Jesus went alone to pray on the Mount of Olives. {273}

Friday, January 19, 31 This morning [Christ] Jesus and a group of disciples went to Jerusalem, first visiting the house of Joanna Chuza. Around ten in the morning, [Christ] Jesus went to the Temple and taught there without arousing any opposition. After sharing a small meal with his disciples in the early afternoon at the house of Joanna Chuza, [Christ] Jesus and the disciples went to the pool of Bethesda, where he imparted instructions to the sick, healing a number of them. On the way out, he healed a paralyzed man who had been ill for thirty-eight years (John 5:1–15). By then, the Sabbath had already begun. So [Christ] Jesus went to the Temple and taught there again. In the evening, around sunset, John the [Baptizer's] body was buried at Juttah, in the vault of Zecharias, the disciples having returned from Machaerus with it the day before. {273}

Saturday, January 20, 31 [Christ] Jesus and the disciples healed the sick this morning at the Coenaculum on Mount Zion. That afternoon they ate there, and [Christ] Jesus went to the Temple. Once again, he was able to teach there without encountering any opposition. That evening he and the disciples ate at the house of Simon the Pharisee in Bethany. (Afterward, at Lazarus' castle,) [Christ] Jesus said goodbye to **Lazarus**, Martha, and Mary Magdalene. {274}

Friday, January 26, 31 Capernaum was full of visitors who had come from far and wide to hear [Christ] Jesus. In addition, a group of sixty-four Pharisees had also gathered, having come from all around to investigate the carpenter's son from Nazareth. [Christ] Jesus visited the homes of Zorobabel, Cornelius, and Jairus. The latter had lost his position as chief elder at the synagogue and had been persecuted because of his contact with [Christ] Jesus. Now Jairus committed himself wholly to the service of [Christ] Jesus. He then began healing and continued to heal throughout the morning. Around midday, [Christ] Jesus withdrew to a hall to preach. Then, as the Sabbath began, he went to the synagogue. He had to make his way through a great crowd before he could begin to teach. When the Pharisees asked him if it was allowed to heal on the Sabbath, he answered by healing a man with a withered hand (Matthew 12:9) and by driving out a devil from one who was deaf, mute, and possessed, and whose hearing and speech were immediately restored. Witnessing this, the Pharisees accused [Christ] Jesus of being in league with the devil. [Christ] Jesus, however, defended himself with the words he spoken in Matthew 12:33–37. Amid the uproar, [Christ] Jesus and his disciples withdrew. That night, [Christ] Jesus stayed at Peter's house. {275}

Sunday, January 28, 31 Many people had followed [Christ] Jesus from Capernaum to Bethsaida. As a result, early this morning, a large crowd had assembled at Matthew's custom house. They had come to hear [Christ] Jesus speak. Still more people came from the surrounding area, bringing with them the sick and possessed. In the afternoon, after healing and teaching, [Christ] Jesus dismissed the crowd, saying that he would teach the next morning on the mountain near Bethsaida-Julias. [Christ] Jesus, the twelve, and the seventy-two disciples then withdrew to a shaded, solitary place. [Christ] Jesus gave them instruction along the lines of Matthew 10:1–42. He arranged them in ranks as follows: the twelve [disciples] two by two, headed by Peter and **John [the son of Zebedee]**; the older disciples formed a circle around them, and then came the younger ones according to the rank he assigned to them. He set the [first twelve disciples] over the [later] disciples, saying that the former should send and call the latter, just as he sent and called the original twelve disciples]. {275}

Monday, January 29, 31 Today a large crowd of some five thousand people assembled on the [Mount of Beatitudes] near Bethsaida-Julias. It was here [on November 28, 30], that [Christ] Jesus had started to teach the "Sermon on the Mount." In the [intervening time Christ] Jesus had continued to teach the beatitudes and the Our Father prayer. Now [Christ] Jesus taught and healed; and the [disciples] baptized many people. And again, the main content of Christ Jesus' teaching was the beatitudes and the Lord's Prayer. Between four and six o'clock in the afternoon, there took place the miraculous feeding of the five thousand (John 6:5–15 and Mark 6:35–45). In the evening [Christ] Jesus withdrew alone (Matthew 14:22–23), while the [disciples] sailed on Peter's ship back toward Bethsaida. A great storm arose on the Sea of Galilee, and there then took place the second miracle of the walking on the water (Matthew 14:25–33), which had taken place for the first time on the night of [December 7, 30]. {276}

Tuesday, January 30, 31 At sunrise, Peter's ship landed near Dalmanutha (Mark 8:10). Here [Christ] Jesus healed and continued his teaching concerning the beatitudes and the Lord's Prayer.... {276}

Wednesday, January 31, 31 Early this morning, [Christ] Jesus and the disciples landed again between Matthew's custom house and Little Chorazin, where [Christ] Jesus addressed a crowd of about a hundred people. About noon he sailed back towards Bethsaida. On landing, he went to Peter's house. Here [Christ] Jesus was greeted by **Lazarus**, who had come to see him. Veronica's son Amandor and one or two others had also come. Then [Christ] Jesus went to a place on the road leading into Bethsaida, where a group of people had gathered. Here he began his great teaching concerning the eucharistic bread of life, which is summarized in John 6:25–34. On this occasion, [Christ] Jesus did not however say that he himself was the bread of life. {276}

Thursday, February 1, 31 [Christ] Jesus continued the teaching on the bread of life at the same place on the road leading into Bethsaida, this time saying quite plainly that he was the bread of life (John 6:35–51).[17] Some two thousand people were present. {276}

Friday, February 2, 31 Still at the same place on the road to Bethsaida, [Christ] Jesus taught on the same theme as the "Sermon on the Mount" (Matthew 5:3–12; 6:9–13). He spoke of the beatitudes and the Lord's Prayer. In the evening, with the start of the Sabbath, he went to the synagogue. As he was teaching, he was interrupted with the question, "How can you call yourself the bread of heaven come down from heaven, since everyone knows where you come from?" [Christ] Jesus then taught again concerning the bread of life (John 6:52–59). This caused a great uproar. The Pharisees cried out, "How can he give us his body (flesh) to eat?" [Christ] Jesus replied that he would give them the food of which he spoke "in its own time" (in 113 weeks). {276–77}

Saturday, February 3, 31 Today [Christ] Jesus taught in the synagogue [at Bethsaida] concerning the sixth and seventh petitions of the Our Father and the first beatitude. He was questioned about his discourse of the day before on the bread of life, concerning the eating of his flesh and the drinking of his blood. He repeated in strong and precise terms all that he had said about this. Then even some of his disciples began to complain: "This saying is hard, and who can bear it?" (John 6:60). [Christ] Jesus replied that they should not be scandalized, and that they would witness quite other things. He also predicted that he would be persecuted, that even his most faithful disciples would desert him, and that he would be put to death. Yet, he added, he would not desert them. His spirit would be with them (John 6:61–65). As he was leaving the synagogue, the Pharisees

---

17. It should be emphasized that Sister Emmerich makes a point to separate into accounts occurring on four different days what is a continuous passage in John's Gospel. One should also note that this discussion of the bread of life precedes the institution of the Eucharist at the Last Supper by some fifteen months!

and certain disloyal disciples tried to detain him with further questions, but the ... loyal disciples surrounded him and escorted him from the synagogue amid much noise, shouting, and confusion.... {277}

Sunday, February 4, 31 Following an invitation from Nathanael (the bridegroom of the wedding at Cana), [Christ] Jesus, the [first] twelve [disciples] and the loyal disciples set off for Cana, on the first stage of a journey through Galilee (John 7:1).[18] {277}

Monday, February 5, 31 While they were walking this morning in the neighborhood of Gischala, [Christ] Jesus revealed to the twelve the disposition and character of each, and arranged them correspondingly in three groups or rows: in the first row—Peter, Andrew, **John** [the son of Zebedee], James the Greater[,] and Matthew; in the second row—Judas Thaddeus, Bartholomew, and James the Lesser; and in the third row—Thomas, Simon, Philip, and Judas Iscariot. Judas Barsabbas stood at the head of the remaining disciples, nearest to the twelve, and [Christ] Jesus then placed him in the second row together with Thaddeus, Bartholomew, and James. {277–78}

Friday, February 9, 31 This morning [Christ] Jesus healed and taught in various homes in Elkasa. As the Sabbath started, he taught in the synagogue, speaking of the building of Solomon's Temple. Afterward, the Pharisees invited him to a meal in the town hall. There a dispute broke out. The Pharisees complained to [Christ] Jesus that his disciples did not observe the Law, because they did not wash their hands before coming to the table (Mark 7:1–13). [Christ] Jesus replied with the words recorded in Mark 7:14–16. Later, [Christ] Jesus explained to the disciples the nature of the Pharisees' spiritual impurity (Matthew 15:12–20). {278}

Monday, February 12, 31 In the company of Peter, **John** [the son of Zebedee], and James the Greater, [Christ] Jesus healed the sick at many homes in Dan. He was followed by an old pagan woman from Ornithopolos, who was crippled on one side. [Christ] Jesus seemed to ignore her, for he was concerned solely with healing Jews. Nevertheless, she begged him to come and heal her daughter, who was possessed. [Christ] Jesus replied that it was not yet time, that he wanted to avoid giving offense, and that he would not help the pagans before the Jews. Later that afternoon, the Syrophoenician woman from Ornithopolos approached [Christ] Jesus and again begged

---

18. "... the twelve [disciples]" includes **John the son of Zebedee**.

him to drive the unclean spirit out of her daughter. There then followed the exorcism of her daughter, as described in Matthew 15:21–28.... That evening, [Christ] Jesus and the disciples dined at the home of an old man of the Nazarite sect, a friend of Lazarus and Nicodemus. It was the celebration of the New Moon festival at the start of the month of Adar. {279}

Sunday, February 25, 31 After teaching in the synagogue [at a village on Phiala Lake], [Christ] Jesus and the disciples visited various shepherd dwellings scattered around the lake. In the evening accompanied by **John [the son of Zebedee]**, Bartholomew, and another disciple, [Christ] Jesus went south toward Nobah and stayed there at an inn frequented by Pharisees. {281}

Monday, February 26, 31 Today [Christ] Jesus taught and prepared a number of people for baptism. **John [the son of Zebedee]** and Bartholomew then performed the baptism. [Christ] Jesus was well received in Nobah by the people, but at a banquet given that evening in the public hall the Pharisees began to argue with him about his disciples' conduct. During the discussion, [Christ] Jesus told the parable of the laborers in the vineyard (Matthew 20:1–6) and also that of the rich glutton and poor Lazarus (Luke 16:19–31).[19] Finally, [Christ Jesus] reproached the Pharisees for not having invited the poor, and sent out the disciples to bring them to the banquet. Today the Purim festival began. {281–82}

Wednesday, March 14, 31 Early this morning, [Christ] Jesus and the disciples went to a mountain northeast of the Mount of the Beatitudes. A considerable crowd had assembled to hear him. [Christ] Jesus spoke concerning the last two beatitudes. He spent the night on Peter's ship. {284}

Thursday, March 15, 31 Today [at the mountain northeast of the Mount of Beatitudes Christ] Jesus delivered the so-called "Sermon on the Mount" (Matthew 5:1-7; 29), signifying the conclusion of his presentation of the beatitudes, which he had begun on the Mount of Beatitudes on [November 28, 30]. Then toward evening took place the feeding of the four thousand (Matthew 15:32–39). [Christ] Jesus took leave of the people, who shed tears of thanks. He made his way back to the lake with the disciples.... 284}

---

19. This Lazarus is not the same person as Lazarus of Bethany.

Sunday, March 18, 31 [Christ] Jesus and the disciples left Bethsaida-Julias and journeyed to Sogane, where he taught and healed until late afternoon. Then he went to a hill outside of the town, and [Christ] Jesus taught the disciples and listened to their accounts of the experiences they had undergone on their missionary travels. That night, [Christ] Jesus withdrew alone to pray. {285}

Monday, March 19, 31 Before dawn, [Christ] Jesus returned to the disciples and they prayed together. The twelve stood around him in a circle and the other disciples around them.[20] [Christ] Jesus asked, "Who do the people say I am?" The reply to this question is recorded in Matthew 16:13–14. Then [Christ] Jesus asked: "But who do you say that I am?" Peter, taking a step forward, declared: "Thou art Christ, the Son of the living God!" At this very moment the Sun was rising, and [Christ] Jesus spoke the words recorded in Matthew 16:17–20. He told the disciples that he was the promised Messiah, applying all the relevant passages from the prophets to himself. He announced that now the time had come for them to journey to Jerusalem for the [Festival of the] Passover. Traveling through the day, that evening they arrived at Bethulia. Here **Lazarus** was waiting for [Christ] Jesus. **Lazarus** had come to warn him that an insurrection against Pontius Pilate was planned and that this threatened to disrupt the [Festival of the] Passover. The revolt would be led by Judas of Gamala, who had the support of a large number of Galileans. **Lazarus** said that it would therefore be advisable for [Christ] Jesus to hold back from the celebrations in Jerusalem. But [Christ] Jesus replied that this uprising would be the forerunner of a far greater one that would take place at a later time, meaning that which would accompany his future trial and persecution. {285–86}

Tuesday, March 20, 31 [Christ] Jesus and the disciples split up into different groups for the journey to Bethany. [Christ] Jesus was accompanied by Simon, Judas Thaddeus, Nathanael Chased, and Judas Barsabbas. They made rapid progress, arriving that night at Lazarus' estate near Ginnim. {286}

Friday, March 23, 31 As [Christ] Jesus and the disciples were approaching Ephron, they were met on the way by Mary Magdalene and the widow Salome, who had come together from Bethany to greet [Christ] Jesus. After resting and talking with the two women, [Christ] Jesus and the four disciples continued on their way. (The two women returned to Bethany by

---

20. "The twelve" includes **John the son of Zebedee.**

another route.) When [Christ] Jesus arrived at Bethany, they were welcomed by **Lazarus**. The [Blessed Virgin Mary] was also there, and other disciples and friends had already arrived. That evening, [Christ] Jesus and all those gathered together in Bethany celebrated the Sabbath in the great hall of the castle. He spoke much about the paschal lamb and about his future suffering. {286}

Tuesday, March 27, 31 Today, [Christ] Jesus and his friends and disciples walked together on the Mount of Olives. Meanwhile, the healed man from the pool of Bethesda continued to go around telling the Pharisees it was [Christ] Jesus who had cured him. The Pharisees then determined to take [Christ] Jesus into custody. In the afternoon, the slaughter of the paschal lambs in the Temple began—at [three and not at twelve-thirty in the afternoon] as was the case on the day of the crucifixion. (On the day of the crucifixion the earlier start was conditioned by the onset of the Sabbath a few hours later.) That evening all [Christ] Jesus' friends and disciples gathered in the great hall at Lazarus' castle to share the Passover feast.[21] During the meal, [Christ] Jesus spoke of the Son of Man as the true vine and referred to his disciples as the grapes on the vine (John 15:1–8). The festivities, with singing from the Psalms lasted until late into the night. {287–88}

Wednesday, March 28, 31 Early this morning [Christ] Jesus and the disciples went to the Temple.[22] They stood among the crowd from sunrise to about eleven o'clock. Then there was a pause in the reception of the offerings. [Christ] Jesus went up to the great teacher's chair in the court before the sanctuary. A large crowd gathered around, including many Pharisees and also the man who had been healed at the pool of Bethesda. The Pharisees accused [Christ] Jesus of breaking the Sabbath because he had healed this man on the Sabbath. [Christ] Jesus replied that the Sabbath was made for humanity, not humanity for the Sabbath. He then recounted the parable of the [rich] man and poor Lazarus.[23] This so outraged the Pharisees that they pressed around and sent for the Temple guards to take [Christ] Jesus into custody. At the height of the uproar, it suddenly grew dark. [Christ] Jesus looked up to heaven and said, "Father, render testimony to thy Son!" A loud noise like thunder resounded and a heavenly voice proclaimed: "This is my beloved son in whom I am well pleased!" [Christ]

21. "... all [Christ] Jesus' friends" includes **Lazarus**, and "... disciples" includes **John the son of Zebedee**.
22. "... and the disciples" includes both **Lazarus** and **John the son of Zebedee**.
23. Not Lazarus of Bethany.

Jesus' enemies were terrified. The disciples then escorted [Christ] Jesus from the Temple to safety.... {288}

Saturday, March 31, 31 After healing many people yesterday in Atharot, [Christ] Jesus was invited to the home of the widow whom he had healed the day before. Later, some of the disciples were spotted plucking ears of corn as they walked. This was reported to the Pharisees and led a few days later [April 4 and 5, 31], to [renewed attacks on Christ] Jesus in Dothaim and Capernaum (Matthew 12:1–2). After the Sabbath had ended, [Christ] Jesus and the disciples went to Lazarus' estate near Ginnim and stayed there overnight. {289}

Tuesday, April 3, 31 From the inn at Hadad-Rimmon where he had been staying [Christ] Jesus went to Kisloth at the foot of Mount Tabor. Here he taught and healed. Around three o'clock in the afternoon, he went with Peter, **John [the son of Zebedee]**, and James the Greater up Mount Tabor. Around midnight, the transfiguration took place (Matthew 17:1–8). {289–90}

Wednesday, April 4, 31 Early in the morning, [Christ] Jesus and the three disciples came down the mountain and met up again with the other disciples. There then followed the healing of the possessed boy whom the disciples had been unable to heal (Mark 9:14–27). After healing several more people, [Christ] Jesus and the disciples continued on their way until they reached Dothaim. As they walked, the three disciples who had witnessed the transfiguration asked [Christ] Jesus questions concerning what he had said about the resurrection of the Son of Man and the words in the scripture about Elijah. [Christ] Jesus answered them as recorded in Matthew 17:9–13 and Mark 9:9–13. He also taught the disciples as stated in Luke 12:22–53. In Dothaim, they met up with some other disciples who had already arrived. As these listened to the account of the healing of the possessed child whom the disciples could not heal, the question arose as to why they were unable to do so. [Christ] Jesus replied as found in Matthew 17:19–21. That evening, [Christ] Jesus and the disciples were guests at a meal given by the Pharisees, who attacked them for breaking the Sabbath, that is, for plucking ears of corn on the Sabbath. [Christ] Jesus replied in the words given in Matthew 12:2–8. {290}

Thursday, April 5, 31 This morning, after teaching at Dothaim, [Christ] Jesus made his way to Capernaum. There he and the disciples were guests at a feast in honor of their homecoming. Some Pharisees were also present. These Pharisees again accused [Christ] Jesus of sanctioning the violation of long-established customs, charging that the disciples had broken the Sabbath, plucked corn, neglected handwashing, and so on. {290}

Wednesday, April 18, 31 At about ten in the morning [Christ] Jesus arrived at the mountain near Gabara where the new "Sermon on the Mount" was to begin. Many Pharisees, Sadducees, and Herodians were among the people gathered there to hear him. After beginning with a prayer, [Christ] Jesus began to teach about prayer and the love of one's neighbor (Matthew 5:38–6:8). He also warned against the Pharisees and false prophets. [Christ] Jesus taught without interruption until evening. Then he descended the mountain to return to where he was staying. Among those who came to meet him there were **Lazarus**, Martha, Dina the Samaritan, Mara the Suphanite, Maroni of Nain, and [the Blessed Virgin] Mary. {292–93}

Thursday, April 19, 31 Today, [Christ] Jesus continued his "Sermon on the Mount." The Pharisees began to proclaim [Christ] Jesus as a "disturber of the peace," saying that they had the Sabbath, the festival days, and their own teaching, and they did not need the innovations of this upstart. They threatened to complain to Herod—who would certainly put a stop to [Christ] Jesus' activities. [Christ] Jesus answered that he would continue to teach and heal, in spite of Herod, until his mission was complete. Eventually, the pressure of the crowd forced the Pharisees to leave so that [Christ] Jesus could continue his teaching undisturbed. After the sermon had ended and the crowd had dispersed, [Christ] Jesus taught the disciples concerning the character of the Pharisees and how they should conduct themselves in relation to them.[24] That evening, as [Christ] Jesus and the disciples ate together, **Lazarus** told of the journey the women had made to Machaerus from Hebron and Jerusalem. Indeed, one of them, Joanna Chuza, had just succeeded in recovering the head of John the [Baptizer] from Herod's castle. {293}

Friday, April 20, 31 This morning, [Christ] Jesus and the twelve [disciples] healed the sick who were gathered at the foot of the mountain.[25] The remaining disciples dispensed food and clothing to the poor. This was the cause of much joy and thanksgiving. Afterward, the people dispersed to return to their home towns in time for the Sabbath. [Christ] Jesus and the

---

24. "... the disciples" includes **John the son of Zebedee.**
25. "... the twelve [disciples]" includes **John the son of Zebedee.**

disciples then made their way to Garisma. On the way, they passed through Capharoth. In Capharoth, some Pharisees, who were well disposed to [Christ] Jesus, warned him that Herod was out to imprison him and deal with him as he had with John the [Baptizer]. [Christ] Jesus replied that he had nothing to fear from "the fox," and that he would do what his Father had sent him to do (Luke 13:31–33). Reaching Garisma, [Christ] Jesus and the disciples went to the synagogue for the start of the Sabbath. {293}

Wednesday, May 16, 31 [While visiting Cyprus, Christ] Jesus taught again today about the Feast of Weeks, about the giving of the Law on Mount Sinai, and about baptism. The Feast of Weeks began that evening. There was a torchlight prayer-procession, which [Christ] Jesus joined. Afterward, he retired to pray alone. {298}

Friday, May 18, 31 [Christ] Jesus and the disciples visited the homes of various people [on Cyprus] to teach comfort and heal. He spoke with several women about their marriage difficulties. That evening, with the beginning of the Sabbath, [Christ] Jesus spoke in the synagogue with tremendous power and earnestness. He spoke of the breaking of commandments and of adultery. Afterward, he prayed alone all night. {298}

Monday, June 11, 31 After teaching in the synagogue at Azanoth, [Christ] Jesus walked to Damna, where he was greeted by **Lazarus** and the two nephews of Joseph of Arimathea. [Christ Jesus] spoke at length with **Lazarus** about accommodating those who would be coming from Cyprus. {302}

Tuesday, June 12, 31 [Christ] Jesus, together with **Lazarus** and the disciples, visited the village belonging to the Centurian Zorobabel of Capernaum, where there was an inn that had been put at the disposal of [Christ] Jesus and the disciples. At the inn, [Christ] Jesus was met, among others, by Nathanael of Cana. Later, Zorobabel and Cornelius came and took a walk with [Christ] Jesus before they returned to Capernaum. Then [Christ] Jesus and the accompanying disciples went to the house of [the Blessed Virgin] Mary.... He dined alone with her and told her of his journey to Cyprus. The [Blessed Virgin Mary] spoke of her concern for his future. [Christ] Jesus said she should think only of God's plan, which he would fulfill. {302–03}

Wednesday, June 20, 31 Many friends and relatives came to see [Christ] Jesus in Cana. They warned him of the bitterness of the Pharisees toward him, saying that it was becoming more and more dangerous for him to continue teaching. [Christ] Jesus then taught them about his mission. He said that he would do nothing except follow the will of his Father. Then with the nine [disciples] and some [other] disciples, he went to Mount Tabor, where they were reunited with the three remaining [disciples]— Thomas, **John [the son of Zebedee]**, and Bartholomew—who had now returned from their missionary journeys. They all went back to Cana together and dined at the house of Israel, the father of the bride at the wedding (John 2:1–11). Present were: the twelve [disciples], the seventy disciples who had been sent out together with the [disciples] on their missionary journeys, the holy women, and many other friends and relatives. It was a kind of feast of remembrance of the wedding at Cana, and it was a great joy for all to be together again. {304}

Thursday, June 21, 31 [Christ] Jesus went with the ... disciples to a hill about two hours' walk from Cana in the direction of Gabara. [He] asked them to tell what they had experienced on their missionary journeys. [Christ Jesus] said: "Now will be seen who has loved me—and, in me, my heavenly Father—and who has spread the word of salvation and healed, not for his own sake, and not for the sake of vain renown, but on my account." As Peter spoke enthusiastically about casting out demons from those possessed, [Christ] Jesus bade him to be silent and, looking up to heaven, spoke the words recorded in Luke 10:18–20. As [Christ] Jesus spoke, [Sister Emmerich] saw a cloud of light shining around him; he prayed joyfully and addressed the disciples ... with the words recorded in Luke 10:21–24.... {304–05}

Thursday, June 28, 31 This morning, [Christ] Jesus took leave of most of the remaining ... disciples. Only Peter, James, **John [the son of Zebedee]**, Matthew, and a few disciples remained with him. They went to Matthew's custom house. Here several friends from Capernaum (Jairus, Zorobabel, Cornelius, and some others) were waiting for him. [Christ] Jesus taught and consoled them before traveling on by boat to Dalmanutha, where he taught that evening. {306–07}

Friday, June 29, 31 Today, accompanied by Peter, James, and **John [the son of Zebedee]**, [Christ] Jesus went to Edrai. With the beginning of the Sabbath they went to the synagogue, where he taught. {307}

Tuesday, July 3, 31 In Nobah, [Christ] Jesus healed many people who were possessed. Peter, James, and **John [the son of Zebedee]** also taught and healed. {307}

Friday, July 6, 31 Before noon, [Christ] Jesus and his traveling companions left Salcha and walked westward along what is called the "Way of David" on account of David's having hidden himself in this region near Mizpeh (1 Samuel 22). [Christ] Jesus told his companions how Abraham had approached the promised land along David's Way and the procession of the three holy kings had also traveled the same path. Then, after a time, they left the Way of David and went southward to the town of Thantia, arriving there at the onset of the Sabbath. In the synagogue, [Christ] Jesus spoke of Balaam and the star of Jacob (Numbers 24:17) and of Micah's prophecy concerning Bethlehem (Micah 5:2). {308}

Sunday, July 8, 31 [Christ] Jesus traveled from Thantia to Datheman, where there was a ruined citadel, used in the war of the Maccabees (1 Maccabees 5:9). Nearby was the mountain where Jephthah's daughter and her twelve maiden-companions had lamented for two months before [she] was put to death (Judges 11:29–40). Balaam had also been on this mountain when he was summoned by the King of Moab (Numbers 22:4–5). [Christ] Jesus ascended the mountain and taught. That evening, he went to Datheman. {308}

* * *

AUTHOR'S NOTE: The above vision recorded by Clemens Brentano on January 8, 1824, was the last vision that he entered into his notebooks. Although she continued to live in visions the day-by-day life of Christ Jesus, due to unspeakable suffering, Sister Emmerich was unable to communicate anything further. She died on February 9, 1824. There is a gap between this date and May 17, 32, when the daily chronicle of Christ Jesus' ministry resumes based on earlier communications to Clemens Brentano. For further details of this 313-day gap, consult pages 308–09 of Powell 1996.

* * *

Saturday, May 17, 32 Accompanied by Peter, James, and **John [the son of Zebedee]**, [Christ] Jesus went to Bethabara, where he was joined by Matthew and another [disciple]. A large crowd had gathered. [Christ] Jesus healed a great many people. It was here that [Christ] Jesus spoke of marriage, blessed the children brought to him (Matthew 19:10–15), and advised the rich youth (Matthew 19:16–26). This last incident was followed by the exchange of words between Peter and [Christ] Jesus recorded in Matthew 19:27–30. Then, toward evening, [Christ] Jesus went to dine in a house where about ten of the holy women were gathered. These included Martha, Mary Magdalene and her maid servant Marcella, Mary Salome, Mary Cleophas, Veronica, and Mary Mark of Jerusalem. [Christ] Jesus continued to teach. {310}

Saturday, May 31, 32 Today, [Christ] Jesus taught in the synagogue in Jericho. After the close of the Sabbath, he and the [disciples] went to Zacchaeus' house, where they dined. [Christ] Jesus told the parable of the fig tree (Luke 13:6–9) and other parables. He then stayed the night with Zacchaeus. It was about this time that Lazarus became deathly ill. {312}

Friday, June 6, 32 After healing a woman with an issue of blood this morning, [Christ] Jesus taught concerning repeated and constant prayer. Later messengers came from Bethany requesting [Christ] Jesus to go there and heal Lazarus. But [Christ] Jesus replied that the time was not yet ripe and that he would travel to Samaria. {312}

Thursday, June 12, 32 Not far from the village [north of Jericho] were ten lepers in a tent. [Christ] Jesus healed them, but only one ran after [Christ] Jesus to thank him (Luke 17:11–19). The leper who ran after [Christ] Jesus later became a disciple. Shortly afterward, as they passed along, a man came out of a shepherd settlement and begged [Christ] Jesus to come because his daughter had just died. [Christ] Jesus, accompanied by Peter, James, and **John [the son of Zebedee]**, went with the shepherd to his house. His daughter, who was about seven years old, lay dead. Looking up to heaven, [Christ] Jesus placed one hand on her head and one on her breast and prayed. The child then rose up, alive. [Christ] Jesus told the [disciples] that—in his name—they should do as he did. {313}

Wednesday, June 25, 32 [Christ] Jesus sent off most of the ... disciples. He left the village [in the mountains near Juttah] and went north to Bethain, where he taught under a tree. {314}

* * *

AUTHOR'S NOTE: Here is another gap. This one is only of thirteen days. See page 314 of Powell 1996 for further details.

* * *

Wednesday, July 16, 32 [Christ] Jesus, accompanied by some [disciples] returned to the little village [in Samaria], where the three holy women were waiting for him. Together they received the news of Lazarus' death. It was here that [Christ] Jesus spoke the words: "Our friend Lazarus has fallen asleep" (John 11:7–13). {315}

Saturday, July 19, 32 After the close of the Sabbath, [Christ] Jesus and the [disciples] returned to Lazarus' estate [near Ginnim]. Mary Magdalene came to meet [Christ] Jesus on the way. She lamented over the death of Lazarus, saying that if [Christ] Jesus had been there he would not have died. [Christ] Jesus replied that his time had not yet come. They then ate at Lazarus' estate and [Christ] Jesus taught. He asked Martha and Mary Magdalene to allow all of Lazarus' effects to stay in Bethany, saying that he would come there in a few days. It was now that he told the [disciples] that Lazarus was dead (John 11:14–16). {315}

Tuesday, July 22, 32 Toward evening they reached the inn of a little place near Bahurim. Here [Christ] Jesus taught concerning the laborers in the vineyard (Matthew 20:1–16). Mary Salome, the mother of James and John [the son of Zebedee] approached [Christ Jesus] to request that her two sons be allowed to take a place beside him in his kingdom (Matthew 20:20–21). {316}

Thursday, July 24, 32 In this little place near Bahurim there were Pharisees who reported back to Jerusalem concerning [Christ] Jesus. Mary Salome again approached [Christ] Jesus on account of her two sons, James and John [the son of Zebedee], but he rebuked her sternly. {316}

Saturday, July 26, 32 In the early hours of the morning, [Christ] Jesus went to Lazarus' grave. He was accompanied by the [disciples], seven holy women, and many other people. He went into the vault where Lazarus' tomb was. Lazarus had been dead for several days, and his corpse had lain for some days before being entombed, for it had been hoped that [Christ] Jesus would come and wake him from the dead. As [Christ] Jesus instructed the [disciples] to remove the stone from the grave, Martha said: "Lord, by this time there will be an odor, for he has been buried for four days." There then took place the raising of **Lazarus** from the dead, as described in John 11:38–44. After the cloths and winding-sheet had been removed, **Lazarus** climbed out of his coffin and came out from the tomb. He tottered on his feet and looked like a phantom. He went past [Christ] Jesus through the door of the vault. His sisters and the other holy women stepped back, as if he were a ghost. [Christ] Jesus followed him from the vault into the open air, went up to him, and took hold of both his hands in a gesture of friendship. A great crowd of people, who beheld **Lazarus** in fear and wonder, thronged around. [Christ] Jesus walked with **Lazarus** to his house. The [disciples] and the holy women went with them. A great tumult arose among the crowd. Inside the house, the women went to prepare a meal, leaving [Christ] Jesus and the [disciples] alone with **Lazarus**. The [disciples] formed a circle around [Christ] Jesus and **Lazarus**. **Lazarus** knelt before [Christ] Jesus, who blessed him, laying his right hand on **Lazarus'** head and breathing on him seven times.[26] *Thus, he consecrated [the **Apostle**] Lazarus to his service, purifying him of all earthly connections and infusing him with seven gifts of the Holy Spirit, which the [disciples] would only receive later at [Pentecost]* (emphasis added). Afterward, all dined together. [Christ] Jesus taught, and [the **Apostle**] **Lazarus** sat next to him. Because there was a great commotion outside, [Christ] Jesus sent the [disciples] to disperse the crowd. He continued to teach that evening. {316–17}

Sunday, July 27, 32 Before daybreak, [Christ] Jesus, accompanied by **John** [**the son of Zebedee**] and Matthew, went to Jerusalem to the house on Mt. Zion where the Last Supper would take place. This house belonged to Nicodemus. [Christ] Jesus remained there for the whole day and that night. Mary Mark, Veronica, and about a dozen other friends came to visit him. He taught and consoled them. Meanwhile, a meeting of the Pharisees and high priests was being held to discuss the raising of [the Apostle] Lazarus by [Christ] Jesus. The Pharisees feared that [Christ] Jesus might awaken all the dead and that this would lead to great confusion. In Bethany, a great tumult arose. [The **Apostle**] **Lazarus** was forced to hide and the ten [disciples] left. {317}

Thursday, August 7, 32 This morning, [Christ] Jesus traveled on in a southeasterly direction. He and the three young shepherds stayed the night with some shepherds they met on the way. [Sister Emmerich] tells that there had been a great uproar in Jerusalem about the raising of Lazarus and that [Christ] Jesus had left Judea in order to be forgotten. The journey [to Chaldea and Egypt], accompanied by only three shepherd youths, was not recorded, as no disciple was present, and no one really knew where he was. {319}

Monday, September 1, 32 [In Sichar Christ] Jesus taught further today concerning marriage. He spoke of David, who had fallen into sin on account of the superabundance of forces within him, which he should have consumed within himself. He added that nothing is lost through continence, but rather through wastefulness. This afternoon he went about one hour

---

26. In recognition of his new status, Lazarus will now be called the Apostle Lazarus.

east of Sichar to the house of a rich herd owner who had died suddenly in one of his fields. His wife and children were very sad and had sent for [Christ] Jesus, begging him to come to the funeral. He came accompanied by the three shepherd youths, by Salathiel and his wife, and about twenty-five people from Sichar. After sending away the people of Sichar, apart from Salathiel and his wife, [Christ] Jesus spoke with the wife of the dead man, whose name was Nazor. He said that if she and her son and daughter would believe in his teaching and follow him, and if they would keep silence in the matter, Nazor would be raised to life again. For, he said, Nazor's soul had not yet passed on to be judged but was still present over the place where he had died. [Christ] Jesus then went with them to the field. Praying, he called Nazor back into his body, saying to those present: "When we return, Nazor will be alive and sitting upright!" They then returned to the house to find Nazor sitting upright in his coffin, wrapped in linen cloths and with his hands bound. After being freed from the wrappings, Nazor climbed out of the coffin and cast himself down at [Christ] Jesus' feet. [Christ] Jesus told him to wash and purify himself, stay hidden in his room, and say nothing about being raised from the dead, until he ([Christ] Jesus) had left the region. [Christ] Jesus and the five people with him then stayed there overnight. {323}

Friday, September 12, 32 [Christ] Jesus and his three young traveling companions made rapid progress on their way [to Arabia]. Around the onset of the Sabbath, they arrived at a well not far from a shepherd settlement. Here they prayed together and held the Sabbath. Here [Sister] Emmerich remarked that the accusation on the part of the Pharisees that [Christ Jesus] did not sanctify the Sabbath simply was not true. {325}

Sunday, September 14, 32 [Christ] Jesus taught the shepherds again today. He spoke of the creation of the world and of the Fall and of the promise of the restoration of all. During this discourse something wonderful took place. He appeared to catch a sunbeam with his right hand, and he made a luminous globe light from it. It hung from the palm of his hand on a ray of light. While he was talking, the shepherds could see all the things he was describing in the globe of light. The Holy Trinity itself appeared there. At the end of the discourse, the globe of light disappeared, and the shepherds cast themselves down in sorrow. [Christ] Jesus later taught them a wonderful prayer and how to worship God, the creator of all. {325–26}

Sunday, September 21, 32 Today [Christ] Jesus went to the tent city of Mensor and Theokeno. As he approached, Mensor came to greet him, riding on a camel, accompanied by about twenty men. They were filled with joy as they went up to [Christ] Jesus. Mensor climbed down from the camel, handed [Christ] Jesus his royal scepter, and cast himself down before him. [Christ] Jesus gave him his hand and raised him up. Mensor asked [Christ] Jesus about the King of the Jews, believing [Christ] Jesus to be an envoy of that king. They all went back to the tent city, where they dined together. {327}

Saturday, September 27, 32 This evening, at the close of the Sabbath, [Christ] Jesus went into the Temple, where there was an idol of a dragon. As one of the women cast herself down before this idol to worship it, [Christ] Jesus said: "Why do you cast yourself down before Satan? Your faith has been taken possession of by Satan. Behold who you worship!" Instantly there appeared before her, visible to all, a slender, redfox-colored spirit with a hideously pointed countenance. All were horrified. [Christ] Jesus pointed to the spirit and indicated that it was this spirit which had woken the woman from sleep each morning before the break of day. The woman had arisen each morning and cast herself down to pray in the direction of the dragon. [Christ] Jesus said: "This awoke you. However, every person also has a good angel, who should wake you, and before whom you should cast yourself down and follow his advice." All then saw a radiant figure at the woman's side. At this approach of the good angel, the satanic spirit withdrew.... {328}

Friday, January 2, 33 Around four o'clock this afternoon [Christ] Jesus and his traveling companions arrived at Heliopolis. Here they met some Jews who had been friends of the [Solomon] Holy Family during their stay in Heliopolis. With the onset of the Sabbath, [Christ] Jesus was escorted to the synagogue by an aged man. In the synagogue, [Christ] Jesus taught and prayed. {332}

Tuesday, January 13, 33 Today, at daybreak, [Christ] Jesus arrived at Jacob's well, accompanied by sixteen young disciples, four having joined him in Bethain. [Sister Emmerich] suddenly called out in ecstasy: "O, he has arrived! How joyful they are to see him! He is at Jacob's well. They are washing his feet and also the feet of the young disciples with him. There are about twelve of them, shepherd sons, who were with him as he went to Cedar—also Peter, Andrew, **John [the son of Zebedee]**, James, Phillip, and one other! They were expecting him here." [Christ] Jesus and his disciples stayed the day at Jacob's well. In the evening, he spoke of his approaching path of suffering. {333–34}

Friday, January 16, 33 Accompanied by the three shepherd youths—Eluid, Silas, and Eremenzear—[Christ] Jesus returned to Sychar, leaving the other thirteen disciples with the shepherds at the settlement. [Christ] Jesus commanded the three youths not to tell anyone where they had been with him or what had taken place on this journey. Peter and **John [the son of Zebedee]** came to meet them on the way. Six more [disciples] were waiting for him at the entrance to Sychar. Together, they all went to a house in the town. At the beginning of the Sabbath, they went to the synagogue, but [Christ] Jesus did not teach or do anything to draw attention to himself. {334}

Saturday, January 17, 33 The [disciples] wanted to hear from the three shepherd youths where they had been with [Christ] Jesus for the past five months. They were very much vexed when the youths refused to say anything. The [disciples] turned to [Christ] Jesus and said that he should express himself more clearly, as they did not understand him. They also said that he should go to Nazareth once again to demonstrate his power through miracles there. [Christ] Jesus replied that he did not want to do this, saying that miracles were of no use if people did not mend their ways. Peter and **John [the son of Zebedee]** agreed with him, but the others were unsatisfied by this reply. [Christ] Jesus then said that he would go to Jerusalem and teach in the Temple. That evening, after the meal, [Christ] Jesus and all the disciples went to the synagogue. Here [Christ] Jesus taught. Some of the Pharisees who were there were much vexed at his teaching and sent messengers to Jerusalem to report that [Christ] Jesus was active again in Sychar. {334}

Sunday, January 18, 33 The Pharisees at Sychar threatened to take [Christ] Jesus into custody and deliver him to Jerusalem. [Christ] Jesus replied that his time had not yet come. He said he would go to Jerusalem of his own accord.... {335}

Tuesday, January 20, 33 In the morning, the three silent disciples [Eliud, Silas, and Eremenzear] were sent by [Christ] Jesus to the holy women to announce his coming. In the afternoon, [the Blessed Virgin Mary], Mary Magdalene, Martha and a few women, accompanied by the three youths, came to greet [Christ] Jesus. They waited for him at a well on the way to Ephron. He came with Peter, Andrew, and **John [the son of Zebedee]**, arriving at the well about two hours before sunset. The women cast themselves down before him and kissed his hand. They then returned to the inn together and [Christ] Jesus spoke with all the women and also taught.... {335}

Wednesday, January 21, 33 This morning, [Christ] Jesus taught and healed in Jericho…. There was a great throng of people in Jericho, as word spread that [Christ] Jesus was there. The Pharisees were greatly disturbed by this and sent messengers to Jerusalem to report [Christ] Jesus' presence in Jericho. [Christ] Jesus, however went to the place of baptism on the Jordan, accompanied by Peter, Andrew, and James the Lesser. [Christ] Jesus healed many, and then as the throng of people grew, he and the [disciples] left and went to Bethel. They arrived in Bethel that evening and were met at an inn by [the **Apostle**] **Lazarus**, Martha, Mary Magdalene, Nicodemus, and John Mark. {336}

Thursday, January 22, 33 After healing many people in Bethel, [Christ] Jesus went to a place north of Jericho, accompanied by Andrew, James the Lesser, and **John [the son of Zebedee]**. [Christ] Jesus healed several people on the way. {336}

Monday, February 9, 33 (Early this morning, while it was still dark, [Christ] Jesus arrived at Lazarus' property south of Alexandrium.) Here he met [the **Apostle**] **Lazarus**, Nicodemus, Joseph of Arimathea, John Mark, and Jair. They ate a meal together. {338–39}

Thursday, February 19, 33 In the morning, [Christ] Jesus, accompanied by [the **Apostle**] **Lazarus**, left Alexandrium and went to Bethany. In the evening, [Christ] Jesus went to the Temple in Jerusalem. He was accompanied part of the way by [the Blessed Virgin Mary]. [Christ] Jesus told her that the time was drawing near when Simeon's prophecy—that a sword would pierce her soul—would become fulfilled. He stayed overnight in Jerusalem in the house of Mary Mark, the mother of John Mark. {339}

Friday, March 6, 33 This afternoon [Christ] Jesus came from Bethany to Jerusalem before the onset of the Sabbath. He ate at the home of John Mark. The holy women and [the **Apostle**] **Lazarus** were also present. But [the **Apostle**] **Lazarus** did not go with [Christ] Jesus to the Temple when the Sabbath began. Later [Christ] Jesus returned to Bethany. {341}

Saturday, March 7, 33 [Christ] Jesus taught in the Temple again this morning and, after a short pause around midday, he continued teaching. He said that one should not hoard up perishable treasures (Matthew 6:19–21). He spoke, too, of prayer and fasting and of the danger of hypocrisy in those practices (Matthew 6:5, 6:16). He referred to his approaching end, indicating that he would make a triumphal entry into Jerusalem beforehand. Addressing the [disciples], he revealed to them something of their future tasks. Peter, **John [the son of Zebedee]**, and James the Lesser would remain in Jerusalem; the others were to spread out and teach in various lands, e.g., Andrew in the region of Galaad, and Philip and Bartholomew around Gesur. [Christ] Jesus told them that they would all meet again in Jerusalem three years after his death, and that **John [the son of Zebedee]** and [the Blessed Virgin] Mary would then go to Ephesus. He taught many other things as well. The Pharisees were enraged by what they heard and wanted to stone [Christ] Jesus as he made his way out of the Temple. [Christ] Jesus, however, managed to elude them and returned to Bethany. After this, he did not teach in the Temple again for about three days. {341}

Monday, March 16, 33 Today [Christ] Jesus taught for about four hours in the Temple. Once again, he described what would happen to him and how many of the disciples would forsake him. He spoke of his forthcoming triumphant entry into Jerusalem and said that he would remain with them for fifteen days. The disciples did not understand the "fifteen days" and believed that he meant a longer period. [Christ] Jesus repeated "three times five days." {342}

Wednesday, March 18, 33 Today, in a basement room in Lazarus' house, [Christ] Jesus told [the **Apostle**] **Lazarus**, Peter, James, and **John [the son of Zebedee]** that tomorrow would be the day of his triumphant entry into Jerusalem. The remaining [disciples] came, and when all were gathered together, [Christ] Jesus spoke with them at length. Then he went to a room where [the Blessed Virgin] Mary and six other holy women were gathered. He told them a parable. Afterward, they all ate. {343}

Thursday, March 19, 33 Early this morning, [Christ] Jesus instructed Silas and Eremenzear to go to Jerusalem, not by the main road, but along a secondary route via Bethpage. He told them to clear the way. He said they would find a donkey and a foal in front of an inn at Bethpage and that they should tether the donkey to a fence. If asked what they were doing, they should reply that [Christ] Jesus had need of these animals (Matthew 21:1–6). After the youths had been gone for a time, [Christ] Jesus divided the disciples into two groups. Sending the older disciples on ahead, [Christ] Jesus followed with the [other] disciples. [The Blessed Virgin] Mary, accompanied by six other holy women, followed at a distance. When they arrived at Bethpage, the two youths brought the donkey and the foal to [Christ] Jesus. He took his seat on one of them. The [disciples] and disciples bore branches from palm trees. They began to sing. Thus they made their way into Jerusalem. The news spread quickly of the procession of [Christ] Jesus and the disciples into the city, and people came from everywhere to see it. There was great jubilation. [Christ] Jesus wept, and the [disciples] also wept, when he said that many now rejoicing would soon mock him. He wept too in beholding Jerusalem, which soon would be destroyed (Luke 19:41–44). When he arrived at the city gate, the jubilation grew and grew (Matthew 21:10–11). [Christ] Jesus rode up to the Temple and dismounted there.... The holy women returned to Bethany that evening, followed later by [Christ] Jesus and the [disciples] (Matthew 21:17). {343}

Friday, March 20, 33 Today, as [Christ] Jesus and the [disciples] made their way to Jerusalem, [Christ] Jesus was hungry. This was a hunger to convert and to fulfill his mission. As he passed by a fig tree, he cursed it when he saw that it had no fruit (Matthew 21:18–19). The fig tree symbolized the old Law and the vine the new Law. Then [Christ] Jesus went to the Temple. Many vendors were again selling their wares in the forecourt. [Christ] Jesus drove them all out (Matthew 21:12–13). He taught in the Temple. At this time, some travelers from Greece told … Philip that they wished to see [Christ] Jesus. Philip spoke with Andrew, who told [Christ] Jesus. [Christ] Jesus continued his teaching. With his hands folded, he gazed up to heaven. From a cloud of light, a ray descended upon him, and a voice like thunder resounded: "I have glorified him, and I will glorify him again" (John 12:20–36). Later, [Christ] Jesus left the Temple and disappeared into the crowd. He went into John Mark's house, where he met and spoke with the travelers from Greece. They were good and well-respected people. Hearing [Christ] Jesus' words, they were converted. In fact, these Greeks were among the first to become baptized by the disciples after Pentecost. [Christ] Jesus then went to Bethany for the beginning of the Sabbath and ate a meal with the disciples at the inn of Simon the leper, whom Christ [Jesus] had earlier healed of his leprosy. At the end of the meal, Mary Magdalene came up to [Christ] Jesus from behind and poured a vial of costly ointment upon his head and feet. She then dried his feet with her hair and left the room. Judas was incensed by this, but [Christ] Jesus excused Mary Magdalene on account of her love. That very night, Judas ran to Jerusalem to Caiaphas' house. This was Judas' first step toward the betrayal of [Christ] Jesus. {343–44}

Saturday, March 21, 33 This morning, as [Christ] Jesus and some of the disciples made their way from Bethany to Jerusalem, the disciples were astounded to find the withered fig tree that [Christ] Jesus had cursed the day before. **John [the son of Zebedee]** and Peter paused to look at the fig tree more closely. As Peter expressed his astonishment, [Christ] Jesus said that if the disciples had faith, they would accomplish more than this, that even the mountains would cast themselves into the sea at their command (Mark 11:20–25). While he was teaching in the Temple this morning, some priests and scribes came up and asked [Christ] Jesus: "by what authority are you doing these things?" [Christ] Jesus answered: "I will also ask you a question; and if you tell me the answer, then I will tell you by what authority I do these things." He then addressed them as recorded in Matthew 21: 23–32. During the afternoon he taught parables about the vineyard owner and the rejection of the cornerstone by the builders (Matthew 21:33-46). The Pharisees were enraged at [Christ] Jesus' words and wanted to capture him, but they did not do so because of the people. That evening, after the close of the Sabbath, [Christ] Jesus returned to Bethany. {344–45}

Monday, March 23, 33 After teaching in Bethany, [Christ] Jesus went to the Temple to teach there. He was approached by five men who were in league with the Pharisees and Herodians. They asked him if they were allowed to pay tax to the emperor. [Christ] Jesus replied as in Matthew 22:16–22.... That evening, [Christ] Jesus and the [disciples] dined with [the **Apostle**] **Lazarus**, and he taught until late that night.[27] {345}

Tuesday, March 24, 33 [Christ] Jesus taught in Bethany and then went to the Temple. This morning the Pharisees were not present and he was able to teach the ... disciples undisturbed. [28] They asked him about the meaning of the words: "Thy kingdom come." [Christ] Jesus spoke at length about this. He also said that he and the Father were one (John 10:30) and that he would be going to the Father (John 16:16).... That afternoon a great many scribes and Pharisees were present. [Christ] Jesus spoke the words recorded in Matthew 23:2–9. He added: "You do not lay hands on me yet, as my hour has not yet come." At this the Pharisees left the Temple. It was already dark when [Christ] Jesus made his way back to Bethany. {345–46}

Wednesday, March 25, 33 Today, [Christ] Jesus spent the whole day with [the **Apostle**] **Lazarus** and the holy women and the twelve [disciples].[29] During the morning, he taught the holy women. Then, around three o'clock in the afternoon, there was a meal, after which they prayed

---

27. "... [disciples]" includes **John the son of Zebedee**.
28. "... disciples" certainly includes **John the son of Zebedee** and may also include the **Apostle Lazarus**.
29. "... twelve [disciples]" includes **John the son of Zebedee**.

together. [Christ] Jesus spoke of the nearness of the time of delivery of the Son of Man, saying, too, that he would be betrayed.... He said that he had come in the flesh for their salvation and that there was something material in his influence upon them, that the body works in a corporeal manner, and for this reason they could not understand him. However, he would send them the [Holy] Spirit who would open up their understanding.... He taught until late into the night. That night Nicodemus and one of Simeon's sons came secretly from Jerusalem in order to see him. {346}

Tuesday, March 31, 33 Today, [Christ] Jesus taught for the last time in the Temple. He spoke of the truth and of the necessity of fulfilling what one teaches. He wished to bring his teaching to fulfillment. It was not enough to believe; one must also practice one's faith. Thus he would bring his teaching to fulfillment by going to the Father.... He also said that [the Blessed Virgin] Mary would remain with them for a number of years after his ascension to the Father. As he left the Temple that evening, he took leave of it, saying that he would never enter it again in this body. This was so moving that the ... disciples cast themselves down on the ground and wept. [Christ] Jesus also wept. It was dark as he made his way back to Bethany. {348}

Wednesday, April 1, 33 Early this morning many disciples assembled at the home of [the **Apostle**] **Lazarus** in Bethany to hear [Christ] Jesus teach. In all about sixty people were gathered together. Toward three o'clock that afternoon, tables were prepared for a meal at the house of Simon the leper. At the meal, [Christ] Jesus and the [disciples] served. [Christ] Jesus going from one table to the other, exchanging words with the disciples as he went. [The Blessed Virgin] Mary was indescribably sad, as [Christ] Jesus had told her that morning of the nearness of his approaching death.... At the end of the meal, while [Christ] Jesus was teaching, Mary Magdalene entered the room bearing a costly ointment that she had bought in Jerusalem that morning. She cast herself down at [Christ] Jesus' feet, weeping, and anointing his feet with the costly ointment. Then she dried his feet with her hair. [Christ] Jesus broke off what he was saying, and some of the disciples were irritated by this interruption. [Christ] Jesus said: "Do not take offense at this woman!" Then he spoke quietly with her. Mary Magdalene took the remaining ointment and poured it upon his head and the fragrance filled the room. Some of the [disciples] muttered at this. Magdalene, who was veiled, wept as she made her way from the room. As she was about to walk past Judas, he held out his arm and blocked the way. Judas scolded her on account of the waste of money, saying it could have been given to the poor. However, [Christ] Jesus said that she should be allowed to go, adding that she had anointed him in preparation for his death and burial, and that afterwards she would not be able to do so again. He said that wherever the Gospel would be taught, her deed and the disciples' muttering would be remembered (Matthew 26:13). Judas was quite furious and thought to himself that he could no longer put up with this kind of thing. He withdrew quietly and then ran all the way to Jerusalem. It was dark, but he did not stumble. In Jerusalem the high priests and Pharisees were gathered together. Judas went to them and said that he wanted to give [Christ] Jesus over into their hands. He asked how much would they give him and he was offered thirty pieces of silver. After concluding this agreement by shaking hands, Judas ran back to Bethany and rejoined the others. That night Nicodemus came from Jerusalem to speak with [Christ] Jesus, and he returned to Jerusalem before the break of day. {348–49}

Thursday, April 2, 33 Today, so-called Maundy Thursday, being Nisan 13 in the Jewish calendar, was the day prior to the Day of Preparation for the [Festival of the] Passover. Shortly before daybreak [Christ] Jesus called Peter and **John [the son of Zebedee]** and gave them instructions concerning the preparation for the Passover feast in the Coenaculum (Luke 22:7–13). They went to Heli, the brother-in-law of the deceased Zacharias of Hebron, who had rented the Coenaculum, which belonged to Nicodemus and Joseph of Arimathea. Heli showed Peter and **John [the son of Zebedee]** the room for the Last Supper. The two [disciples] then went to the house of the deceased priest Simeon, and one of Simeon's sons accompanied them to the marketplace, where they obtained the four lambs to be sacrificed for the meal. They also went to Veronica's house and fetched the chalice to be used that evening by [Christ] Jesus at the institution of the Holy Communion. Meanwhile [Christ] Jesus spoke again to the disciples about his imminent death, and—in taking leave of her—talked at length alone with [the Blessed Virgin Mary]. In Jerusalem Judas met again with the Pharisees and made the final arrangement for the betrayal of [Christ] Jesus. Around mid-day, after taking final leave of [the Blessed Virgin] Mary, the other holy women, and [the **Apostle] Lazarus**, [Christ] Jesus went to Jerusalem with the remaining … disciples. The disciples went to the Coenaculum to help with the preparation there, while [Christ] Jesus walked with the nine [disciples], teaching as he went, from the Mount of Olives to Mount Calvary and back again to the Valley of Josaphat. Here they were met by Peter and **John [the son of Zebedee]**, who summoned them to the Passover feast. Judas arrived just before the meal began. [Christ] Jesus dined with the twelve [disciples] in the main hall of the Coenaculum; two groups of twelve [other] disciples, each with a "house father," ate in separate side rooms. The house father of the first group, comprising the older disciples, was Nathanael, and that of the second group was Eliachim, a son of Cleophas and Mary Heli. All subsequent events on this evening of the Last Supper, and the following events that night on the Mount of Olives, are described in each of the four Gospels. {349–50}

Friday, April 3, 33 As described by [Sister] Emmerich, the Moon was not quite full as [Christ] Jesus accompanied by the eleven [disciples], walked through the Valley of Josaphat up to the Mount of Olives. She recounted in detail the experiences undergone by [Christ] Jesus in the Garden of Gethsemane, where his suffering began. Here he lived through, in his soul, all the future suffering of the … disciples, and friends of the early church; and he also underwent the temptation which he overcame with the words: "Not my will, but thine, be done" (Luke 22:42). Around midnight Judas arrived at the Garden of Gethsemane accompanied by twenty soldiers and six officials. Judas went up to [Christ] Jesus and kissed him, saying: "Hail Master!" [Christ] Jesus replied: "Judas, would you betray the Son of [Man] with a kiss?" (Luke 22:47–48). There then took place the capture of [Christ] Jesus. Thus began Good Friday, the last day in the earthly life of [Christ Jesus]. The sequence of events summarizing his suffering (Passion) and culminating in his death on the cross was described by [Sister] Emmerich as follows:

> The capture of [Christ] Jesus shortly before midnight; [Christ] Jesus presented to Annas around midnight; the trial by Caiaphas; Peter's denial; [Christ] Jesus in the prison at Caiaphas' court; the sentencing of [Christ] Jesus by Caiaphas; the suicide of Judas; [Christ] Jesus presented to Pontius Pilate at around six o'clock that morning; [Christ] Jesus presented to Herod Antipas; [Christ] Jesus presented again to Pilate; the scourging of [Christ] Jesus, which lasted about three quarters of an hour and was over by about nine o'clock that morning; the crowning with thorns; Pilate handed over [Christ] Jesus to be crucified and pronounced the death sentence upon him about ten o'clock that morning; the carrying of the cross to Golgotha on Mount Calvary; after [Christ] Jesus had fallen three time under the weight of the cross, Simon of Cyrene was compelled to help him carry the cross; Veronica came to mop the blood and sweat from the face of [Christ] Jesus with her veil; [Christ] Jesus fell to the ground for the fourth and fifth times—the fifth time in the presence of the "weeping daughters" of Jerusalem; [Christ] Jesus, on

his way up Mount Calvary, fell to the ground a sixth time, and then a seventh time shortly before reaching the summit — at this seventh time it was about 11:45 A.M. Jerusalem time; [Christ] Jesus was disrobed for the crucifixion—at noon a reddish darkening appeared before the Sun; [Christ] Jesus was nailed to the cross about 12:15 P.M.; then the cross was raised up; and at 12:30 P.M. the trumpets sounded forth from the Temple announcing the slaying of the Passover lambs; the two criminals were crucified—the repentant one to [Christ] Jesus' right and the unrepentant one to his left; dice were cast for [Christ] Jesus' clothes; [Christ] Jesus, after being mocked, spoke the words: "Father, forgive them, for they know not what they do!"; shortly after 12:30 P.M., a darkening of the Sun took place, and the heavens grew darker and darker; the repentant criminal said: "Lord, let me come to a place where you may save me; remember me when you come into your kingdom," to which [Christ] Jesus replied: "Truly, I say to you, today you will be with me in paradise!"; [Christ] Jesus spoke the words to [the Blessed Virgin] Mary, "Woman, behold, this is your son; he will be more your son than if you had given birth to him," and to John he said, "Behold! This is your mother!";[30] toward three o'clock that afternoon [Christ] Jesus called out in a loud voice: "Eli, Eli, Lama Sabachtani!" which means: "My God, my God, why hast thou forsaken me!"; [Christ] Jesus spoke the words: "I thirst!"; the soldier Abenadar reached a sponge soaked in vinegar up to [Christ] Jesus' mouth; [Christ] Jesus spoke the words: "It is fulfilled!" followed by the words; "Father, into thy hands I commend my spirit!"; at these words [Christ] Jesus died—it was just after three o'clock on that Good Friday afternoon, and an earthquake rent a gaping hole in the rock between [Christ] Jesus' cross and that of the criminal to his left; the heavens were still darkened, and the radiant being of [Christ] Jesus descended into the gaping hole in the ground—thus began his decent into hell. {351–52}

The final entry in Dr. Powell's summary of Sister Emmerich's visions states as follows: "At the resurrection at dawn on Easter Sunday, April 5, [C.E.] 33, exactly thirty-three and one-third years less one and one-half days had elapsed since the birth of the [Nathan] Jesus just before midnight on Saturday/Sunday. December 6/7, 2 [B.C.E.]"

---

30. The Powell text quotes Sister Emmerich as saying John, and tradition has it that this was **John the son of Zebedee**. As developed in Chapters 10 through 12, there is a likelihood that the **Apostle Lazarus** was also involved in this event, whether in the flesh or in the spirit.

APPENDIX 5

THREE EXCERPTS FROM *DIE DREI JÜNGER JOHANNES* (THE THREE DISCIPLES CALLED JOHN)

(This translation is contributed by Dr. Robert Powell; emendations to preserve the Consistent Nomenclature effort of the treatise have been added in square brackets.)

The Gospels speak of three human beings who bore the name John. They speak of John the [Baptizer], known as the preparer of the way for Christ [Jesus]. They speak of a second John, the brother of James and son of Zebedee, who belonged to the circle of the twelve disciples. And they speak of a third John. He wrote *The Revelation to John* and the gospel named after him. He is the one who bore the name Lazarus and who was called back to life by Christ [Jesus] after having undergone several days of death. For this new life he received a new name. He became the disciple whom the Lord loved, which means that he had reached the perfect condition of discipleship. *The name for someone who could live discipleship perfectly was John.* Lazarus-John had already undergone the experience of death and since then was able to live consciously in two worlds. For him the abyss between this world and the yonder world no longer existed. Christ [Jesus] was able to say of him that he would not taste death and that he would remain independent of the body until the second coming of Christ. Thus there are: John the [Baptizer]; John [the son of] Zebedee, one of the twelve disciples; and Lazarus[-John], [also called John] the Evangelist....[1]

For him, since then [having been raised from the dead], the spiritual world was no longer separate from the physical world. He could spiritually participate in earthly events, without being physically present. This occurred on the Thursday when the twelve disciples experienced how Christ [Jesus] celebrated the Last Supper with them and gave them bread

---

1. Irene Johanson *Die Drei Jünger Johannes* (*The Three Disciples Called John*) (Stuttgart: Urachhaus Verlag, 1997) pp. 9–10.

as his body and wine as his blood. This transformation did not take place in the earthly bodily sense but in the realm of life forces, in the etheric. The bread remains bread, but it is penetrated by the divine stream of the Word to become bearer of the Logos, bearer of the Christ [Being], his body. Similarly the juice of the vine—penetrated by his devotion, his power of love—becomes his life blood.

What remained hidden to the eyes of those physically present was experienced by the disciple whom the Lord loved, who perceived the etheric streams that were communicated by [Christ] Jesus through word and touch to the bread and wine, and who rested spiritually on the Lord's breast. And from this place of rest he was taken up into the process of transformation that then began and worked on through all the Christ-permeated disciples. The words spoken by Christ [Jesus] following the Last Supper [John 14–17] bear witness that he had experienced the etheric streams of Christ [Jesus]'s words as something that transforms all life. Just as in the beginning the creation was summoned forth from the Spirit of God, called into the world through the Word, and thus began the process of crystallization from the Spirit to matter, so through Christ [Jesus]'s words in that holy act—in which in each sacrament the spirit was called forth from the world of substance—a seed was awakened for a new heaven and a new earth. Since the Last Supper this process of the Christianization of matter continues as a creation in the realm of the etheric in which— since the Ascension—[the Risen] Christ holds sway and is active. [Lazarus-]John was the first to consciously participate in this....[2]

As individuals the twelve disciples were not capable, prior to the death of their Lord, to become "John" human beings [in the sense of the words italicized above]. But in their twelvefoldness they were able to bear [Lazarus-]John within them, to feel the disciple whom the Lord loved in their midst. Thus he was in their midst on the last evening [the evening of the Last Supper]. Only *The Gospel According to John* speaks of this. John the Evangelist was wholly permeated with the inspiring genius (John the [Baptizer]) of the group of disciples. He experienced in beholding and writing his gospel the earthly events from the spiritual realm. He beheld the twelve gathered around their Lord, the twelve around the thirteenth, just as is shown to us by the archetype of the twelve signs of the zodiac around the Sun. He also beheld resting on the Lord's breast the disciple whom the Lord loved united with the inspiring genius of the twelve, John

---

2. Johanson 1997 pp. 45–46.

the [Baptizer]. He experienced himself in spiritual union with the inspiring genius, the group spirit of the twelve. Just as Grünewald [in his painting *The Isenheim Altar*] portrays John the [Baptizer] at the foot of the
cross, where he could never have stood physically, as he had already been
beheaded, so have some painters portrayed the disciple whom the Lord
loved as a thirteenth disciple on the painting of the Last Supper, although
he was not physically present. Spiritually, however, he was present in their
midst and lay at the heart of [Christ] Jesus.

Only *The Gospel According to John* relates—upon [Christ] Jesus saying,
"One of you will betray me"—that Peter asks the disciple whom the Lord
loves to ask who it is. Mark reports that each of the disciples asks, distressed, "Is it I?" Matthew records that Judas asks, "Is it I?" and that
[Christ] Jesus replies, "You have said so." The earthly aspect is that each
disciple feels deeply impacted. The spiritual aspect is that the spirit of their
community puts the question, "Who is it?" And the disciple whom the
Lord loves is one with this spirit. He experienced this event spiritually, not
on the earthly plane.

In the Christian tradition the accounts from *The Gospel According to
John* and from the other three Gospels [the Synoptic Gospels] have
become interwoven. For example, most artists have painted the institution
of the sacraments of bread and wine as the Synoptic Gospels portray it,
and added in the disciple on the Lord's breast as recounted by John, who
does not describe the Last Supper but does speak of the morsel of bread
that Judas is given. On these paintings the inspiring genius of the twelve
remains invisible, but he is represented through the one who lay on the
Lord's breast. He is the one who belonged to the twelve from the beginning and who also bears the name of John, the son of Zebedee, who par-
took of the Last Supper as representative of the disciple whom the Lord
loved. The latter was spiritually united with the inspiring genius of their
community and was spiritually present in their midst. This conception has
lived on through the centuries of Christianity. Thus it came about that
John [the son of] Zebedee was identified with the disciple who lay at the
Lord's breast at the Last Supper, and only a few had any idea about the
mystery of "the disciple whom the Lord loved," which was revealed by
Rudolf Steiner.... [3]

---

3. Johanson 1997 pp. 32–34.

GLOSSARY[1]

Ahriman name given to the personification of evil in the *Zoroastrian religion* of ancient Persia (Gaynor 1953). In *Anthroposophy*, Ahriman is considered one of two powerful spiritual beings who are not evil of themselves, but who attempt to exert undesirable influences on *humanity*. See also *Christ Being* and *Lucifer*.

ahrimanic beings as used by Dr. Steiner, refers to a class of beings that are above *humanity* in their spiritual development, but below the higher angelic choirs. Dr. Steiner rejects the concept that these beings are "evil," although they are the source of evil in human evolution. See Steiner 1991a pp. 33-34.

Akasha a celestial ether, or astral light, that fills all space. Every thought and action that takes place in the *material world* is recorded in this *spiritual medium*. See also Gaynor 1953.

Akashic record "For *spiritual science*, the only true source is the everlasting Akashic record, which allows us to understand past events without recourse to physical documents."[Steiner 2001 p. 27] "… a mighty spiritual panorama in which all past world-processes are recorded." [Steiner 1972 p. 105]

anthroposophy a content of knowledge about the nature of the *spiritual world* and how it relates to the humanity that lives in the *material world*. See also *spiritual science* and the discussion by Smith 2000 p. xv, who calls anthroposophy "the wisdom of the soul of the human being."

Anthroposophical Society an organization founded by Dr. Steiner in 1913. The world headquarters of this society are located in Dornach, Switzerland.

Apostle John part of the *Consistent Nomenclature effort* (see Table 6). This term is used to refer to *John the son of Zebedee* after *Pentecost*, at which time, because of the descent of the *Holy Spirit* upon the twelve disciples, they all became apostles (see Acts 2).

Apostle Lazarus part of the *Consistent Nomenclature effort* (see Table 6). This term is used to refer to *Lazarus* of Bethany who became an apostle when he was *initiated* by *Christ Jesus* (see Part Three).

astral body the third of the seven *constitutional components* of the human being (as listed by the author in Chapter 1). As a rock has only a *physical body*

---

1. Words and word groups in *italic font* are also defined in this Glossary.

and a living plant has both a *physical body* and an *ether body,* an animal has all three of the lowest *constitutional components.*

B.C.E. stands for Before the Common Era, an alternative for B.C., which stands for Before Christ. This nomenclature is preferred in order not to offend those who do not believe in the divinity of *Christ Jesus.*

bilocation term used to refer to the ability of an individuality to be in two different places at the same time (see also Gaynor 1953). This requires initiation at a very high level (see Chapter 11).

Blessed Virgin Mary part of the *Consistent Nomenclature effort.* Name used to refer to the *Solomon Mary* after certain changes have taken place at the time immediately preceding the baptism of *Jesus of Nazareth* in the River Jordan (see Chapter 6).

body used in two ways: 1) a theoretical term (as defined by Dr. Steiner in Steiner 1994 p 21) that is not intended to have any preconceived meaning; and 2) equivalent to the term *physical body,* the first of the seven *constitutional components* of the human being (as defined by the author in Chapter 1).

C.E. stands for Common Era, an alternative for A.D., which stands for Anno Domino—Latin for Year of our Lord. This nomenclature is preferred in order not to offend those who do not believe in the divinity of *Christ Jesus.*

Christ Being part of the *Consistent Nomenclature effort.* The terms Christ, *Christ Jesus,* Jesus, Jesus Christ, *Messiah,* and Son of God have been used specifically in other sources. This term is reserved for indicating the portion of the *Godhead* that has special responsibility for the Earth Planetary Evolution (see Chapter 1) and who came from the *spiritual world* to dwell in human form in the *material world.* The Christ Being holds in balance the undesirable forces of materialism (*Ahriman*) and pride (*Lucifer*).

Christ Jesus part of the *Consistent Nomenclature effort* (see Table 3). This term is used only to refer to that portion of the life of Jesus between the baptism in the Jordan River and the crucifixion.

Christian used as an adjective, this word usually connotes conformity with the religion Christianity. However, as used in this book, it has a broader meaning relating to *the Incarnation* of the *Christ Being* without implying conformity to any specific doctrine or faith tradition.

Christian Community name of the faith tradition that provides liturgical support for worship based on *anthroposophy.*

Christians used as a noun, refers to those who are adherents of any of the various *Christian* denominations. See also *ecumenical.*

clairvoyant one who possesses *organs* of spiritual sight. See also *initiate* and *seer.*

Coenaculum as described in the visions of Sister Emmerich, the central structure in a large estate in Jerusalem belonging to Nicodemus and Joseph of Arimathea. It was used by *Christ Jesus* and his disciples for celebrating the *Festival of the Passover* on the day before the crucifixion. In the New Testament this space is called "a large room upstairs" or, in earlier translations, "an upper room."

Consistent Nomenclature effort used throughout the treatise, this title refers to an effort made to avoid the use of synonyms in the names of persons; this is especially important if the name is deliberately changed when the person undergoes a change in status. Also a general attempt to avoid using more than one name for a given activity, e.g., *Pentecost* and Whitsun are synonymous names for the same event, but only *Pentecost* is used.

constitutional component as used in Chapter 1, this term refers to one of the seven elements that make up the human being. Three of these components are part of the perishable *material world,* and the other four are part of the eternal *spiritual world.*

cosmos refers to the farther reaches of the *material world* but, as used in this book, includes the spiritual components, which are not visible to ordinary human vision.

Earth used in two ways: 1) to refer to the planet earth as described in the conventional astronomy of the *material world* and 2) the fourth of seven cosmic *planetary cycles of evolution* (see Chapter 1), which includes other planetary bodies and *spiritual world* elements not visible to ordinary human vision.

ecumenical refers to a broad perspective or to unity among faith divisions; the more restricted usage—unity among various *Christian* denominations—is preferred. The term *interfaith* should be employed when cooperation among various world religions is under consideration.

eschaton connotes the final destiny of *humanity.* For those who do not have the broader anthroposophical frame of reference, it signifies the last day of existence for the *material world.*

esoteric refers to a body of knowledge; a broad interpretation such as "knowledge that is restricted to a small group" is preferred over the narrower definition "knowledge understood only by the specially initiated."

esotericist a student of *spiritual science* or one especially interested in *esoteric* lore.

ether body the second of the seven *constitutional components* of the human being (as listed by the author in Chapter 1). Although it is an oversimplification, a plant differs from a rock because it is alive; those differences are related to the presence of an ether body in addition to the presence of a *physical body* in a living plant. See Chapter 1 for synonyms.

Fall, the used in two distinct ways: 1) refers to an alienation between God and a group of angels who became too impressed with themselves and were thrown out of heaven; this is related to the War in Heaven, which is an important part of Milton's *Paradise Lost*, see also Tradowsky 1998; and 2) refers to a similar alienation between God and humanity as represented, metaphorically, by the story of Adam and Eve in Genesis, the first book of the Old Testament.

Festival of the Passover a Hebrew festival used to commemorate the saving of the Jews in Egypt. It was an obligation of devout Jews to attend this festival in Jerusalem on an annual basis.

Fifth Post-Atlantean Epoch characterized as the European-American Epoch, this is the name for the portion of the current *Post-Atlantean Age*. See Figure 1 for actual years.

Fourth Post-Atlantean Epoch characterized as the Greco-Roman-Christian Epoch, this is the name for the period of time between 747 B.C.E. and 1413 C.E. This is the epoch in which the events that are the subject of this discourse took place.

Godhead a term that refers to the highest level of the *spiritual world* responsible for the current *planetary cycle of evolution* called *Earth* (see Chapter 1). Synonyms include God, Divinity, and Holy Trinity. See also Steiner 1996 pp. 152–53.

human, humanity for the most part this word refers to beings of flesh and blood on planet earth; however the word can also refer to a level of self-consciousness that has been achieved in earlier cosmic planetary cycles by beings, such as archangels, who were human at an earlier time and are now at a higher level in the *spiritual world* than ordinary mortals. See also Steiner 1996 pp. 52–64.

Incarnation, the refers to the descent of the *Christ Being* into human form after a suitable preparation. See Chapter 6 for details and also Chapter 1, note 5.

individuality part of the *Consistent Nomenclature effort*. This term is used for the fourth of the seven *constitutional components* of the human being. This is the central core of the human being. Although human beings are not directly conscious at this level, it has also been called the seat of the personality. It is the lowest of the *constitutional components* that return to the eternal *spiritual world* after a death in the *material world* and the basis for continuity from one life in the *material world* to the next, but only *clairvoyants* are able to be aware of earlier incarnations. See Chapter 1 for synonyms.

initiate used as a noun, this word implies an individual who has achieved a higher level of cognition than ordinary human beings. Initiate implies a higher level of spiritual development than the related term *clairvoyant*. See also Steiner 1997 pp. 6–15; Steiner 1994 p. 194; and especially Steiner 1991b pp. 45ff. Used as a verb, this word indicates the process whereby a human being achieves a higher status. See Table 6.

interfaith refers to cooperation between two or more world religions. Contrast with *ecumenical*, where the cooperation is restricted to different *Christian* denominations.

Jesus of Nazareth part of the *Consistent Nomenclature effort* (see Table 3). This term is used only to refer to that part of the life of Jesus between the *Festival of the Passover* in 12 C.E. and the baptism in the Jordan River. See Chapter 6 for further details.

Johannine tradition having to do with the authorship of *The Revelation to John, The Gospel According to John,* and/or the *Letters of John.*

John the Baptizer part of the *Consistent Nomenclature effort*. This term replaces the earlier usage John the Baptist.

John the Divine a term used to refer to the author of *The Revelation to John* at a time when it was not known who the author might have been. In this treatise, the term *Presbyter John* with its appropriate identification is used by preference (see Part Three).

John the Evangelist a term used to refer to the author of *The Gospel According to John* at a time when the authorship was attributed to *John the son of Zebedee.* In this treatise, the term *Presbyter John* with its appropriate identification is used by preference (see Part Three).

John the son of Zebedee part of the *Consistent Nomenclature effort*. Because there has been confusion over the name John, the author has been careful to use this longer name for the sake of clarity. Like others in this treatise, this individual undergoes more than one status; at *Pentecost* he becomes the *Apostle John* (see Table 6).

karma a term derived from Hindu tradition, where *reincarnation* is a well-established belief. The concept refers to the sum total of good and bad actions that have occurred in previous incarnations (earth lives).

Lazarus used to refer to two different persons: 1) *Christ Jesus* tells a parable about a rich man and a sick beggar whose name is Lazarus, see Luke 16:19–31; and 2) a wealthy supporter of *Jesus of Nazareth* and later *Christ Jesus,* who had a substantial home in Bethany. According to the visions of Sister Emmerich, he was the brother of *Martha, Mary Magdalene,* and *Silent Mary.* Lazarus was brought back from the dead as described in John 11:38–44. As part of the *Consistent Nomen-*

clature effort (see Table 6) and in recognition of this substantial change in his status, Lazarus, for the time after he was *initiated* by *Christ Jesus,* is referred to as the *Apostle Lazarus.* At a later time, he becomes *Presbyter John.*

Lazarus-John although this term is frequently used in the relevant literature to refer to *Lazarus* of Bethany after his being *initiated* by *Christ Jesus,* in this treatise as part of the *Consistent Nomenclature effort,* he will be called the *Apostle Lazarus* for the relevant portion of his life. See also *Presbyter John.*

lore used in the sense of "a body of knowledge." Although the term refers to the realm of the *esoteric* (see Introduction), it is intended as a neutral term and should be accepted without preconceptions relating to validity.

Lucifer name for a fallen archangel who has become the personification of evil in early *Christian* documents (see Gaynor 1953). In *anthroposophy,* Lucifer is considered as one of two powerful spiritual beings who are not evil of themselves but who attempt to exert both desirable and undesirable influences on humanity. See also *Christ Being* and *Ahriman.*

luciferic beings as used by Dr. Steiner, refers to a class of beings that are above *humanity* in their spiritual development, but below the higher angelic choirs. Dr. Steiner rejects the concept that these beings are "evil," although they are the source of evil in *human* evolution. See Steiner 1991a pp. 33–34.

Martha the sister of *Lazarus* of Bethany.

Mary Magdalene although this association is not made in the gospels, according to the visions of Sister Emmerich, Mary Magdalene is the sister of *Lazarus* of Bethany.

Mary-Sophia part of the *Consistent Nomenclature effort* (see Table 6 and note 5). Name used to refer to the *Blessed Virgin Mary* after the change in her status that took place at the time of *Pentecost.*

material world refers to the perishable physical world that has been created by the eternal *spiritual world.* See also Steiner 1996 pp. 15–20.

Messiah refers to the historical figure prophesied in the Hebrew tradition and also to *Christ Jesus* who is considered by *Christians* to be the fulfillment of those prophecies.

monism of thinking the philosophical position of Dr. Steiner who rejected materialism, spiritualism, and all forms of dualism. See Steiner 1995.

Mysteries refers to what was taught in the various *mystery schools* that have been present since the beginning of recorded history at various locations. See also Steiner 1997.

mystery a broad interpretation such as "that which is not yet completely understood" is preferred over the narrower view (a religious truth that one can know only be revelation and that one cannot fully understand). See also Steiner 1997 pp. 1–6.

mystery schools refers to sites, often in temples and other secluded spots, where those seeking knowledge of the spiritual world would gather and undergo an extended, rigorous mode of life that included fasting, isolation, ordeals, and meditative techniques. Such a mode of life was a prerequisite to being conducted into the life of the spirit and beholding a higher world order, i.e., being initiated. See Steiner 1991b pp. 45ff.

Nathan Jesus part of the *Consistent Nomenclature effort* (see Table 3). This name is used only to refer to the second of the two Jesus children from his birth in 2 B.C.E. to the *Festival of the Passover* in 12 C.E.

Nathan Joseph part of the *Consistent Nomenclature effort*. This name is used to refer to the descendant of King David, through his son Nathan, who became the spouse of the *Nathan Mary*. She gave birth to the *Nathan Jesus* in 2 B.C.E. under circumstances described in *The Gospel According to Luke*. See Chapter 6.

Nathan Mary part of the *Consistent Nomenclature effort*. Born on July 17, 17 B.C.E., the Nathan Mary, the spouse of the *Nathan Joseph*, lived only twenty-eight years; she died on August 4, 12 C.E.

Old Moon the third of seven *planetary cycles of evolution*. See Chapter 1.

Old Saturn the first of seven *planetary cycles of evolution*. See Chapter 1.

Old Sun the second of seven *planetary cycles of evolution*. See Chapter 1.

organs refers both to the sense organs that enable *human* beings to experience the *material world* and also to special organs, not yet developed in most individuals, that enable seeing and hearing in the *spiritual world*.

Pentecost originally a festival of the Hebrews to celebrate a period fifty days after the *Festival of the Passover*. On May 24, 33 C.E., fifty days after the Resurrection, the *Holy Spirit* descended on the disciples and the *Blessed Virgin Mary* and altered their status: the disciples became apostles and had new powers of healing, and the *Blessed Virgin Mary* became united with Sophia (see *Mary-Sophia*).

planetary cycle of evolution refers to great cosmic eras that predate our present *Earth* planetary cycle of evolution and will occur after the present cycle is no more. See Chapter 1.

physical body the lowest of the seven *constitutional components* listed in Chapter 1. One way to distinguish these elements, although it is an oversimplification, is to suggest that a rock has only a physical body.

Post-Atlantean Age fifth of seven ages within the *planetary cycle of evolution* called *Earth*.

Presbyter John part of the *Consistent Nomenclature effort* (see Table 6). This name is used to refer to *Lazarus* of Bethany upon his return to Ephesus circa 66 C.E.

Radiant Star see Zaratas.

reincarnation the concept that the *individuality*, a non-perishable entity of the *human* being, alternates between life in the *spiritual world* and life in the *material world*. See also Steiner 1994 p. 76.

Risen Christ part of the *Consistent Nomenclature effort*. The term refers to the *Christ Being* after the Resurrection on April 5, 33 C.E.

seer one who has developed the spiritual *organs* of hearing and sight.

Silent Mary according to the visions of Sister Emmerich, another sister of *Lazarus* of Bethany. Several interactions with *Christ Jesus* are described in Appendix 4.

Solomon Jesus part of the *Consistent Nomenclature effort* (see Table 3). This name is used only to refer to the first of the two Jesus children from his birth in 6 B.C.E to the *Festival of the Passover* in 12 C.E. The Solomon Jesus died on June 4, 12 C.E. after his individuality was transferred to the *Nathan Jesus*. See Chapter 6.

Solomon Joseph part of the *Consistent Nomenclature effort*. This name is used to refer to the descendant of King David, through his son Solomon, who became the spouse of the *Solomon Mary*. She gave birth to the *Solomon Jesus* in 6 B.C.E. under circumstances described in *The Gospel According to Matthew*. See Chapter 6.

Solomon Mary part of the *Consistent Nomenclature effort* (see Appendix 3). Born on September 7, 21 B.C.E., the spouse of the *Solomon Joseph* as determined by the priests of the Temple in Jerusalem (see Chapter 7). Following the death of the *Solomon Joseph* and the *Nathan Mary*, she married the *Nathan Joseph* and became the stepmother of the *Nathan Jesus* (see Chapter 6: The Second Merger). Later, she underwent two significant changes in her spiritual status: 1) after *the Incarnation* of the *Christ Being*, due to a merger of the *individuality* of the *Nathan Mary* with her own being, virginity was restored and in recognition she was called the *Blessed Virgin Mary*; and 2) at the time of *Pentecost*, an alliance with the heavenly Sophia is acknowledged by referring to her as *Mary-Sophia* (see Chapter 10). The Solomon Mary died in Ephesus on August 15, 44 C.E. at the age of sixty-five.

soul used in two ways: 1) a theoretical term (as defined in Steiner 1994 p. 21) that is not intended to have any preconceived meaning; and 2) equivalent to the terms *ether body* and *astral body* collectively, two of the seven *constitutional components* of the human being (as defined by the author in Chapter 1).

special individuality also the sister soul of Adam, the individuality that incarnated into the *Nathan Jesus* (see Chapter 6).

spirit used in three ways: 1) a theoretical term (as defined in Steiner 1994 p. 21) that is not intended to have any preconceived meaning; 2) equivalent to the term *individuality*, the fourth of the seven *constitutional components* of the human being (as defined by the author in Chapter 1); and 3) when speaking of the threefold nature of the human being, the term includes not only the *individuality*, but also the three higher components above it.

spiritual science a synonym for *anthroposophy*, observation of spiritual processes in *human* life and in the *cosmos*. See also Steiner 1994 p. 18.

spiritual world refers to the eternal realm that has created the perishable *material world*.

Theosophical Society refers to a spiritual philosophical movement founded in the nineteenth century under the leadership of Helena Blavatsky. Dr. Steiner was a lecturer for the Society at one time and even became the founder and General Secretary (equivalent of President) of the German Section of the Society in 1902, but he disassociated himself from it to found the *Anthroposophical Society* in 1913.

Zaratas name of Chaldean King or Magus who was the leader of an advanced group of priestly kings. He was called "Radiant Star." Dr. Steiner affirms not only that he was the teacher of Pythagoras but also that he was a reincarnation of *Zarathustra* (Steiner 2001 p. 107).

Zarathustra a significant personage in the ancient Persian culture. According to Steiner 2001 p. 107, the *individualities* of two of Zarathustra's pupils became the Egyptian Hermes and the Hebrew Moses. A later incarnation of Zarathustra was called *Zaratas*, who became a teacher in Chaldea and who was called by the Magi "Radiant Star." This is the individuality that incarnated in the *Solomon Jesus* (see Chapter 6).

Zoroastrian Religion name of the Persian religion founded by *Zarathustra* in the sixth century B.C.E. He was also called Zoroaster.

BIBLIOGRAPHY

Almon, Clopper *A Study Companion to* "An Outline of Esoteric Science" (Great Barrington, MA: Anthroposophic Press, 1998).

Archiati, Pietro *Reincarnation In Modern Life: Towards a New Christian Awareness* Six lectures given in Rome 22–25 April 1994 (trsl. Pauline Wehrle, London: Temple Lodge, 1997).

Arenson, Adolf *The History of the Childhood of Jesus: A Study of the Spiritual Investigations of Rudolf Steiner* (trsl. and ed. H. Collison, London: Anthroposophical Publishing, 1922).

Bock, Emil *The Childhood of Jesus: The Unknown Years* (trsl. Maria St. Goar, Edinburgh: Floris Books, 1997).

Book of Common Prayer, The: and Administration of the Sacraments and Other Rites and Ceremonies of the Church (New York: Church Hymnal Corporation and Seabury Press, 1979).

Birgitta of Sweden: Life and Selected Revelations (ed. Marguerite Tjader Harris, New York: Paulist Press, 1990).

Butkovich, Anthony *Revelations: Saint Birgitta of Sweden* (Los Angeles: Ecumenical Foundation of America, 1972).

du Buysson, Philippe Decouvoux *The Saint Baume: A Mountain Steeped in Geological and Religious History* (Marseille: Editions PEC, 1995).

Catechism of the Catholic Church (2nd Edition of the English translation, Saint Charles Borromeo Catholic Church web site, 1997).

Edwards, Ormond *When Was Anno Domini?: Dating the Millennium* (Edinburgh: Floris Books, 1999).

Emmerich, Anne Catherine *Das Leben Unseres Herrn Und Heilande Jesu Christi* ("The Life of Our Lord and Savior Jesus Christ") (Regensburg, 1885–1860, in three volumes).

Emmerich, Anne Catherine *The Life of the Blessed Virgin Mary* (trsl. Sir Michael Palairet, Springfield, IL: Templegate, 1954a; also reprinted, Rockford, IL: TAN Books, 1970).

Emmerich, Anne Catherine *The Life of Our Lord and Saviour Jesus Christ combined with The Bitter Passion and The Life of Mary* (trsl. anonymous, arr. and ed. The Very Reverend Carl E. Schmöger, C.SS.R., Fresno, CA: Academy

Library Guild, 1954b; also reprinted under the title *The Life of Jesus Christ and Biblical Revelations: From the Visions of the Venerable* Anne Catherine Emmerich *as recorded in the journals of Clemens Brentano*, Rockford, IL: TAN Books, 1986, in four volumes).

Eusebius *Historica Ecclesiastica* III, 39, 3 in Johannes Hemleben *Johannes Der Evangelist (John the Evangelist)* (Hamburg: Rowohlt Verlag, 1972).

Eusebius *Historica Ecclesiastica* III, 39, 3ff. in Gerd-Klaus Kaltenbrunner *Johannes Ist Sein Name (John Is His Name)* (Zug, Switzerland: Die Graue Edition, 1993).

Fahsel, Helmut *Der Wandel Jesu in Der Welt (The Travels of Jesus in the World)* (Basel, Switzerland: Ilionverlag, 1942).

Filson, Floyd V. "Who Was the Beloved Disciple?" *Journal of Biblical Literature* 68: 83–88, 1949.

Gaynor, Frank *Dictionary of Mysticism* (New York: Philosophical Library, 1953).

Haskins, Susan *Mary Magdalen: Myth and Metaphor* (New York: Riverhead Books, 1995).

Heidenreich, Alfred *The Unknown in the Gospels* (London: Christian Community Press, 1972).

Heidenreich, Alfred "Preface." in Rudolf Steiner's *The Last Address* (London: Rudolf Steiner Press, 1967).

Hemleben, Johannes *Johannes Der Evangelist (John the Evangelist)* (Hamburg: Rowolt Verlag, 1972).

Holy Bible, The: The New Revised Standard Version (Nashville, TN: Thomas Nelson Publishers, 1989).

Interpreters Dictionary of the Bible, The (Nashville, TN: Abingdon, 1962).

Irenaeus *Adversus Haereses* V, 33, 4 in Gerd-Klaus Kaltenbrunner *Johannes Ist Sein Name (John Is His Name)* (Zug, Switzerland: Die Graue Edition, 1993).

Jarvis, Samuel Farmer *A Chronological Introduction to the History of the Church: A New Inquiry into the True Dates of the Birth and Death of Our Lord and Saviour Jesus Christ* (New York: Harper, 1845).

Johanson, Irene *Wie Die Jünger Christus Erlebten (How the Disciples Experienced Christ)* (Stuttgart: Urachhaus Verlag, 1992).

Johanson, Irene *Die Drei Jünger Johannes (The Three Disciples Called John)* (Stuttgart: Urachhaus Verlag, 1997).

Kaltenbrunner, Gerd-Klaus *Johannes Ist Sein Nammen (John Is His Name)* (Zug, Switzerland: Die Graue Edition, 1993).

Ketzel, Albert Ryle "Translator's Foreword" in *Birgitta of Sweden: Life and Selected Revelations* (ed. Marguerite Tjader Harris, New York: Paulist Press, 1990).

König, Karl *The Mystery of John and the Cycle of the Year* (trsl. G. F. Mier, ed. Gregg Davis and Nicholas Poole, Great Britain: Camphill Books, 2000).

Krause-Zimmer, Hella *Die Zwei Jesuknaben in Der Bildenden Kunst (The Two Jesus Children in Pictorial Art)* (Stuttgart: Verlag Freies Geistesleben, 1969).

McDermott, Robert A., ed. *The Essential Steiner: Basic Writings of Rudolf Steiner* (New York: HarperCollins, 1984).

McDermott, Robert A. "Introduction: Approaching Rudolf Steiner's Lectures on the Gospel of Luke" in Rudolf Steiner's *According to Luke: The Gospel of Compassion and Love Revealed* (trsl. Catherine E. Creeger, Great Barrington, MA: Anthroposophic Press, 2001).

Morris, Bridget *St Birgitta of Sweden* (Woodbridge, Suffolk, UK: Boydell Press, 1999).

Nag Hammadi Library, The (ed. J. M. Robinson, Leiden-New York: E. J. Brill, 1988).

New Century Encyclopedia of Names (ed. C. L. Barnhart; Englewood Cliffs, NJ: Prentice Hall, 1954, in three volumes).

New Complete Works of Josephus, The (trsl. William Whiston, Grand Rapids, MI: Kregel Publications, 1999).

New Oxford Annotated Bible, The: With the Apocryphal / Deuterocanonical Books New Revised Standard Edition (eds. Bruce M. Metzger and Roland E. Murphy, New York: Oxford University Press, 1991).

Ovason, David *The Two Children: A Study of the Two Jesus Children in Literature and Art* (London: Century, 2001).

Pagels, Elaine *Adam, Eve, and the Serpent* (New York: Vintage Books, 1989).

Pagels, Elaine *Beyond Belief: The Secret Gospel of Thomas* (New York: Random House, 2003).

Powell, Robert *Christian Hermetic Astrology: The Star of the Magi and the Life of Christ* 1991 (reprinted Hudson, NY: Anthroposophic Press, 1998).

Powell, Robert *Chronicle of the Living Christ The Life and Ministry of Jesus Christ: Foundations of Cosmic Christianity* (Hudson, NY: Anthroposophic Press, 1996).

Powell, Robert *The Most Holy Trinosophia and the New Revelation of the Divine Feminine* (Great Barrington, MA: Anthroposophic Press, 2000).

Powell, Robert (Personal communication dated October 10, 2001).

Powell, Robert (Personal communication dated September 1, 2002).

Reincarnation: The Phoenix Fire Mystery (eds. Joseph Head and S. L. Cranston, New York: Crown Publishing, 1977).

Schmöger, Carl E. *The Life of Anne Catherine Emmerich* (trsl. Michael Palairet, Rockford, IL: TAN Books, 1986, in two volumes).

Smith, Edward Reaugh *The Burning Bush* (Hudson, NY: Anthroposophic Press, 1997).

Smith, Edward Reaugh *The Disciple Whom Jesus Loved: Unveiling the Author of John's Gospel* (Great Barrington, MA: Anthroposophic Press, 2000).

Steiner, Rudolf *Gospel of St. John* (trsl. Maud B. Monges, Hudson, NY: Anthroposophic Press, 1962).

Steiner, Rudolf *Christ and the Spiritual World: The Search for the Holy Grail* (trsl. C. Day and D. Osmond, London: Rudolf Steiner Press, 1963).

Steiner, Rudolf *The Last Address* (trsl. George Adams, London: Rudolf Steiner Press, 1967).

Steiner, Rudolf *The Etherization of the Blood: The Entry of the Etheric Christ into the Evolution of the Earth* (trsl. Arnold Freeman and D.S. Osmond, London: Rudolf Steiner Press, 1971).

Steiner, Rudolf *An Outline of Occult Science* (trsl. Maud and Henry B. Monges and revised by Lisa D. Monges, Hudson, NY: Anthroposophic Press, 1972).

Steiner, Rudolf *From Jesus to Christ* (trsl. Charles Davy, Sussex, England: Rudolf Steiner Press, 1991a).

Steiner, Rudolf *Gospel of St. Mark* (trsl Conrad Mainzer, ed. Stewart C. Easton, Hudson, NY: Anthroposophic Press, 1986).

Steiner, Rudolf *The Spiritual Guidance of the Individual and Humanity: Some Results of Spiritual-Scientific Research into Human History and Development* (trsl. Samuel Desch, Hudson, NY: Anthroposophic Press, 1991b).

Steiner, Rudolf *Theosophy* (trsl. Catherine E. Creeger, Hudson, NY: Anthroposophic Press, 1994a).

Steiner, Rudolf *Mysterienwahrheiten Und Weinachtsimpulse* (*Mystery Truths and Christmas Impulses*) (Dornach, Switzerland: Rudolf Steiner Verlag, 1994b).

Steiner, Rudolf *Intuitive Thinking as a Spiritual Path: A Philosophy of Freedom* (trsl. Michael Lipson, Hudson NY: Anthroposophic Press, 1995a).

Steiner, Rudolf *The Fifth Gospel: From the Akashic Record* (trsl. A.R. Meuss, London: Rudolf Steiner Press, 1995b).

Steiner, Rudolf *The Spiritual Hierarchies and the Physical World: Reality and Illusion* (trsl. R.M. Querido and Jann Gates, Hudson, NY: Anthroposophic Press, 1996).

Steiner, Rudolf *Christianity as Mystical Fact* (trsl. Andrew Welburn, Hudson, NY: Anthroposophic Press, 1997).

Steiner, Rudolf *From the History and Contents of the First Section of the Esoteric School, 1904–1914* (Great Barrington, MA: Anthroposophic Press, 1998).

Steiner, Rudolf *Autobiography: Chapters in the Course of My Life: 1861–1907* (trsl. Rita Stebbing, ed. Paul M. Allen, Hudson, NY: Anthroposophic Press, 1999).

Steiner, Rudolf *According to Luke: The Gospel of Compassion and Love Revealed* (trsl. Catherine E. Creeger, Great Barrington, MA: Anthroposophic Press, 2001).

Stjerna, Kirsi Irmeli *St. Birgitta of Sweden: A Study of Birgitta's Spiritual Visions and Theology of Love* (Unpublished doctoral dissertation, Boston University, Graduate School, 1995).

Tomberg, Valentin *Covenant of the Heart: Meditations of a Christian Hermeticist on the Mysteries of Tradition* (trsl. Robert Powell and James Morgante, Rockport, MA: Element, 1992).

Tradowsky, Peter *Christ and Antichrist: Understanding the Events at the End of the Century and Recognizing Our Tasks* (trsl. John M. Wood, London: Temple Lodge, 1998).

de Voragine, Jacobus *The Golden Legend: Readings on the Saints* (trsl. William Granger Ryan, Princeton: Princeton University Press, 1993, in two volumes).

Welburn, Andrew *The Beginnings of Christianity: Essene Mystery, Gnostic Revelation and the Christian Vision* (Edinburgh: Floris Books, 1991).

Welburn, Andrew "Introduction" in Rudolf Steiner's *Christianity As Mystical Fact* (trsl. Andrew Welburn, Hudson, NY: Anthroposophic Press, 1997).

Wetmore, James "Foreword" in Robert Powell's *Chronicle of the Living Christ The Life and Ministry of Jesus Christ: Foundations of Cosmic Christianity* (Hudson, NY: Anthroposophic Press, 1996).

Whicher, Olive *Sun Space: Science at a Threshold of Spiritual Understanding* (London: Rudolf Steiner Press, 1989).

INDEX

basis of failed excorcism, 153
Ezekiel, 43, 135
  Jesus of Nazareth reinterprets the
    vision of Ezekiel, 182

F
Fahsel, Helmut, cartographer, 177
  detailed maps of Christ Jesus'
    travels, 139, 140, 177
Father, 23, 24, 147, 151, 153, 156,
    160–162, 166, 187, 195, 200,
    210, 213, 214, 221, 222, 233,
    234, 237
  Christ Jesus request his Father to
    render testimony, 152, 218
Feast
  of Lights, 207
  of the Passover, 50, 183, 195, 218,
    235
  of Tabernacles, 75, 201
  of Weeks, 161, 221
Feeding of the multitudes
  five thousand, 143, 158, 213
  four thousand, 143, 216
Festival
  of Purim, 216
  of the New Moon, 191, 193, 197,
    207, 216
  of the Passover, 14, 30, 38, 53, 55,
    81, 83, 91, 137, 138, 152, 155,
    156, 194, 196, 217, 235, 242,
    244, 246, 247, 248
Fig tree without fruit, a symbol of the
    old Law, 232
Filson, Floyd V., 74, 74 n. 2
First merger
  of Solomon Jesus and Nathan
    Jesus, 54, 55, 57, 165, 179
Flamske, Germany, 170
Flemish School, 22, 33
Flight to Egypt, 28, 56, 149, 193
Fotheringham, J. K., 15
Frames of Reference
  nature of human being, 6–7
  time-dependent, 3–6
Future tasks of the disciples assigned,
    230, 231

G
Gabara, 220, 222
  home of Simon Zabulon, 146, 203
Gadara, 138
  exorcising the Priestess of Moloch,
    137, 151
  Christ Jesus taught in the synagogue,
    136, 201
Galgala, 143, 207
Galilee, 29, 47, 75, 101, 105, 119,
    136, 139, 150, 185, 188, 191,
    196, 200, 203, 215
Gap in the record of the visions, 91,
    137, 138, 144, 156, 161, 171,
    172, 223, 224
Garisma, 221
Garden of Gethsemane, *see* also
    Mount of Olives, 84, 87, 98,
    100, 103, 104, 160–162, 236
Gaynor, Frank, 12 n. 2, 241, 242, 245
Genealogic Charts
  Matthew, 26
  Luke, 27
Gennabris, 188
  Christ Jesus taught in the synagogue,
    189, 200
  home of Nathanael Chased, 189,
    192
German-Austrian Oberufer Cycle
  Kings' Play, 25
  Shepherds' Play, 25
Gethsemane, 84, 88, 162
  garden of, *see* also Mount of Olives,
    87, 98, 100, 103, 104, 160, 162,
    236
  see also Significant Events That
    Occurred More than Once
Gilgal
  Joseph of Arimathea and Lazarus
    present at synagogue, 75, 186
Gill, Penny, xvi
Ginnim, site of a villa owned by Lazarus,
    147, 193, 198, 217, 219, 225
Gischala, 136, 137, 203
  birthplace of three men of zeal,
    136, 203
  placing the disciples in rows, 215

Moon, phases of, 16
Mount Attarus, site of temptations by
  Satan, 160, 187, 188
Mount beyond Gabara, 220, 222
  site of conversion of Mary
    Magdalene, 203
Mount Ephraim, 185
  nearby cave, 186
  Mount of Olives, 53, 84, 88, 98,
    211, 218
  cave in Garden of Gethsemane,
    160, 161
  place where Christ Jesus prayed
    alone, 161, 197, 198, 212
  place where Christ Jesus took disci-
    ples on Good Friday, 236
  valley of Josephat, 235, 236
Mount of the Beatitudes, 204, 205,
  216
  site of some but not all portions of
    the Sermon on the Mount, 141–
    143
Mount Quarantania, 135, 160, 187
Mount Tabor, 203, 209, 219, 222
Mozian in Iraq, 139
"My hour has not yet come." said by
  Christ Jesus at Cana, 145, 190 n.
  10
"My hour has not yet come." said by
  Christ Jesus in the Temple, 233
Mystery
  school, xx, 78, 247
  tradition, 78
Mystery of
  Beloved Disciple, 9, 69, 70, 79, 93,
    94, 96, 98, 102, 103, 165, 240
  Golgotha, x, xiii, 10, 94, 108, 109,
    113, 114, 121, 122, 125
  the Incarnation, 10, 64, 131, 132,
    134, 163
  two Jesus children, 8, 12, 19, 21,
    30, 59, 61, 64, 94

N
Naboth's vineyard, 137
Nag Hammadi Library, The, 120 n. 28
Nain, 151, 203, 205, 220

healing of the daughters of the
  widow Lais, 151, 202
raising from the dead of Martialis,
  203
Nathan, son of David, 13, 26, 27, 61,
  246
Nathan Jesus, 19, 20, 22, 28–30, 33,
  34, 36–38, 42, 48, 49, 51–55,
  57, 61, 138, 165, 176, 247, 248
  adoration of the shepherds, 19, 178
  birth date, 16, 25, 50, 51, 55, 178,
    237, 247
  birth location, 29, 47
  first visit to the Temple in 8 C.E.,
    30, 53
  presentation to the Temple, 29, 53,
    178
  return to Nazareth, 29, 47, 178
  transfer of Zarathustra individual-
    ity from Solomon Jesus, 19, 30,
    31, 38, 53–57, 165, 179, 248
Nathan Joseph, son of Heli, 36, 51,
  52, 56, 179, 186, 247, 248
  childlike nature and obedience to
    God, 65
  genealogy, 13, 27, 48, 247
  merger of two families, 55–57,
    179, 248
Nathan Mary, 13, 36, 37, 51, 52, 64,
  117, 165, 183, 186, 247
  birth date, 178, 247
  death date, 56, 179, 247
  transfer of individuality to
    Solomon Mary, 57, 179, 248
  visit to her cousin Elizabeth, 178
Nathanael Chased, 23, 24, 148, 189,
  189 n. 6, 191, 192, 217, 236
Nathanael of Cana, 101, 189–191,
  196, 215, 221
Nazara
  Christ Jesus multiplied bread in his
    hands to feed the poor, 149,
    193
Nazarene environment, 64, 65
Nazareth, 13, 23, 28–32, 47, 53–56,
  74, 140, 149–151, 158, 178,
  183, 195, 209, 212, 229

CHARLES S. TIDBALL was born in 1928 in Geneva, Switzerland. At age seven his family moved to the United States of America, where later he earned a B.A. in Chemistry from Wesleyan University, an M.S. in Pharmacology from the University of Rochester, a Ph.D. in Physiology from the University of Wisconsin-Madison, and an M.D. from the University of Chicago. Following two years of post-graduate clinical training, he joined the faculty of the School of Medicine of The George Washington University in Washington, DC, in 1959, where, subsequently, he became Professor and Chair of the Department of Physiology. In 1967 he received the Washington Academy of Science Award for Scientific Achievement in the Biological Sciences. In addition to the duties of managing the Department, he maintained an active research program while directing the education of medical students, graduate students, and the further training of post-doctoral fellows.

In 1973, Dr. Tidball founded the Office of Computer Assisted Education at the Medical Center, and additionally pioneered the online training of medical library personnel in computerized citation retrieval. For more than ten years he participated in the Association for the Development of Computer-based Instructional Systems both as incorporator and officer of the Health Education Network, Inc., sponsored by the National Library of Medicine. While on sabbatical leave in 1978–79, he was consultant to the Deputy Director of the Clinical Center of the National Institutes of Health where he developed a multi-media training program to assist physicians in learning computerized patient management. Starting in 1980, he developed, for the Department of Education at GWU, an Educational Computing Technology Program which he directed, while on leave from the School of Medicine during 1982–84. Dr. Tidball then returned to the Medical Center as Professor of Computer Medicine and as staff physician for the Medical Center's Multitest Facility. He had supervisory responsibility for administering a medical computing proficiency requirement for all medical students at GWU, and was instrumental in developing patient management software for the GWU Department of Neurological Surgery. In 1992, The George Washington University designated him Professor Emeritus of Computer Medicine and of Neurological Surgery.

Since 1987, Dr. Tidball has continued his service to the Washington National Cathedral as Volunteer Manager of the Cathedral Information Systems Program. This group of volunteers has developed a computer database of the works of art that have been crafted into the building along with a companion database containing biographical information on those who have been responsible for bringing about the Cathedral's structure and its programs.

Recently, Dr. Tidball has been engaged in collaborative research with his wife, Professor M. Elizabeth Tidball. In 1994 they were both appointed Distinguished Research Scholars at Hood College where they are Co-Directors of the Tidball Center for the Study of Educational Environments. He is a co-author, with his wife and two other colleagues, of *Taking Women Seriously: Lessons and Legacies for Educating the Majority* (Washington: American Council on Education/Oryx Press, 1999). In 1994, Wilson College, Chambersburg, PA, awarded him the Doctor of Humane Letters degree, and in 1999 Hood College honored him with a Doctor of Science degree.

Dr. Tidball has had a lifelong interest in anthroposophy. He visited the Goetheanum in Dornach, Switzerland, in 1948 and again in 1970. Since his retirement he has been able to devote more time to the study of Dr. Steiner's writings. He has been an active member of the Rudolf Steiner Study Group of the Anthroposophical Society Greater Washington Branch for twelve years. Encountering Dr. Powell's *Chronicle of the Living Christ* encouraged him to expand his interests to include the contributions of revelations in furthering an understanding of biblical texts. Portions of the present book were delivered as illustrated lectures in Baltimore, MD, (2001) and in Washington, DC, (2002 and 2004).